D1067370

MARK & HELEN OSTERLIN LIBRARY
NORTHWESTERN MICHIGAN COLLEGE
TRAVERSE CITY, MICHIGAN 49686-3061

Reference Book - Room Use Only

CURRICULUM
AND INSTRUCTION

DEBATING ISSUES
in American Education

EDITORIAL BOARD

Editors-in-Chief

Charles J. Russo
University of Dayton

Allan G. Osborne, Jr.
Principal (Retired), Snug Harbor Community School,
Quincy, Massachusetts

Volume Editor

A. Jonathan Eakle
The Johns Hopkins University

Advisory Board

Francine DeFranco
Homer Babbidge Library, University of Connecticut

Ralph D. Mawdsley
Cleveland State University

Martha M. McCarthy
Loyola Marymount University and Indiana University

Mark E. Shelton
Monroe C. Gutman Education Library, Harvard University

CURRICULUM
AND INSTRUCTION

VOLUME EDITOR

A. JONATHAN EAKLE

THE JOHNS HOPKINS UNIVERSITY

2

VOLUME

DEBATING ISSUES
in American Education

SERIES
EDITORS

CHARLES J. RUSSO
ALLAN G. OSBORNE, JR.

⑤SAGE reference

Los Angeles | London | New Delhi
Singapore | Washington DC

Los Angeles | London | New Delhi
Singapore | Washington DC

FOR INFORMATION:

SAGE Publications, Inc.
2455 Teller Road
Thousand Oaks, California 91320
E-mail: order@sagepub.com

SAGE Publications Ltd.
1 Oliver's Yard
55 City Road
London EC1Y 1SP
United Kingdom

SAGE Publications India Pvt. Ltd.
B 1/I 1 Mohan Cooperative Industrial Area
Mathura Road, New Delhi 110 044
India

SAGE Publications Asia-Pacific Pte. Ltd.
3 Church Street
#10-04 Samsung Hub
Singapore 049483

Copyright © 2012 by SAGE Publications, Inc.

All rights reserved. No part of this book may be reproduced or utilized in any form or by any means, electronic or mechanical, including photocopying, recording, or by any information storage and retrieval system, without permission in writing from the publisher.

Printed in the United States of America.

Library of Congress Cataloging-in-Publication Data

Curriculum and instruction/volume editor, A. Jonathan Eakle.

p. cm.—(Debating issues in American education ; v. 2)

Includes bibliographical references and index.

ISBN 978-1-4129-8808-7 (cloth : alk. paper)

1. Curriculum planning—United States. 2. Public schools—Curricula—United States. I. Eakle, A. Jonathan, 1957-

LB2806.15.C6923 2012
375'.001—dc23   2011039049

Publisher: Rolf A. Janke
Acquisitions Editor: Jim Brace-Thompson
Assistant to the Publisher: Michele Thompson
Developmental Editors: Diana E. Axelsen, Carole Maurer
Production Editor: Tracy Buyan
Reference Systems Manager: Leticia Gutierrez
Reference Systems Coordinator: Laura Notton
Copy Editor: Megan Markanich
Typesetter: C&M Digitals (P) Ltd.
Proofreader: Jennifer Thompson
Indexer: Mary Mortensen
Cover Designer: Janet Kiesel
Marketing Manager: Carmel Schrire

SUSTAINABLE FORESTRY INITIATIVE
Label applies to the text stock
Certified Sourcing
www.sfiprogram.org
SFI-00341

12 13 14 15 16 10 9 8 7 6 5 4 3 2 1

CONTENTS

ABOUT THE EDITORS-IN-CHIEF

Charles J. Russo, JD, EdD, is the Joseph Panzer Chair in Education in the School of Education and Allied Professions and an adjunct professor in the School of Law at the University of Dayton. He was the 1998–1999 president of the Education Law Association and 2002 recipient of its McGhehey (Achievement) Award. He has authored or coauthored more than 200 articles in peer-reviewed journals; has authored, coauthored, edited, or coedited 40 books; and has in excess of 800 publications. Russo also speaks extensively on issues in education law in the United States and abroad.

Along with having spoken in 33 states and 25 nations on 6 continents, Russo has taught summer courses in England, Spain, and Thailand; he also has served as a visiting professor at Queensland University of Technology in Brisbane and the University of Newcastle, Australia; the University of Sarajevo, Bosnia and Herzegovina; South East European University, Macedonia; the Potchefstroom Campus of North-West University in Potchefstroom, South Africa; the University of Malaya in Kuala Lumpur, Malaysia; and the University of São Paulo, Brazil. He regularly serves as a visiting professor at the Potchefstroom Campus of North-West University.

Before joining the faculty at the University of Dayton as professor and chair of the Department of Educational Administration in July 1996, Russo taught at the University of Kentucky in Lexington from August 1992 to July 1996 and at Fordham University in his native New York City from September 1989 to July 1992. He taught high school for 8½ years before and after graduation from law school. He received a BA (classical civilization) in 1972, a JD in 1983, and an EdD (educational administration and supervision) in 1989 from St. John's University in New York City. He also received a master of divinity degree from the Seminary of the Immaculate Conception in Huntington, New York, in 1978, as well as a PhD Honoris Causa from the Potchefstroom Campus of North-West University, South Africa, in May 2004 for his contributions to the field of education law.

Russo and his wife, a preschool teacher who provides invaluable assistance proofreading and editing, travel regularly both nationally and internationally to Russo's many speaking and teaching engagements.

Allan G. Osborne, Jr. is the retired principal of the Snug Harbor Community School in Quincy, Massachusetts, a nationally recognized Blue Ribbon School of Excellence. During his 34 years in public education, he served as a special education teacher, a director of special education, an assistant principal, and a principal. He also served as an adjunct professor of special education and education law at several colleges, including Bridgewater State University and American International University.

Osborne earned an EdD in educational leadership from Boston College and an MEd in special education from Fitchburg State College (now Fitchburg State University) in Massachusetts. He received a BA in psychology from the University of Massachusetts.

Osborne has authored or coauthored numerous peer-reviewed journal articles, book chapters, monographs, and textbooks on legal issues in education, along with textbooks on other aspects of education. Although he writes and presents in several areas of educational law, he specializes in legal and policy issues in special education. He is the coauthor, with Charles J. Russo, of five texts published by Corwin, a SAGE company.

A past president of the Education Law Association (ELA), Osborne has been an attendee and presenter at most ELA conferences since 1991. He has also written a chapter now titled "Students With Disabilities" for the *Yearbook of Education Law,* published by ELA, since 1990. He is on the editorial advisory committee of *West's Education Law Reporter* and is coeditor of the "Education Law Into Practice" section of that journal, which is sponsored by ELA. He is also on the editorial boards of several other education journals.

In recognition of his contributions to the field of education law, Osborne was presented with the McGhehey Award by ELA in 2008, the highest award given by the organization. He is also the recipient of the City of Quincy Human Rights Award, the Financial Executives Institute of Massachusetts Principals Award, the Junior Achievement of Massachusetts Principals Award, and several community service awards.

Osborne spends his time in retirement writing, editing, and working on his hobbies: genealogy and photography. He and his wife Debbie, a retired elementary school teacher, enjoy gardening, traveling, attending theater and musical performances, and volunteering at the Dana Farber Cancer Institute in Boston.

ABOUT THE
VOLUME EDITOR

A. Jonathan Eakle is an associate professor in The Johns Hopkins University School of Education. He teaches and mentors advanced graduate students and conducts research on cross-cultural and international studies in education; out-of-school and in-school literacies; and the interrelations of the plastic arts, printed texts, and other communication forms in museums and classrooms. He supervises clinical practicum at Johns Hopkins. Eakle's work includes translating empirical data to sensible products using novel qualitative research methods. He serves on the faculty editorial advisory board of the The Johns Hopkins University Press—the oldest running academic press in the United States. He has contributed in various ways to international education organizations, major education journals, and high-profile publications. Eakle's coedited book on secondary school literacy is the third volume of a 50-year-old series published by the National Council of Teachers of English. His research on Mexico City museums, identity, power, and education is forthcoming. He resides with his family in the Washington, D.C., metro area.

ABOUT THE CONTRIBUTORS

Donna E. Alvermann is a University of Georgia Appointed Distinguished Research Professor of Language and Literacy Education. Her research focuses on young people's media literacies in digital environments. Her books include *Adolescents and Literacies in a Digital World; Reconceptualizing the Literacies in Adolescents' Lives* (3rd ed.); and *Adolescents' Online Literacies: Connecting Classrooms, Digital Media, & Popular Culture.*

Elizabeth B. Bernhardt is the John Roberts Hale Director of the Language Center and professor of German studies at Stanford University. She has spoken and written on second-language reading, teacher education, and policy and planning for foreign- and second-language programs. She earned her PhD at the University of Minnesota.

Stergios G. Botzakis is an assistant professor of adolescent literacy in the Theory and Practice in Teacher Education Department at The University of Tennessee. His research interests include content-area literacy, middle grades instruction, secondary instruction, and graphic novels, as well as working with struggling adolescent readers.

Linda E. Brody directs the Study of Exceptional Talent at the Johns Hopkins Center for Talented Youth. She earned her doctorate in gifted education at Johns Hopkins and has published widely on effective interventions for talented students and on special populations including extremely gifted students, gifted females, and twice-exceptional students.

John Castellani is an associate professor in the School of Education at The Johns Hopkins University. He is currently coeditor for both the *Journal of Special Education Technology* of the Technology and Media Division of the Council for Exceptional Children and the *New Horizons for Learning* quarterly journal. His teaching and research interests are in the areas of data mining, online and virtual learning, assistive and instructional technology, as well as educational technology leadership.

Gina Cervetti is an assistant professor in the School of Education at the University of Michigan. Her work focuses on the interface of literacy and content-area learning. Dr. Cervetti completed her doctoral work at Michigan State University in educational psychology and served as a postdoctoral scholar at the University of California, Berkeley.

Rosa Aurora Chávez-Eakle is a psychotherapist, creativity researcher, and founder of the Washington International Center for Creativity where she has her practice. After graduating from the Universidad Nacional Autonoma de Mexico, she was a visiting scholar at the Torrance Center for Creative Studies becoming E. P. Torrance's last student.

Jamie Colwell is a PhD candidate in curriculum and instruction at Clemson University. Her specific areas of interest and research are adolescent literacy and teacher education.

Bonnie Cramond is the director of the Torrance Center for Creative Studies and Talent Development in the College of Education, as well as a professor, and the graduate coordinator in the Department of Educational Psychology and Instructional Technology at the University of Georgia.

Margie W. Crowe spent 30 years teaching general and special education in public and private schools before joining the special education faculty at the University of Southern Mississippi. Her interests include assistive technology, differentiating instruction, and curriculum design.

Marcia H. Davis is an associate research scientist at the Center for Social Organization of Schools at The Johns Hopkins University. Her research interests include the development of interventions to improve content-area literacy in high school classrooms and whole-school interventions to improve student engagement in learning.

Laurie U. deBettencourt is a professor and chair of the Special Education and Teacher Preparation Departments at The Johns Hopkins University. Currently, she is coeditor of *TESE,* the journal of the Teacher Education Division of Council for Exceptional Children and has coauthored six textbooks. She has spent 27 years teaching and supervising graduate students in the field of education.

Jeanne Gilliam Fain is an assistant professor of elementary education and special education at Middle Tennessee State University. She received her MEd from Arizona State University and her PhD in language, reading, and culture from the University of Arizona. Fain's essay in this volume reflects the complexities of teaching practice and English-Only policies.

Margaret J. Finders is a professor in the Department of English at the University of Wisconsin–La Crosse. Her research interests focus on early adolescence, gender, and sociopolitical dimensions of teaching and learning. Her published work focuses on how self and relationships are constituted and reconstituted through friendship, family, school networks, and the role of literacy.

Latisha Hayes taught students with reading disabilities in the primary through middle grades as a special educator and reading specialist. She is currently an assistant professor at the Curry School of Education at the University of Virginia and teaches courses on the diagnosis and remediation of reading difficulties. In addition, she is the coordinator of the McGuffey Reading Center.

George G. Hruby is the executive director of the Collaborative Center for Literacy Development for the Commonwealth of Kentucky and an assistant research professor of literacy education at the College of Education, University of Kentucky. His scholarly works center on theoretical analysis, most recently of educational neuroscience related to literacy development.

Marcia Invernizzi is the Henderson Professor of Reading at the University of Virginia's Curry School of Education where she also serves as director of the McGuffey Reading Center. She is the principal investigator of Phonological Literacy Screening (PALS), a founder of Book Buddies, and a coauthor of *Words Their Way.*

Jennifer Jones is an associate professor of literacy education in the College of Education & Human Development at Radford University in Virginia. Her research has been published in many journals and has received teaching and scholarly activity awards within her college and university.

Christopher Knaus is an associate professor in the College of Education at California State University, East Bay. In addition to developing urban youth voice, Knaus creates educator pipelines that develop culturally responsive urban educators of color. Knaus earned his PhD at the University of Washington.

Judith T. Lysaker is an associate professor of literacy and language education in the Department of Curriculum and Instruction at Purdue University. Her research focuses on reading as a dialogic, relational process and how reading fosters the development of social imagination in children.

Ralph D. Mawdsley holds a JD from the University of Illinois and a PhD from the University of Minnesota. He has authored over 500 publications on the subject of education law. Mawdsley was president of the Education Law Association in 2001 and was awarded that organization's Marion A. McGhehey Award in 2004. He has received two Fulbright Awards, one to South Africa and one to Australia.

Carol J. Mills is the senior director for Research and Counseling Services at the Center for Talented Youth at The Johns Hopkins University where she received her doctorate in psychology. The author of many scholarly articles, Mills's research includes cognitive and personality development, education of highly gifted students, and twice-exceptional children.

Timothy E. Morse is an associate professor at the University of Southern Mississippi, where he directs the Mississippi Department of Education's Autism Project. In addition to having taught undergraduate and graduate special education courses at the university, he has worked as a public school special education administrator and teacher.

P. David Pearson is a professor at the University of California, Berkeley. He has authored numerous seminal articles and books and edited *The Handbook of Reading Research* and *Reading Research Quarterly*. Pearson has been presented with prestigious awards in education for his contributions to literacy education research and practice.

Katharine Rasch currently serves as Unit Assessment Research Director at Delta State University. She is dean and professor emerita at Maryville University–St. Louis and has worked with accreditation for 25 years both at her institutions and chairing two of three of the National Council for Accreditation of Teacher Education's (NCATE) boards during her service. Her research focuses on partnerships and professional practice.

David Reinking is the Eugene T. Moore Professor of Teacher Education at Clemson University where he provides leadership in pursuing the institution's goal to enhance its national standing. In that role, he has observed how current approaches to national accreditation inhibit authentic innovation and improvement in programs of teacher education.

Loukia K. Sarroub is an associate professor of education at the University of Nebraska–Lincoln whose work focuses on literacy, linguistic anthropology, and youth cultures. She is the author of *All American Yemeni Girls: Being Muslim in Public Schools* and has published her research in journals such as *Harvard Educational Review, Reading Research Quarterly,* and *Ethnography & Education.*

Marc L. Stein is an assistant professor at The Johns Hopkins University School of Education. His research focuses on the social context of education and educational policy. Specifically, his research interests include the social and organizational contexts surrounding public school choice, summer learning, and teachers' instructional practice.

Lisa Patel Stevens is an associate professor of education at Boston College. Her work is with recently immigrated youth and draws on participatory action research knowledge frames and approaches to explore themes of race, education, and capital. Prior to working in academia, Stevens was a high school teacher, a journalist, and a state-level policymaker.

Mark A. Templin is an associate professor of education specializing in science and middle grades education at the University of Toledo. His research interests focus on understanding relationships among political theory, philosophy of science, and science teaching practices.

Peggy Whalen-Levitt is the director of the Center for Education, Imagination and the Natural World where she coordinates the center's co-research program for educators, The Inner Life of the Child in Nature: Presence and Practice. She holds a PhD in language in education from the University of Pennsylvania.

Ellen Winner is professor and chair of psychology at Boston College and senior research associate at Harvard Project Zero. Her research focuses on the arts and cognition. In 2000, she received the Rudolf Arnheim Award for Outstanding Research by a Senior Scholar in Psychology and the Arts from Division 10 of the American Psychological Association (APA).

Michelle Zoss is an assistant professor of English education at Georgia State University. Her research in education focuses on integration of visual arts and literacy for secondary students and teachers, an enterprise that began with her experiences teaching visual art and English language arts in elementary and high school classrooms.

INTRODUCTION

EDUCATION AND THE DESIGN, PRODUCTION, AND ENACTMENT OF CURRICULUM AND INSTRUCTION

Education in the United States is multifaceted. It can be an object of politics and law and a stage of different cultural values and conflict. Education is a means of employment for people in various occupations and settings. Public schooling provides many children with the few good meals that they are served each week, and schools can be their refuge from harsh weather. Similarly, schools strive to keep children safe—sometimes from dangers of surrounding neighborhoods where crime and violence are wide ranging. Nonetheless, although schools can mean many different things to many people, when all is said and done, education is about the learning that takes place among teachers and students.

The volume in hand is about this learning—the what, how, and by whom knowledge circulates and is dispersed in local education settings. This diffusion of knowledge (e.g., of subject-specific content and strategic learning processes, ways of conduct, cultural rules) formally unfolds under the umbrella phrase *curriculum and instruction*—the overarching topic of and in some cases the point of departure for the following chapters. The goal of these chapters is to present a few key issues in curriculum and instruction that take place in contemporary schools in the United States and different perspectives on those issues.

Curriculum is a blueprint, design, or plan of a course of study that is to take place. Typically, it includes concepts, procedures, and processes deemed important by a government institution, school administration, education community, and so forth, for teachers to teach and for students to learn during a particular period of time and in a specific place. To set the foundation for subsequent chapters, in the following pages, theories of curriculum and instruction of U.S. public education are briefly examined. Over the years, there have been diverse conceptual camps bearing different names that have come out of these theories. For the present purpose, it is convenient to think of curriculum and instruction operating in a continuum between two poles. At an extreme end of this continuum, there is the tendency to hold fast to, preserve, maintain, or recapture what is believed to be the traditional dimensions of curriculum and instruction; often promoters of these practices advocate to conserve ideas that have stood the test of time.

The other extreme of the curriculum continuum is a progressive one. Sponsors of this side insist that the goal of curriculum and instruction is to advance education beyond what is already known. In the subsequent section, theoretical sketches are provided to situate the reader in reading the remains of the volume. The sketches function in a middle zone between the two extremes of progress and conservation yet draw from each side. That section is followed by one about how the reader may use the concepts from the sketches to examine the current state of curriculum and instruction in the United States and subsequent chapters of the present volume.

THEORIES OF EDUCATION AND ITS DESIGN AND PRACTICE

Although at first blush there might seem to be a degree of uniformity in U.S. curriculum, untangling how it is actually conceptualized and implemented shows its many fragments. One source of this fragmentation is the different stances in the field of education in general and the formation and application of curriculum in particular (Ornstein, 2007). These diverse perspectives sometimes reflect historical developments; for example, some standpoints echo the education practices of the Ancient Greeks, as reinterpreted through more contemporary points of view. For instance, deductive analysis—Socratic inquiry typically guided by a knowledgeable elder—and instruction in traditional values are general hallmarks taken from antiquity by educators. Further, from the Greeks and through the subsequent waves of humanism and the establishment and evolution of national and local laws and policies eventually came notions of contemporary education in the United States, which at its root is based in democratic concepts.

Democratic Education

Education in the United States has not always been wedded to the basic constitutional principles of liberty, equality, and justice. Until the 20th century, education was principally for economically privileged white males, yet as society and cultural values in the United States changed, so too did its education practices. A democratic approach to curriculum and instruction that reemerged during modern times that was appropriated from the Greeks and incorporated Socratic inquiry is Paideia, which in its modern form borrowed from the progressive education theories of John Dewey. A central tenet in Paideia is equality, and it provides for a general and shared liberal arts curriculum for all citizens (Adler, 1982). The democratic notion of the Paideia curriculum, as with its Greek predecessors, was a reaction against distinct schooling tracts paralleling different socioeconomic strata and workplaces, which marked hegemonic periods of Greek culture as well as those of the Industrial Revolution, among other times.

Rather than placing children in one track that was directed toward higher education and a relative life of leisure and another track that was designed for laborers who needed to be taught manual skills useful in settings such as a factory or farm, a democratic education curriculum purportedly makes all possibilities—and the material assets that come along with those possibilities—available to all students regardless of their backgrounds and stations in life. In short, Paideia curriculum, akin to the founding ideas and documents of the U.S. Republic, set forth an education system which valued a broad foundation in the arts and sciences and cultivated individual qualities alongside a responsibility of the individual to the local community, nation, and beyond.

In its pure, utopian form, Paideia curriculum from antiquity to present is based on assumptions of freedom and equality. This made the express idea of Paideia align well with the notions associated with various civil rights movements, school desegregation, the Great Society, and other progressive notions of the latter half of the 20th century. These historical developments contributed to the formation of dozens of schools, a national center, and so forth that explicitly follow Paideia concepts and pedagogies.

One of the hallmarks of how Paideia curriculum unfolds is through its practice of dialogic seminars, which have at least three general characteristics: (a) teachers relinquish much, if not all, instructional authority; they may, nonetheless, facilitate discussions with open-ended questions or serve as coaches to encourage seminar participant perspectives or to help them articulate their ideas; (b) the choices of what is deemed as important to the topics at hand during the Paideia seminar are not fixed and are decided upon by all discussants; and (c) an understanding of materials under discussion is developed by the seminar groups, not given by the teachers to the students (Billings & Fitzgerald, 2002). As suggested by this framework, freedom and equality are notions threaded through the participant roles, format, and delivery of the Paideia curriculum, which more often than not are composed of open curricular content grounded in an authentic purpose, such as, for example, questions revolving around the benefits, drawbacks, and challenges of green technologies or the uses and abuses of virtual reality schooling environments.

This fundamental utopian notion of democracy in curriculum and instruction of U.S. schooling has crystallized through other ways and in other places and at other times. The open, egalitarian approach embedded in Paideia's core, for instance, was taken literally and to extremes in what is known as the open school movement. It, too, professed qualities of equality and freedom in curriculum and encouraged instruction that displaced authority to center on the child rather than on the adult teacher. In addition, part of this decentralization involved breaking open classroom containers where children could be free to explore, exchange a free flow of ideas, and move about large open spaces unfettered by walls and other obstacles (Proshansky & Wolfe, 1974). Nevertheless, the result of these open arrangements was often chaos, and although the reasons for the disorder had been debated, in the end the open school movement fizzled.

Similarly, other dimensions of what was once considered to be hallmarks of democratic education in the United States, such as free play and hands-on inquiry, have also sputtered—a theme that threads through many of the subsequent essays of the present volume. To be sure, in rhetoric this is not the case. Conservative education movements have turned words such as the word *reform* that were once the battle banners of progressive educators toward their own purposes. In this vein, who could, for instance, divorce equality and justice from statements such as "no child left behind"? These issues are some of the most salient ones in current education policy and practice and are taken up in earnest in the essays found in the chapters that follow.

Yet beyond the reform rhetoric, there are great undemocratic divides that have arguably widened in recent years through U.S. public education policy, education funding, and the resulting curriculum and instruction of all of the nation's children. Nel Noddings (2005) suggested that education reform as it is presently conceived limits education to only a slim portion of what it could actually be. In fact, many education scholars and practitioners argue that the pedagogical slice that is being most effectively promoted by reformists is the one that concentrates on limited proficiencies in limited subject areas (e.g., math and reading), which are measured in limited ways. The education of the whole child—a popular term that suggests qualities beyond just cognitive ones—instead involves notions that have been touchstones of democratic education during most of the 20th century: "(1) health; (2) command of the fundamental processes; (3) worthy home membership; (4) vocation; (5) citizenship; (6) worthy use of leisure; and (7) ethical character" (Kliebard, 1995, as cited by Noddings, 2005, p. 10). In addition, educating the whole child has more often than not involved dimensions that are elusive to scientific measurement or not easily determinable by other means. For example, Waldorf Education, an admired and widespread pedagogical approach especially in parts of Europe, works to cultivate qualities of soul and spirit, dimensions that in the least escape the quantitative research criteria professed by some scientists and the new education reformers. To be sure, these matters are at the heart of what it means to be human, and aspects of what counts as democratic dimensions of education, how it is defined and is practiced, or not, are touchstones to following essays of the present volume.

Education and Privilege

The liberal arts curriculum and its democratic rhetoric that have been at the core of most modern U.S. public schooling are evident through various levels of society and its institutions. Nonetheless, how it is actually implemented greatly differs depending on context. A great divide in U.S. schooling is based on economics, and often economics create other spatial divides, such as school and housing districts separated by barriers that mark territories of racial difference (Eakle, 2007). In short, and well outside democratic concepts, there have been flights to schooling alternatives based on class, race, national origin, and so forth, especially since landmark legislation was created that was designed, in the abstract, to end inequalities and create, as Lyndon Johnson described it, a Great Society.

Flights to public education alternatives can take many different paths. Some flights are motivated by ideological or religious purposes and the curriculum that goes along with such purposes. To be sure, sometimes choices among curricula are complicated ones. For instance, Svi Shapiro (1996), a Jewish leftist academic in education leadership who supports critical pedagogies and public education, when faced with the dilemma of enrolling his daughter in public or religious school chose the latter. In this vein, and as suggested in the previous section, the education of what is known as the whole child leads some parents to curriculum such as Montessori. As a rule, being able to select specialized education curriculum is tied to the ability to pay for it. However, as detailed extensively in other volumes of the present series, payment notions have crept into education through school vouchers, tax credits, and so forth. And along with capital concepts and the ability to pay for education comes privilege and elitism.

An exemplar of privilege in public education is found through the Boston Latin School (BLS), the country's oldest public school and a longtime feeder school to Harvard University. Established in 1685, BLS boasts of prestigious students, which include Samuel Adams, George Santayana, and Joseph Kennedy. Over the years, the school's curriculum has centered on the humanities with emphasis on rhetoric and classical subjects, and up to this day, the school requires years of study in Latin and exercises in declamation (oral recitation compositions and practices). This pedagogical discourse—squarely embedded in BLS's curriculum—has prepared scores of its students for entry into Ivy League professional schools, among others. It is also a discourse of wealth and privilege; and, despite its efforts in achieving a diverse student body the school has educated a disproportionally upper-class student body (Katnami, 2010).

The issue of class is not a new one in schools such as BLS. Alluding to his own BLS experience, an adolescent Benjamin Franklin (1722) wrote about a passage through the temple gate of education that was attended by a porter of *"Riches* . . . [and] many who came even to the very Gate, were obliged to travel back again as ignorant as they came, for want of this necessary Qualification" (para. 5). Arguably since its inception there has been at least two distinct tracks in U.S. schooling—one traveled by those who have and the other by those who have not and curriculum in one way or the other has been designed to accommodate these two pathways.

The BLS population shows other, and sometimes related, tracks of U.S. schooling—ones that are divided along racial, ethnic, and gender lines. Not surprisingly given the colonial times that BLS came into being, it was exclusively composed of white male students and faculty, which was a practice generally carried forward well into the 20th century; it was not until the 1970s that coeducation was practiced at BLS. Additionally, BLS as well as many other affluent schools has been disproportionately composed of white students and teachers. To combat this inequality, in 1976, as reported by Samar Katnami (2010), BLS was ordered to reserve 35% of its seats for black and Latino students, a practice it continued years after the courts had relinquished control of the school's quota system. However, over a decade ago, other court rulings against affirmative action caused BLS to abandon its practice of minority quotas; thus, its minority population has plummeted. It is reasonable to assume that in part this is because a main criterion for school admission is the ability to score well on standardized exams that are often shown to be biased against minorities (Unzueta & Lowery, 2010). Therefore, to this day, the rigorous, classical liberal arts curriculum and resources of BLS, and schools like it, are in large part the exclusive property of families from majority groups.

Mentorship, Education, and Disciplinary Knowledge

A well-rounded liberal arts education curriculum is deemed by most educated people in the United States as important to prepare children for university and beyond. Certainly, if K–12 curriculum and instruction is in lockstep with that of higher education this makes sense. Nonetheless, an underlying assumption of this historical continuity is not without criticism. Another way to think about education is that it should foster creativity and innovation—arguably one of the most important education tasks to meet the challenges of contemporary life. As addressed later in the present volume, one way in which creativity can be cultivated is through a modified curriculum that offers accelerated content to students who are determined to be capable of managing it. In this vein, constructivist curriculum and instruction is an approach wherein students are taught at a level that is challenging to them. However, to those who have advanced this idea (e.g., Piaget, 1976; Vygotsky, 1978) to discover what is demanding, yet not too difficult nor too easy, for students is not simply something that can be derived from a formula or a test that can be applied to all children. It requires a good teacher who has the resources and background to determine and meet his or her students' needs and to help them discover their talents and interests.

Howard Gardner (1999), a Harvard scholar well known for his theory of multiple intelligences popularized in the 1980s, drew on these classical notions when describing various disciplines (e.g., of science, art, religion) and discipleship. From these stances, which have roots in the rites and practices of tribal cultures, classical antiquity, and the centuries-old craftsman guilds of Asia and Europe, he argued that students often learn best when engaged in domain-specific and authentic experiences provided under the guidance of an experienced mentor. For instance, during a time long past, aspiring attorneys would seek out a willing mentor lawyer who would take them under wing and allow the novice to "read the law" in their library. The master would oversee their fledgling's arguments in court until they were ready to leave the mentor's nest and practice law on their own. Providing such authentic support experiences remains a hallmark of good teaching practices in some U.S. schools; budding educators are taught by experienced practitioners in teacher preparation programs, complete internship experiences under the watchful guidance of a certified teacher leader, and then are paired with teacher mentors as they assume their first classroom assignments with children.

Discipline and Control Models of Curriculum and Instruction

Also in the vein of experience, John Dewey (1902), who was trained in the first national psychology lab at The Johns Hopkins University, suggested that experience is not only a quality possessed by adults in an educator role. In fact, for an educator to teach a prescribed set of concepts and procedures reduced to the memorization of minutiae, according to Dewey, pitches the interest of the child *against* the curriculum. In such cases, curriculum operates through an absolute teacher authority that holds and dispenses the knowledge of basic skills to pupils, such as how to properly pronounce and scribe discrete parts of speech and successfully accomplish basic processes, such as, for example, how to correctly group numbers into various sets. Curriculum and instruction of this ilk represents that which is commonly referred to today as traditional, back-to-basics, teacher-centered pedagogy. Of this, and as suggested in subsequent chapters of the present volume, the teacher center has, as of late and in some cases, evolved into a mere conduit function, where the core of the curriculum is actually displaced to a spot far from the classroom to a central county administration, or a state or national office. And, routinely, these government offices receive their marching orders from think tanks and authoritative resources that profess purportedly neutral "what works" scientific practices (see Institute of Education Sciences, 2011). In short, the teacher is sometimes cast by government and neoacademic authorities to the role of a puppet, who merely delivers a one-size-fits-all script of discrete facts to, borrowing from Karl Popper (1972), fill the empty buckets of children's minds.

Implicit in puppet and bucket modes of education, the words *disciples* and *discipline* take on other meanings in the settings where some contemporary U.S. schooling takes place. By definition, a disciple is a follower. If following is consistent with many steadfast notions of learning, then the teacher's goal is to sooner or later give some degree of freedom to the pupil. On the other hand, strict discipleship models can be a means of simply producing faithful and permanent followers. Rather than freedom, instruction can be targeted to meet compliance standards and other objectives. This can function in several ways under the watchful eyes of school and government authorities (cf. Foucault, 1975/1977). For example, through rules and repetition, physical bodies are controlled, such as by the arrangements of desks in neat classroom rows and by formations of military-like lines where students are expected to follow decorum when moving from one setting to another, among other times.

In turn, the actual content of learning material can be restricted to control students, as well. For instance, history can be slanted to highlight some points while casting other matters to the side; a common example of this is why wars were fought and how wars were won. In addition, the level of complexity that is provided in content-area material and curricula can also assure followers as well as leaders. Divisions based on privilege and rank, as described in earlier sections of the present introduction, can translate to some students being challenged with ideas and problems that prepare them to advance toward higher education curriculum and to occupy top rungs of employment. All too often divisions of curricular content mirror the resources of the immediate community; as a result, the rich get richer and the poor, poorer.

As suggested earlier in this section, the delivery of the curriculum in a disciplinary model of education can be a depleted one in various ways, and children are not the only ones affected. Teachers, administrators, and local education offices are increasingly required to do more with less, especially those people who serve in the most challenging school and community environments. For example, as student to teacher ratios are increased to remarkably high levels, as has been the case since the recent U.S. economic downturn, control becomes a paramount issue—particularly in places that experience comparatively unrestrained and high levels of crime and violence. As a result and as of late, schools in some high-risk urban areas have begun to resemble prisons with lockdown protocols, surveillance cameras, and armed security officers.

Rounding out the discipline and control approach to curriculum and instruction is the practice of examination. As with a military fitness test or medical assessment, students in public schools are periodically and systematically evaluated to survey their fitness to go forward in academics. On the face, holding children accountable for their learning seems reasonable. However, as suggested by an entire volume of the present book series devoted to standards and accountability, and subsequent chapters of the text in hand, testing is central, frequent, and carries high stakes in contemporary U.S. public schools. The examination can also serve as a means to expose, sort, and control. And current trends are toward increasingly applying similar measures to areas of education besides the child—to teachers, administrators, and those who prepare educators for public service.

Those who advocate for disciplinary and controlling curriculum and instruction frequently level arguments that anything less direct and forceful leads to willy-nilly methods that contribute to ongoing achievement gaps. In this respect, John Dewey (1902) suggested that children, if left strictly to their own experiences and preferences, are more likely than not to meander like will-o'-wisps. On the other hand, much is to be learned from children as they participate in learning activities "on their own" in informal learning environments such as museums (Eakle, 2009). Curriculum can remedy this fleeting aimlessness but only if it sets out in broad strokes what is useful for children to know and is shaped by a teacher to align with a student's specific experiences and needs. Thus, a counterpoint to the arguments for discipline and control in schools is that education should be centered on the student and the transformative dimensions of education rather than merely on competencies in gaining standardized sets of knowledge and processes. In short, rather than producing compliant subjects, education in the hands of wise teachers can lead to divergent thinking, creativity, and innovation.

HOW TO READ WHAT FOLLOWS

The volume is predicated on the assumption that education involves polarizing issues. As with wider cultures and their values, certain topics stimulate bold contrasts while others vary along a scale of gray between black and white. Indeed, there are instances in the subsequent essays that represent salient education issues in intermediate tones that span a broad range. In this vein, sometimes particular points converge to overlap with counterpoints and, at other times, points disperse and move apart. Organizing the essays that follow bearing in mind these possible divergences and convergences across the authors' ideas is one way to read the chapters.

Charting how each essay conforms with or opposes the various curriculum and instruction theories and concepts laid out previously in the present introduction can be a useful means for readers to gain insights from the two debates set forth in the succeeding chapters. For instance, to what extent does the author advocate for freedom or constraint in curriculum and instruction? Is the focus on the individual teacher and student, or is the attention placed on larger units, such as the school district or on widespread education policy? To what extent are cultural and individual differences considered in relation to the topics addressed by the authors? Is the author's viewpoint taken from traditional notions or from novel concepts?

Each piece begins with a short introduction that endeavors an overview of the topic. The overviews are designed to place the reader in the middle ground of the topic, yet, even so, that middle ground is not intended to give the impression that it occupies a strictly neutral zone. In fact, as Brian Street (2003) suggested, all texts are created with a purpose, and the acts of reading and writing texts are social ones, involving not only the background and perspectives of the author but also those of you, the reader. Nonetheless, working from the middle through the overviews affords a tactic for the reader to navigate to the left or right while interpreting the arguments presented in the essays.

While reading from the middle and to either side of the two debates, readers can approach the essays like a juror might do—weighing one side against the other and seeking a preponderance of the evidence that supports the claims of the authors. For those readers of the volume who are new to the field of education, perhaps the essays will help to develop your own perspectives and allow you to have a voice in the matters that you will encounter in the future. For experienced readers of the volume, perhaps what you encounter in the following chapters will help you reaffirm your positions or adopt new ones—or, in the least, show you recent developments surrounding salient education issues.

Education reform is an issue that threads through the present volume, and it is one that likewise ebbs and flows through modern education debates. Thus, a guiding question for the reader of the following chapters is simply, what does reform mean? A reform issue in the 1950s was how cognitive psychological insights could be used in structuring rigorous curriculum to, in part, address

who serve in the most challenging school and community environments. For example, as student to teacher ratios are increased to remarkably high levels, as has been the case since the recent U.S. economic downturn, control becomes a paramount issue—particularly in places that experience comparatively unrestrained and high levels of crime and violence. As a result and as of late, schools in some high-risk urban areas have begun to resemble prisons with lockdown protocols, surveillance cameras, and armed security officers.

Rounding out the discipline and control approach to curriculum and instruction is the practice of examination. As with a military fitness test or medical assessment, students in public schools are periodically and systematically evaluated to survey their fitness to go forward in academics. On the face, holding children accountable for their learning seems reasonable. However, as suggested by an entire volume of the present book series devoted to standards and accountability, and subsequent chapters of the text in hand, testing is central, frequent, and carries high stakes in contemporary U.S. public schools. The examination can also serve as a means to expose, sort, and control. And current trends are toward increasingly applying similar measures to areas of education besides the child—to teachers, administrators, and those who prepare educators for public service.

Those who advocate for disciplinary and controlling curriculum and instruction frequently level arguments that anything less direct and forceful leads to willy-nilly methods that contribute to ongoing achievement gaps. In this respect, John Dewey (1902) suggested that children, if left strictly to their own experiences and preferences, are more likely than not to meander like will-o'-wisps. On the other hand, much is to be learned from children as they participate in learning activities "on their own" in informal learning environments such as museums (Eakle, 2009). Curriculum can remedy this fleeting aimlessness but only if it sets out in broad strokes what is useful for children to know and is shaped by a teacher to align with a student's specific experiences and needs. Thus, a counterpoint to the arguments for discipline and control in schools is that education should be centered on the student and the transformative dimensions of education rather than merely on competencies in gaining standardized sets of knowledge and processes. In short, rather than producing compliant subjects, education in the hands of wise teachers can lead to divergent thinking, creativity, and innovation.

HOW TO READ WHAT FOLLOWS

The volume is predicated on the assumption that education involves polarizing issues. As with wider cultures and their values, certain topics stimulate bold this ilk represents that which is commonly referred to today as traditional, back-to-basics, teacher-centered pedagogy. Of this, and as suggested in subsequent chapters of the present volume, the teacher center has, as of late and in some cases, evolved into a mere conduit function, where the core of the curriculum is actually displaced to a spot far from the classroom to a central county administration, or a state or national office. And, routinely, these government offices receive their marching orders from think tanks and authoritative resources that profess purportedly neutral "what works" scientific practices (see Institute of Education Sciences, 2011). In short, the teacher is sometimes cast by government and neoacademic authorities to the role of a puppet, who merely delivers a one-size-fits-all script of discrete facts to, borrowing from Karl Popper (1972), fill the empty buckets of children's minds.

Implicit in puppet and bucket modes of education, the words *disciples* and *discipline* take on other meanings in the settings where some contemporary U.S. schooling takes place. By definition, a disciple is a follower. If following is consistent with many steadfast notions of learning, then the teacher's goal is to sooner or later give some degree of freedom to the pupil. On the other hand, strict discipleship models can be a means of simply producing faithful and permanent followers. Rather than freedom, instruction can be targeted to meet compliance standards and other objectives. This can function in several ways under the watchful eyes of school and government authorities (cf. Foucault, 1975/1977). For example, through rules and repetition, physical bodies are controlled, such as by the arrangements of desks in neat classroom rows and by formations of military-like lines where students are expected to follow decorum when moving from one setting to another, among other times.

In turn, the actual content of learning material can be restricted to control students, as well. For instance, history can be slanted to highlight some points while casting other matters to the side; a common example of this is why wars were fought and how wars were won. In addition, the level of complexity that is provided in content-area material and curricula can also assure followers as well as leaders. Divisions based on privilege and rank, as described in earlier sections of the present introduction, can translate to some students being challenged with ideas and problems that prepare them to advance toward higher education curriculum and to occupy top rungs of employment. All too often divisions of curricular content mirror the resources of the immediate community; as a result, the rich get richer and the poor, poorer.

As suggested earlier in this section, the delivery of the curriculum in a disciplinary model of education can be a depleted one in various ways, and children are not the only ones affected. Teachers, administrators, and local education offices are increasingly required to do more with less, especially those people creativity can be cultivated is through a modified curriculum that offers accelerated content to students who are determined to be capable of managing it. In this vein, constructivist curriculum and instruction is an approach wherein students are taught at a level that is challenging to them. However, to those who have advanced this idea (e.g., Piaget, 1976; Vygotsky, 1978) to discover what is demanding, yet not too difficult nor too easy, for students is not simply something that can be derived from a formula or a test that can be applied to all children. It requires a good teacher who has the resources and background to determine and meet his or her students' needs and to help them discover their talents and interests.

Howard Gardner (1999), a Harvard scholar well known for his theory of multiple intelligences popularized in the 1980s, drew on these classical notions when describing various disciplines (e.g., of science, art, religion) and discipleship. From these stances, which have roots in the rites and practices of tribal cultures, classical antiquity, and the centuries-old craftsman guilds of Asia and Europe, he argued that students often learn best when engaged in domain-specific and authentic experiences provided under the guidance of an experienced mentor. For instance, during a time long past, aspiring attorneys would seek out a willing mentor lawyer who would take them under wing and allow the novice to "read the law" in their library. The master would oversee their fledgling's arguments in court until they were ready to leave the mentor's nest and practice law on their own. Providing such authentic support experiences remains a hallmark of good teaching practices in some U.S. schools; budding educators are taught by experienced practitioners in teacher preparation programs, complete internship experiences under the watchful guidance of a certified teacher leader, and then are paired with teacher mentors as they assume their first classroom assignments with children.

Discipline and Control Models of Curriculum and Instruction

Also in the vein of experience, John Dewey (1902), who was trained in the first national psychology lab at The Johns Hopkins University, suggested that experience is not only a quality possessed by adults in an educator role. In fact, for an educator to teach a prescribed set of concepts and procedures reduced to the memorization of minutiae, according to Dewey, pitches the interest of the child *against* the curriculum. In such cases, curriculum operates through an absolute teacher authority that holds and dispenses the knowledge of basic skills to pupils, such as how to properly pronounce and scribe discrete parts of speech and successfully accomplish basic processes, such as, for example, how to correctly group numbers into various sets. Curriculum and instruction of but also in other human qualities, such as developing feeling characteristics, ethical practices, and the ability to be empathetic. Highly controlled and scripted programs, which might be well suited for teaching discrete skills, such as memorizing simple number sets or pronouncing words that rhyme, are less likely, she argues, to develop these more profound human qualities.

There is always a program of sorts operating in a school even in schools that claim to have a "deprogrammed" curriculum that emphasizes the freedom of teachers and students to make choices about educational content and processes. A common historical example of a less programmed schooling system is the open education movement of the 1960s; such issues can be seen today in the ongoing education policy debates between progressive versus transmission classrooms (where knowledge is transmitted from a knowledgeable elder to a child who is unaware of that knowledge). The often debated narrative of open schooling is that it evolved into program incoherence and chaos as a result of classrooms without walls and with activities that emphasized free play rather than structured learning. However, Herb Kohl, a founder of the open school movement, reflected that the open school philosophy was grossly misunderstood and misapplied: "Teachers promoted the idea that openness meant feeling, not learning and architects interpreted openness as meaning no walls . . . open architecture and that touchy-feely stuff also had nothing to do with open education" (Scherer, 1998, p. 34). Rather than what Kohl described as the myth of "touchy-feely," two principal hallmarks of open education programs were a human response to students' emotions and the development of their critical thinking and creative capabilities. Many educators believe these are the most valuable dimensions of curriculum, which is taken up in Judith T. Lysaker's counterpoint essay.

On the other end of the program spectrum is the perspective that public school programs need a high level of control, as introduced in the opening words of this introduction. In some schools, such as those in high-crime urban areas, this is for safety reasons, as illustrated in essays in the volume on school safety. That volume also addresses another topic commonly associated with safety: discipline. As Michel Foucault (1975) and other scholars of the past few decades have detailed, schools can, in the extreme, be like prisons or military boot camps designed to produce disciplined and compliant people. In this vein, it is not uncommon to find urban schools with programs that underscore prison-like means of control with supporting disciplinary methods, such as detention areas, armed school officers, and trained attack and drug detection canines. Furthermore, school programs centering on control and discipline approaches can be supported through technologies, such as surveillance cameras, metal detectors, tracking devices, and walkie-talkie communication, among other ways. Punishment is also a part of overall school programs and

Do curriculum and instruction in schools need to be more or less programmatic?

POINT: Marcia H. Davis, *The Johns Hopkins University*

COUNTERPOINT: Judith T. Lysaker, *Purdue University*

OVERVIEW

This chapter addresses a main idea of curriculum design and instructional implementation that ebbs and flows at various intensities during different times in U.S. public schooling: education programs. As detailed subsequently, although programs are numerous and nuanced, a defining characteristic is to what extent they are controlled. The strictest level of control is in cases where teachers are required to adhere precisely to a script. Such scripted instruction can be extreme when teachers are expected to be reading from a specific page of a program's text that addresses a specific concept or strategy on a particular day of the school year. If such a program is faithfully implemented in a school, administrators can be agents of control who walk the hallways to ensure that the curriculum is being enacted properly. On the other hand, in schools underscoring creativity and innovation, teaching and learning is less controlled, and more emphasis is placed on teacher and student decisions to modify curriculum goals.

Education curricula in and of themselves are programmatic—a system of procedures that are targeted for end results, usually, and in the least, for academic achievement and individual growth. From an ideal stance, a program leads to productive individuals who contribute to the general welfare of their families, selves, communities, nation, and so forth. As addressed in Judith T. Lysaker's (Purdue University) counterpoint essay, this type of productivity is based not only in the materials that one might design or create for consumption

Dewey, J. (1902). *The child and the curriculum.* Chicago: University of Chicago Press.

Eakle, A. J. (2007). Literacy spaces of a Christian faith-based school. *Reading Research Quarterly, 42,* 472–511.

Eakle, A. J. (2009). Museum literacies and adolescents using multiple forms of texts "on their own." *Journal of Adolescent & Adult Literacy, 53*(3), 204–214.

Foucault, M. (1977). *Discipline and punish* (A. M. Sheridan Smith, Trans.). New York: Vintage Books. (Original work published 1975)

Franklin, B. (signed Silence Dogood). (1722, May 14). *Letter number 4.* The Franklin Papers Archive. Originally printed in *The New-England Courant.* Retrieved June 6, 2011, from http://www.franklinpapers.org/franklin/framedNames.jsp

Gardner, H. (1999). *The disciplined mind.* New York: Simon & Schuster.

Heath, S. B. (2000). Making learning work. *Afterschool Matters, 1*(1), 33–45.

Institute of Education Sciences. (2011). *What works clearinghouse.* Retrieved July 4, 2011, from http://ies.ed.gov/ncee/wwc

Katnami, S. (2010). Pics, grutter, and elite public secondary education: Using race as a means in selective admissions. *Washington University Law Quarterly, 87,* 625.

Kliebard, H. (1995). *The struggle for the American curriculum 1893-1958.* New York: Routledge.

Noddings, N. (2005). What does it mean to educate the whole child? *Educational Leadership, 63*(1), 8–13.

Ornstein, A. C. (2007). Philosophy as a basis for curriculum decisions. In A. C. Ornstein, E. F. Pajak, & S. B. Ornstein (Eds.), *Contemporary issues in curriculum* (pp. 5–11). Boston: Allyn & Bacon.

Piaget, J. (1976). *To understand is to invent: The future of education.* New York: Penguin Classics.

Popper, K. (1972). *Objective knowledge: An evolutionary approach.* Oxford, UK: Oxford University Press.

Proshansky, E., & Wolfe, M. (1974). The physical setting and open education. *The School Review, 82*(4), 556–574.

Shapiro, S. (1996). A parent's dilemma: Public vs. Jewish education. *Tikkun, 11*(6), 59.

Street, B. (2003). What's "new" in new literacy studies? Critical approaches to literacy in theory and practice. *Current Issues in Comparative Education, 5,* 77–91.

Unzueta, M. M., & Lowery, B. S. (2010). The impact of race-based performance differences on perceptions of test legitimacy. *Journal of Applied Social Psychology, 40,* 1948–1968.

Vygotsky, L. (1978). *Mind in society.* Cambridge, MA: Harvard University Press.

the perceived threat of communism and its military arsenal. Following a national distrust of institutions, Watergate, and the Vietnam War, in the 1970s to 1980s education reform meant the development of "whole" character traits in whole children through holistic curricular design and instructional methods such as whole language and open education. In the 1990s to early 2000s, institutional faith was renewed in some corners of education through the production of scientific truth statements of what is predictably reasonable to assume—or statistically proven to work—in curriculum and instruction, or not, under certain conditions using particular populations. These truth statements have led to reform initiatives with scientifically endorsed standards, education policies, and packaged curriculum and instruction programs that like home appliances carry a scientific seal of approval and that displace the individual in favor of the statistic. Through these various reform movements, however, achievement gaps among the poor and the privileged and among those of different cultural heritage have continued. Therefore, as of late, because the scientific reform movement has purportedly solved some of the curriculum and instruction problems in schooling, it has trained its sights on educators and local administrators and teacher education programs as the sources of the ongoing disparities in schooling. Thus, notions of accountability that were once applied to student performance are now encompassing a wider surveillance of teachers, principals, other frontline educators, and the institutions and manners that educators are prepared for and placed in service.

The ebb and flow of education issues, that have led to debates such as the ones presented in the following chapters, suggests another way to read the text in hand: to transform it for your own purposes. Education reform initiatives, for example, are predicated on assumptions that ideas can be put to practice. By extension, U.S. education is based on concepts that curriculum and instruction is a main source of empowerment in a democratic society and can lead to what Thomas Jefferson identified as life, liberty, and the pursuit of happiness, a bedrock notion underscoring that all texts can be read and ideas transformed that lead to revolutions of thoughts and actions in schools and beyond.

A. Jonathan Eakle
The Johns Hopkins University

FURTHER READINGS AND RESOURCES

Adler, M. J. (1982). *The Paideia proposal: An educational manifesto.* New York: Macmillan.

Billings, L., & Fitzgerald, J. (2002). Dialogic discussion and the Paideia seminar. *American Educational Research Journal, 39*(4), 907–941.

can take place through marked physical treatment in some states (i.e., corporeal punishment), sequester, isolation, denial of privileges, pleasures (e.g., recess), and so forth.

Controlling students is not only central to some school programs; programs can more or less restrain teachers. Sometimes the reasons behind such restraints amount to what has been commonly referred to as "teacher bashing." In this respect, Jeffrey R. Herold (1971) believed that teachers and school administrators are "mindless . . . [and] intellectually and emotionally incapable of doing anything different" (than "managerial" pedagogy) and settle for the "easier textbook approach" (another program means) for delivering their lessons (p. 126). Thus, it is believed by some critics that educators should be precisely orchestrated in the content they teach and how they teach it. This stream of thought about transmitting school content aligns with new education trends reported by *The New York Times* in July 2010: robots with artificial intelligence are presently being tested as public school teachers or teacher assistants in several countries including the United States.

The two extremes of total laxity and complete control of school curriculum and instruction presented in previous paragraphs are rarely, if ever, actually put into practice in schools. One such example is Concept-Oriented Reading Instruction, which balances structured learning from printed texts with exploratory learning that engages students (Guthrie, 2008). In this vein, Marcia H. Davis's (The Johns Hopkins University) point essay describes programs—The Johns Hopkins University's Talent Development Middle Grades and High Schools—that take a middle ground between the two extremes. In these programs, a structure exists that provides materials, sequence, and goals that meet state education mandates, while at the same time allowing teachers freedom to be distinctive—for instance, by supplementing the programs with other materials and experiences that they deem important for their individual classrooms.

With teacher quality coming under increasing scrutiny and academic achievement standards and accountability becoming common themes of U.S. education reform, rigorous, if not controlling-type, programs are presently enjoying increased interest in schools and governments. In part, this is because there is some amount of comfort for school, district, and state administrators to adopt programs that are deemed as "best practice" and "what works" by authorities such as the U.S. Department of Education's (ED) Institute of Education Sciences. However, whether curriculum and instruction in education should be more or less programmatic in schools and what counts as education presently remain a matter of degree, philosophy, and local choice and are topics of the following essays.

A. Jonathan Eakle
The Johns Hopkins University

POINT: Marcia H. Davis
The Johns Hopkins University

M any school boards around the United States are mandating the use of instructional programs in their K–12 schools due partly to the push by federal initiatives for scientifically based instruction. These programs are generally run by companies or universities outside of the school district and come with a sizable cost. The programs supply teachers with instructional materials such as books, lesson plans, and student materials, as well as professional development (PD). To promote their programs, many organizations will claim that their program is research-based, ensures the standardization of instruction, promotes good teaching practices, and is proven to increase achievement. But what does this mean for individual schools and teachers? Are programs with standardized curriculum limiting the originality of teachers, or are they freeing teachers to think about other aspects of instruction? What can a teacher gain from a program over what he or she can do independently? This essay details reasons for the adoption of a solid instructional program and describes the benefits it can bring.

PROGRAMMATIC INSTRUCTION AND THE INEXPERIENCED TEACHER

Teachers just starting out in the field of education need as much support as they can get, and administrators would like to see new teachers receive this support. Teaching is one of the few professions that expects a person to be an expert on the first day on the job. Civil engineers, for example, do not design and supervise major projects such as bridges until they have years of experience with simpler designs developed under strict supervision. However, all teachers, whether it is their 1st year or 30th year on the job, are expected to select materials, create engaging lessons, call parents, provide support for troubled students, individualize instruction, motivate students, assess students' previously acquired and learned knowledge, effectively manage the classroom, participate in school meetings and responsibilities, and do much more. New teachers, not to mention seasoned ones, are often swamped by all of these responsibilities, which they are often expected to complete with little guidance or supervision. Having mentors or experienced teachers to guide inexperienced teachers in at least some of these decisions and tasks can help tremendously. Unfortunately, in most school systems, there is little funding for the extensive in-class support and coaching that many inexperienced teachers need. An association with a particular program—especially a program that requires coaching for teachers using the program—will make it more likely that a school can obtain money for a coach.

Even without coaches, having the materials and curriculum determined for them can help inexperienced teachers get started and free up some of their time to develop their styles of teaching and discipline styles and find ways to deal with the myriad tasks that are involved in the field of teaching. Just like the engineer who receives less and less supervision with more responsibility for larger projects, the experienced teacher can be given more freedom to adapt and select curriculum for his or her students.

EXPERIENCED TEACHERS AS INEXPERIENCED CURRICULUM WRITERS

Although many teachers are experienced with the day-to-day job of instructing students, few are experienced in curriculum writing. Curricula in this case not only include lesson plans but also detail the teaching, students' learning and ways of assessing their learning, and how each of these pieces fit together. Curriculum writers of instructional programs need to do the following:

- Write instruction in accordance with state and federal guidelines.

- Support differentiated instruction to meet the needs of a variety of learners.

- Know and include the latest educational research on learning and motivation.

- Set clear and realistic expectations of teachers and students.

- Indicate where and how assessment can be used throughout the year and each lesson.

- Provide passing guides on when the content needs to be delivered so that no skills or content is overlooked.

One of the more challenging tasks of writing curriculum may be aligning it with current research, and this is one of the major marketing claims made about instructional programs. Educational research is ongoing, abundant, and, at times, conflicting. For example, curriculum writers may ask, should a teacher implement more collaboration in their instruction, and, if so, how often and how many students should make up the collaborative group? Trying to sort through it all to come up with the best approach for a specific school can be a daunting task. This is often why major curricula are generally written by a team of researchers and developers working together. This research focus is often supported by federal government initiatives as well. Only programs that are founded on scientifically based research are eligible for funding through federal initiative, as in the case with Reading First, a federal program authorized under No Child Left Behind (NCLB) (2001) that provides grants for early reading instruction in classrooms.

CONSISTENCY AND COOPERATION AMONG TEACHERS

Content and schoolwide programs can help teachers feel connected with other educators by supporting team planning. Teaming within and across content areas can help build this sense of connection as well as give students the confidence that everyone in the school is working toward the same goal. Consistency of content and instructional methods across classrooms creates a unified approach to teaching and learning. For instance, if two geometry teachers are teaching from two different texts from two different perspectives, they will have a more difficult task collaborating on teaching than if they had the same text and program.

Programmatic instruction and teaming can also lead to more consistency among teachers. In most schools, there are both weak and strong teachers, as well as some who fall in between these two extremes. With a program in place, a principal can at least be assured that the teachers are covering the needed content to meet schoolwide and state standards. Further, if many schools within a district are using the same program, then even in cities where there is high mobility rates of students due to lack of stable housing, employment, and so forth, the students may very likely be able to continue where they left off at their last school with academic content and instruction, without much interruption of their education.

SYSTEMATIC INSTRUCTION

Instructional programs can vary in the amount of autonomy teachers are given to make instructional decisions. Programmatic instruction is generally systematic, meaning that it gives teachers a blueprint to follow in order to make pieces of the instruction work together with consistent language and fidelity to the instructional objectives. Just as a blueprint determines quality in the design and construction of a house, instruction is as good as the blueprint the teacher follows. With systematic instruction, the pieces of education—such as the terminology, objectives, connection among topics, use of technology, and assessment—are all written into the blueprint and work together to build learning.

Scripted instructional programs are the most systematic of all programmatic instruction. Scripted instruction refers to curriculum in which the teacher is told what to say during each minute of class time, and it generally ensures that each minute of a class is being fully used. Although this type of instruction began with reading programs, it has begun to be used in other content areas as well. Some of the major scripted programs are easy to recognize and include programs such as Success for All and Direct Instruction. The major reason for scripting lessons is to standardize learning and leave nothing to chance. At first, teachers often feel very programmed and unable to assert creativity into their teaching. However, as they learn the basics of the program, teachers often realize that even while following the script, there are ways to make their instruction more personalized. Research has indicated that teachers will still make adjustments to programs, even when the program is a highly controlled, scripted one.

Although many school boards are leaning toward selecting scripted programs, not all programs are scripted. Teachers are given more autonomy in less restrictive programs, such as The Johns Hopkins University's Talent Development Middle Grades and High Schools programs, which give teachers freedom to be unique and to supplement with other materials and experiences for their students. For example, in the reading program of Talent Development called Strategic Reading, English teachers can select from a large range of books and materials for their students and are given recommendations on background knowledge instruction, vocabulary building, and discussion questions. With less restriction, teachers are more likely to buy in to the program.

It is generally believed that no program will be able to fit all students. Therefore, teachers and administrators need to choose a program that will be the best possible match with their students, and they should take into account the amount of autonomy teachers are given to adapt it for individual students. When choosing a program, teachers and administrators should look for programs that give the teacher some autonomy, find a program that matches the particular students' needs, keep in mind that teachers will make adjustments and allow room for that, be prepared to offer teachers a lot of support while they are learning to teach with a new program, and include all partners in selecting a program.

PROFESSIONAL DEVELOPMENT

Another benefit of programs is the addition of well-thought-out PD. School-based professional development is often pulled together by experienced teachers and administrators with little or no PD experience, and it is often haphazardly put together. This quick PD is sometimes jokingly referred to as "drive-by PD," in that a new topic is presented to the teachers each week or month with little or no time to contemplate the idea or connect it with the other topics. Although the teachers may be very successful in their profession, being able to implement a successful PD for an entire school takes different skills and knowledge.

Effective PD is job-embedded, connected with the other topics in the entire year of PD, and comprehensive, and it fosters reflective practice and includes time for teachers to make changes to their instruction, which generally takes many weeks or months to reflect and perfect. Those in charge of instructional programs often use district-level specialists skilled in PD who not only deliver PD but also oversee a teacher or school to make sure the program is being run smoothly and with fidelity and to find solutions for teachers when they have difficulty implementing the program. Some programs hire coaches to visit teachers on a set schedule to provide intensive job-embedded PD during the year. Other programs may even include methods that can be tailored to meet the needs of teachers not working directly with the course materials. Or teachers may also learn methods that they can then transfer to their standards-based courses.

Also, at times, with a program comes training for school administrators. A school's administrative leadership is in charge of assigning time for instructional decisions such as team planning time and extended class periods for specific content areas. In school-based PD, administrators are often not involved and therefore may not understand the importance of a specific intervention, instructional procedure, and so on. Problems occur when principals and staff do not understand the importance of practices in a program. For example, if a school saw the necessity and value of weekly team planning meetings, a principal who may not understand the importance of these meetings might either shorten the time teachers have in their meetings or carelessly schedule assemblies and testing time that interfere with the meetings. An administrator who has been invited to the training and assured of the importance of team meetings may very well hold that time sacred for the teachers. Programs offering PD for administration sometimes also provide the administration with information about tools for supporting teachers and evaluating the implementation of the program.

SCHOOL TURNAROUND

The schools that desperately need instructional programs are those not making mandated adequate yearly progress (AYP) goals and that need major reforms to change. The statistics show a grim picture for the fate of many adolescent students across the nation in these low-performing schools. By the time students reach ninth grade in these schools, they may already have formed habits of irregular attendance, problem behavior, and low performance. Often, teachers and administrators blame poor home conditions and students' behavior for their lack of success with their students without considering what they can do to improve. Perhaps many of these administrators and teachers have run out of answers.

One method by which schools have succeeded in meeting progress goals has been the adoption of a research-based school program that has shown to work in similar schools. There are many ways programs can help schools turn around their student achievement. First, many of these schools have a large proportion of students who are struggling academically. Without immediate interventions, these students will eventually drop out once they reach high school. Help from a program can include curriculum that gives students "double doses" of the subject area content they need to learn; transition courses that reteach basic skills and content that is needed for upper-level academics; and twilight school (ones with evening classes) for older students. Further, many of these struggling students thrive on the day-to-day structure that is provided by systematic instruction.

Second, programs can help schools find ways to minimize student misbehaviors such as poor attendance and classroom disturbances by helping teachers and administration to implement intensive interventions at the student and classroom level, as well as global interventions related to school climate and structure. Third, many programs will offer support and advice for finding ways to connect with the family and community of the students in their schools to enhance instruction. These partnerships are critical for getting students to understand the importance of staying in school. Finally, many larger national programs offer conferences, Listservs, and webinars where teachers from across the country can come together to talk about issues that affect all of their schools.

With the help of programs, many schools have had much success changing the achievement rate of their students in even the most challenging school districts. Adopting a program that focuses both on curriculum to improve achievement as well as student, class, and school interventions not only makes sense for the school and the students it serves but it also indicates to the community that changes are being made. The What Works Clearinghouse website established by the U.S. ED Institute of Education Sciences summarizes the research on the effectiveness of many programs and should be examined before deciding on any program.

CONCLUSION

There are many reasons to choose an instructional program for a school or district from the materials that are provided for PD. However, with so many different programs, teachers and administrators need to consider if the program fits their particular students, teachers, and the wider community; what other support and help comes with the program; and how best to gain teacher and other stakeholder approval.

COUNTERPOINT: Judith T. Lysaker
Purdue University

With the enactment of NCLB (2001) legislation, programmatic instruction has increased significantly and has homogenized and standardized American schooling. The use of scripted programs in particular has gained popularity with school districts and administrators interested in raising student performance on standardized tests and avoiding the punitive results of failing to meet AYP goals. Though the degree of control in programs differs significantly and the weight of the mandates about their implementation mitigates the consequences of their implementation, programmatic instruction may derail teaching and learning in important ways. In this counterpoint essay, the argument is advanced that programmatic instruction has the potential to disrupt a sensitive interrelated ecosystem of relationships in which learning occurs. This essay first describes some of the relationships in this ecosystem and suggests ways in which the condition of intersubjectivity within these relationships fosters both responsive instruction and meaningful learning. Next, the entry considers ways in which programmatic instruction can disrupt a classroom's ecosystem of relationships, leading to the erosion of these same intersubjective conditions and disrupted learning. The essay concludes with a brief outline of the larger moral implications of this relational disruption.

ECOSYSTEM OF RELATIONSHIPS AMONG STUDENTS, TEACHERS, AND CURRICULUM

Sociocultural learning theory has long demonstrated that people learn as they jointly participate with others and with the materials of their culture through value-laden sign systems; most commonly, it is known that language learning is mediated by and situated in a complex ecosystem of human relationships. It follows that learning is continuously afforded or constrained by the quality and kinds of relationships available to the learner. A thorough articulation of all the relationships within this ecosystem is beyond the scope of this essay. Thus, the focus will be on three reciprocal relationships through which and within which learning takes place: (1) the teacher–learner relationship; (2) the learner–curriculum relationship; and (3) the teacher–curriculum relationship and its antecedent, the teacher–subject relationship. It is the accomplishment of inter-subjectivity in each of these relationships that makes learning possible. It is these relationships that are most directly disrupted by overly programmed instruction and that likely lessen opportunities for learning.

Teacher–Learner Relationship

Among the relationships that are central to the ecosystem of classroom life, one of the most obvious is the teacher–learner relationship. The teacher–learner relationship is the central context for student learning; it is within this relation-ship that instruction occurs. Sociocultural learning theory often foregrounds this relationship with the notion of scaffolding, a widely used way of describing how a teacher mediates a learning task for a student (Vygotsky, 1978). However, it is important to consider the possibility that a teacher's ability to successfully scaffold—or, in other words, support—student learning depends upon the relationship between the teacher and the student.

Teachers typically adopt a stance of inquiry as they consider how to scaffold student learning. They bring to mind student learning histories, envision stu-dent future growth, and imagine experiences and materials that will provide the context within which to situate their learning. The teacher's desire to know the student and the resultant knowledge of that student and his or her needs, interests, and sensibilities allow the teacher to make informed instructional decisions, carefully choosing materials and experiences as well as calibrating the talk and activities that support student learning. This scaffolding might also be viewed as an act of care in which a teacher seeks to "apprehend the real-ity of the other" and to respond to that reality in a way that promotes good for the other (Noddings, 2003, p. 14). This description suggests that scaffolding is not simply a straightforward set of cognitively determined actions on the part of the teacher. Nor is the student's subsequent learning a straightforward cognitive response. Rather, as Addison Stone has suggested, scaffolding is a subtle interpersonal process, and these interpersonal aspects have consequences for learning (Lysaker, McCormick, & Brunette, 2005). This implies that teachers may need to be personally and subjectively present in order to establish the exchanges between and among the subjectivities of the students and teacher that are the preconditions of meaningful learning and personal transformation.

One way, thus, to understand these consequences is that the presence of emotional qualities results in interpersonal openness making a rich exchange of intersubjectivities possible. In other words, learning may depend on a personal relationship between the student and the teacher and a disruption in that relationship may impede learning.

Learner–Curriculum Relationship

The qualities of trust and attachment in the teacher–student relationship have implications for how students engage in the curricular endeavor as well. In addition to increasing the likelihood that students will allow their own subjectivities to emerge more freely, enhancing the intersubjective relationships they have with their teachers, students may be more willing to be known, to be present in the learning task, to enact a certain vulnerability within the learning event. This emergence of the students' subjectivities breathes life into curricular activity; it becomes personally relevant and meaningful. Moreover, the emergence of student subjectivities leads to the vital presence of difference within the curricular endeavor. That is to say the quality of student–teacher relationships giving rise to the articulation of student subjectivities results in a multivocal, nonhomogeneous classroom environment. Such an environment might be said to be inherently dialogic with contrasts between self and others continually noticed, negotiated, and internalized. From one point of view, the different personal perspectives within the classroom might be described as "simultaneity of difference," which promotes personal transformation (Bakhtin, 1935/1981). Combined, the teacher's caring, inquiring, relational stance, and articulation of nonhomogenized individual student subjectivities promote individually relevant and culturally responsive instruction. Both individual attention and culturally responsive instruction have been shown to promote learning, particularly for students who have experienced learning difficulties or who are marginalized by sociocultural differences.

Like the teacher–curriculum relationship, the learner–curriculum relationship consists of cognitive and affective connections to the tasks and materials of the curricular endeavor. And also like the teacher–curriculum relationship, when a student has a "good" *relationship with the curriculum* and subject area materials, there is a sense of connection among these dimensions. The student has some familiarity with the subject that is being examined and the tasks or texts that link him or her to the current curricular demands. In this case, the learner is *positioned within* the curricular endeavor, not distanced from it; the possibility of an intersubjective relationship between the student and the curriculum exists. This contributes to a sense that the curriculum is relevant and that learning is possible and appealing.

In addition, students have a stance in regard to the curriculum that might be characterized as either inquiring or receptive. When students have an inquiring stance toward a subject, they actively pursue it; there is a sense of motion toward the subject that is being studied, which is fueled by curiosity and the desire to know. Importantly, the learner's position influences this stance. A sense of connection and ownership of the curricular endeavor leads to a desire to know—that is, a sense of inquiry that promotes active engagement in the curricular endeavor. Students seek intersubjective relationships with the subject area topics. On the other hand, students may have a receptive stance that is static and without the desire to know. In such cases, there is a sense of being positioned outside the curricular endeavor; it may seem foreign and distant because the student lacks familiarity with the tasks or texts. As a result, learners may be less connected and less likely to be engaged. For those learners, the possibility of intersubjective connections within the curricular endeavor seem remote and without meaning.

Teacher–Curriculum Relationship

Alongside the teacher–learner and learner–curriculum relationships, there are perhaps less obvious yet important ones. In this section of the present essay, these less obvious and important relationships are detailed—those between the teacher and curriculum and its antecedent: the teacher subject–relationship.

The teacher–curriculum relationship consists of the cognitive and affective connections between the teacher and the learning tasks, as well as the use of language, education materials, and time. When teachers engage in active curricular construction, they often begin with a sense of inquiry about their students and the subject matter at hand. This sense of inquiry is both an intellectual and moral stance as teachers consider how to design responsive curriculum that will support student learning. The process of curricular construction demands complex thinking and a command of subject area matters as well as imagination and care. It is teachers' own thinking—their knowledge, feelings, and hunches—that give rise to the activities, materials, and the use of language and time associated with curricular implementation. Through this personal and constructive process, teachers form a sense of ownership of and commitment to the curricular endeavor; they establish a relationship with the curriculum that then becomes a part of the classroom's relational ecosystem and a critical resource for students.

In addition to the teacher–curriculum relationship, teachers have relationships with their subject area material. Consider history teachers: They know dates, events, and the consequences of events that have meaning for them. This knowledge may evoke strong feelings and lead them to form particular beliefs about humanity. They have read biographies, studied names and places, and been enamored by a particularly eventful lecture; they have developed a love for history. In fact, teachers who care about the subjects in this way have developed a kind of intersubjectivity with their discipline. They meet that subject on an interpersonal plane in which dialogic exchanges between the voices encountered in the study of the subject contribute to the ongoing growth of their knowledge and experience of that subject. Indeed, as Parker Palmer (1983) suggested, the relationship that teachers have with subjects is what students most profoundly grasp in the learning context. In this way, teachers' relationships with their curricula and their subjects mediate and shape students' relationships with that same curriculum and the subject matter that is being investigated.

PROGRAMMED CURRICULUM AND THE DISRUPTION OF THE ECOSYSTEM OF RELATIONSHIPS

Now that the ecosystem of relationships within which learning occurs and arguments for the importance of intersubjectivity within these relationships for student learning has been laid out, the question of what might happen to these relationships with the implementation of programmed curricula will be addressed. The first relationship that is most obviously disrupted by programmatic curriculum is the teacher's relationship to the curriculum. First, because a programmed curriculum is produced by external experts, the teacher's sense of inquiry and subsequent intellectual and creative activity are cut short. Teachers no longer engage in prolonged consideration of important curricular questions about responding to student learning needs such as what kinds of language, activity, and texts might support learning. Instead, the program largely replaces this interpersonal process; the identity of the teacher is displaced to make room for the talk, action, and ideology of a program. The teacher's sense of connection to the curriculum, ways of knowing, sense of competence, curiosity, and caring about the subject as well as a regard for the curricular endeavor as interesting and important are disrupted. This weakens the teacher's relationship with the curriculum and dilutes the potent learning that might come from bringing this relationship into the classroom as a resource for student growth.

A second rupture that may occur when overly programmatic instruction is implemented is the relationship between the student and the curriculum. The students' learning histories, backgrounds, interests, and even language are no longer the starting point of curricular construction and instructional response. This shifts students' relationships with the curriculum in significant ways. Because teachers are no longer building curriculum as a response to students, they are positioned outside of the curricular endeavor, creating a sense of distance between who they are, what they know, and how they learn and what the curriculum asks of them. This positioning of students outside of the curricular endeavor promotes a receptive, passive stance. This is likely to disrupt any possibility for the development of intersubjectivity within the planned learning events of the curriculum.

This claim is supported in the literature on student motivation. As demonstrated through John Guthrie's (2008) work, students' interests in materials, topics, and learning tasks increase the likeliness of student engagement in those tasks. In programmed curricula, the learners' interests are absent from the curricular process, likely reducing the degree of engagement in learning. Student self-efficacy, also linked to learning motivation, is similarly diminished by the disruption of the learner–curriculum relationship. The distance that exists between the curricular task and the learning needs of the students, which is the result of a prescribed set of learning tasks, may significantly reduce students' sense of self-efficacy as they approach tasks that seem unrelated to their own abilities. The teacher's ability to scaffold learning through responsive individual instruction is truncated by rigid prescription to particular learning tasks. In a related way, Allan Wigfield and his colleagues have discovered that students' willingness to engage in learning in the first place is dependent on a sense of self-efficacy. Further, research on student choice suggests that when students choose curricula materials, they gain a sense of ownership that may mediate both interest and self-efficacy (Lysaker, 1997). The reduction or omission of student choice in programmatic instruction would likely further reduce student motivation.

Finally, programmed instruction may damage the relationship between teachers and students. Programmed instruction changes the teacher's presence in several ways, altering what he or she "brings" to students. Teacher interaction with students is no longer a spontaneous exchange but a performative act originating outside of the teacher. In this way, teaching and learning are robbed of the intersubjective potential inherent when teachers construct curriculum in response to their knowledge and care of their students.

CONCLUSION

This essay advanced the argument that curriculum should be less rather than more programmatic. The overarching problem with programmatic approaches to curriculum is that they significantly disrupt the ecosystem of relationships upon which learning depends and within which learning occurs. These relationships—the teacher–learner/learner–teacher, teacher–curriculum, and learner–curriculum relationships—are the sites of rich, dialogic exchange and intersubjectivity that encourage learning and transformation of the person.

Disruption of these relationships through the insertion of an authoritative distant other in the form of predetermined tasks, prescribed use of language, and the control of time and materials diminishes the emergence of both teachers' and students' subjectivities within the curricular endeavor, all of which lead to more homogenized, less dialogic, and thus impoverished discourse in schools.

This, of course, suggests social and moral consequences of programmatic curricula as well. First, because programs are largely constructed and produced by those within dominant discourse communities, they perpetuate current cultural norms that marginalize whole populations of less privileged learners. Second, by controlling such value-laden aspects of human exchange as language and decisions about the use of time and materials (e.g., "How long can I spend with this student? What book might be of interest and support the developing strategy use of this reader?"), programs replace the ethos of a teacher with the ethos of a program. Arguably, the consequences of this replacement are the reproduction of the ethos of the program producers and perhaps, more importantly, the removal of the moral grounding of the teacher from the classroom and from the lives of students.

Programmatic curricula may rupture the ecosystem of relationships within which students develop vitally important human qualities. It risks reducing the opportunities for students to develop their own identities as well as an awareness and valuing of those identities. It can limit students' opportunities to know others in authentic ways and to become aware of and value difference. And, in fact, programmatic instruction has the potential to threaten academic engagement and hence academic accomplishment. Are we willing to risk these reductions in human potential at a time when globalization will likely increasingly demand a generation of people who know themselves; seek out others in empathetic, caring ways; and regard the world with a vibrant sense of inquiry?

FURTHER READINGS AND RESOURCES

Bakhtin, M. M. (1981). *The dialogic imagination.* Austin: University of Texas Press. (Original work published 1935)

Balfanz, R. (2009). Can the American high school become an avenue of advancement for all? *Future of Children, 19*(1), 17–36.

Borman, G. D., Slavin, R. E., & Cheung, A. C. K. (2005). The national randomized field trial of success for all: Second-year outcomes. *American Educational Research Journal, 42*(4), 673–696.

Cole, M. (1996). *Cultural psychology: A once and future discipline.* Cambridge, MA: Harvard University Press.

Duncan-Owens, D. (2009). Scripted reading programs: Fishing for success. *Principal, 88*(3), 26–29.

Foucault, M. (1975). *Discipline and punish: The birth of the prison* (A. Sheridan, Trans.). New York: Vintage.

Guthrie, J. T. (Ed.). (2008). *Engaging adolescents in reading.* Thousand Oaks, CA: Corwin.

Herold, J. R. (1971). The prospects for the remaking of American education. *Education, 92,* 125–130.

Lysaker, J. T. (1997). Learning to read from self-selected texts: The book choices of six first graders. In C. K. Kincer, K. A. Hinchman, & D. J. Leu (Eds.), *Inquiries in literacy theory and practice: The forty-sixth yearbook of the National Reading Conference* (pp. 273–282). Chicago: National Reading Conference.

Lysaker, J. T., McCormick, K., & Brunette, C. (2005). Hope, happiness, and reciprocity: A thematic analysis of preservice teachers' relationships with their reading buddies. *Reading Research and Instruction, 44*(2), 21–45.

Noddings, N. (2003). *Caring: A feminine approach to ethics and moral education* (2nd ed.). Berkeley: University of California Press.

Palmer, P. (1983). *To know as we are known.* New York: Harper and Row.

Scherer, M. (1998). The discipline of hope: A conversation with Herb Kohl. *Educational Leadership, 56,* 8–13.

Vygotsky, L. S. (1978). *Mind in society: The development of higher psychological processes.* Cambridge, MA: Harvard University Press.

COURT CASES AND STATUTES

No Child Left Behind Act of 2001, 20 U.S.C.A. §§ 6301 *et seq.*

Should teachers have a voice in statewide curricula decisions?

POINT: Jennifer Jones, *Radford University*
COUNTERPOINT: Stergios G. Botzakis,
The University of Tennessee

OVERVIEW

The question guiding this chapter involves the delicate balance of governance and democracy in U.S. education. Democracy is a main concept frequently referenced in U.S. political and social life in general and at public education institutions in particular. Yet, in public school curricula, instruction in democracy varies. In some classes such as civics, democracy is described with powerful keywords, such as equality and justice, but is not given the same emphasis as other core subject areas, such as math and reading. At other times, democracy is the topic of intensive professional development (PD) activities for teachers, such as in James Madison University's "We the People" curriculum, which is taken up by some public schools. Even more varied are the ways democracies are put to systemic practice, which involves governance in and by institutions (see School Governance volume of this series for further reading).

With representational democracy on its sleeves, public education in the United States during most of the nation's history has been a matter of governance. School board members are elected by and represent the people of their communities. They hold meetings in public where parents, teachers, school administrators, and other stakeholders can be involved in decisions that face their local schools. This type of grassroots governance leads Michael Resnick and Anne Bryant, officers of the National School Board Association, to claim that school boards are "living democracies." And on their faces, local school boards and their intimate ties to their communities can certainly support the notion of democracy in U.S. education.

However, during recent years, local control of schools has been increasingly wrested from the hands of locals, especially grassroots teachers, and centralized in layers of hegemonic structure. Part of this layering of control came about because of civil rights issues, such as the landmark *Brown v. Board of Education* (1954) ruling, which is lauded for its significant impact on equality and dignity but, according to some people such as the so-called southern Democrats of the time, gave undue control to the federal government on local education issues—in this case, school desegregation. At the same time, the local voices of educators and other community leaders were diminished in light of larger, global issues, such as those associated with the Cold War and the need to produce students who could meet the competitive challenges of the day, such as producing scientific knowledge beyond that of the Soviets.

The top-down influence of the federal government on local schools has continued, in large part, as a result of federal funding. For example, and as shown through many essays in the present book series, monies are granted, or not, to state governments if they accept federal conditions to focus their curriculum and instruction on particular topics and if they target specific benchmark achievement requirements. In part because of these economic issues so too have state departments of education increasingly exercised control over local school boards and their public schools. For example, in some cases only state-sponsored curriculum programs can be enacted in public schools. One such program is *Success for All* (Slavin & Madden, 2001), which, although its effectiveness in student achievement is supported by rigorous randomized studies, is often criticized as hinging on "scripted instruction." In this vein, what has come to be known as "direct instruction" classroom curricula involves clear and precise scripts of what a teacher says, when she says it, and to whom.

Direct instructional approaches are not new, but they have enjoyed resurgences in popularity under the education reform movement of the past decade. In one sense, this is because some schools have not been able to close ongoing achievement gaps among economic groups, and to mechanize instruction with a program deemed effective by scientific means is appealing to educators and administrators who are in the line of fire if their schools do not meet mandated goals. For comparable reasons, traditional teacher education programs are becoming targets for school reformists. Further, the fear of change such as job and benefit loss may result in widespread changes of curriculum and instruction in public schools but not necessarily change for the better.

Fear can also silence opposition and reduce resistance—a counterpoint to democracy but a reality in institutions such as U.S. businesses, governments, and schools. Take, for instance, the diminished voice of teacher unions as teachers experienced reduced benefits, declining work conditions with, for example, class sizes as large as 60 students to 1 teacher, and so forth, since the recent economic downturn of the U.S. economy, which has had particular consequences on state and local government spending in general and schools in particular because of the large proportion of state budgets that are devoted to schooling (as high as 1 in 3 state revenue dollars).

On the other hand, the reform effort could take another turn if teachers' voices were amplified in a democratically inspired environment. Antonio Gramsci (2005) suggested that pedagogy perhaps more democratic than what has been seen in recent U.S. schools could come about as it did in a European school experiment of the past century, which was a "reaction against all types of formula, against dogmatic teaching, against the tendency to make education into something mechanical . . . On the intellectual plane, too, their [student] progress is substantially greater than that of pupils from ordinary schools" (p. 143).

In light of democratic principles and the education reform effort, through the following essays, the issues of teacher voices are taken up. Speaking from a position of teacher experience, Jennifer Jones (Radford University) argues that it is only from the most practical bedrock, the teacher/student/community relationship and bringing teachers' experience to the design of curriculum and instruction that the most important purposes of education can be achieved. Stergios G. Botzakis (The University of Tennessee) takes the other side of the issue, but unlike the current reformists he turns the issue back to the democratic local level and highlights the academic successes of such a focus: Finland's grassroots schooling model and its resulting superior student achievement. Through this, he implies that actual and sustained education reform could be achieved by abandoning the current top-down structures that are driving the reform movement and returning power to teachers and other educators at the local level.

A. Jonathan Eakle
The Johns Hopkins University

POINT: Jennifer Jones
Radford University

Statewide curricula design and accompanying assessments have been on the forefront of American education for decades culminating most recently with No Child Left Behind (NCLB) (2001) legislation, which has heightened the political adoption of standardized curricula and assessment at the state level. As a result of NCLB, and in an effort to adhere to its standards-based requirements, many states have imposed instructional mandates upon schools and teachers. Such mandates include standardized curricula, high-stakes testing, and the use of research-based textbook adoption. Teachers are often asked to teach to fidelity with these materials and curricula (Dewitz, Jones, & Leahy, 2009), and pressures are mounting with federal initiatives such as Race to the Top (RTT), whose funding involves the development of common state standards and high quality assessments to measure the standards. Teacher effectiveness serves as a key component of these initiatives. Regardless of the title placed on it, standards-based curricula and assessment coexist as a main engine driving the decisions currently being made by state departments of education.

Sadly, thus far these large education initiatives have produced meager results. With increased teacher participation and amplified teacher voices in state curriculum decisions, these insufficient results could change.

Indeed, the somewhat political effort to improve the quality of instruction across the United States requires the collective expertise of many stakeholders. Department of Education (ED) experts, district and school administrators, higher education professionals and researchers, and administrators often comprise such decision-making bodies. Inclusion of their voices in the process is logical, as representation of key stakeholders and knowledgeable professionals is necessary for the creation of effective curricula. But where do teachers fit in this process? Too often ignored, teachers should have an active seat at the statewide curricula decision-making table. Teachers' voices should no longer be silenced by bureaucrats who are politically driven and hold little knowledge about learning, curriculum design, and instruction.

In the 1980s, research efforts often focused on teacher participation in decision making, as well as teacher empowerment and voice, showcasing the importance of teacher participation in education processes at many levels within the school. It is important to consider the findings of this body of research when taking the decision-making process to the next level in the

MARK & HELEN OSTERLIN LIBRARY
NORTHWESTERN MICHIGAN COLLEGE
TRAVERSE CITY, MICHIGAN 49686-3061
Reference Book - Room Use Only

system—the state level. A survey conducted in the 1980s gleaned that teachers were rarely asked to participate in key decision-making arenas such as evaluation or design of curriculum at the school level (Conley, 1991). Teacher unions such as the National Education Association (NEA) and the American Federation of Teachers have long served as vehicles for teachers' voices in the shaping of curriculum and policy decisions in districts, states, and even at the national level. The importance of teachers' roles in decision making regarding curricula at the state level cannot be underestimated. Research on teacher participation conducted in the 1980s and 1990s indicates that teacher participation in decision-making processes at the school level appears to be instrumental to school outcome results. In sum, and as detailed in subsequent sections of this essay, for several compelling reasons teachers' voices must be represented in statewide efforts to design and revise curricula if positive results in U.S. public education are to occur.

TEACHERS ARE CONTENT AND PRACTICE EXPERTS

With a minimum of 4 years' college education in child development and learning, as well as specific subject area domains, educators are well equipped to offer a voice of expertise in the design of statewide curricula. In fact, many teachers are educated well beyond 4 years, holding graduate level degrees in various specialty areas in education such as literacy, technology, and special education. The recent NEA's *Status of the American Public School Teacher* report shares demographic information about our nation's teachers via survey findings. In 2006, 36% of teacher respondents held a bachelor's degree, and 60% had earned an advanced degree. Such expertise should not be ignored when decisions are made regarding state-level curricula.

Combine teacher subject area knowledge with knowledge acquired through classroom and other experiences and the result is that teachers not only have intellectual expertise to bring to the decision-making table but powerful elements to share about the practical application of education research and theory to students' learning. A median of 15 years' teaching experience was reported in the NEA survey, with 56% of teachers continuing to add to their knowledge through earning further college credit during the past 3 years. In other words, teachers are *in line professionals* and have the keen ability to consider what curriculum decisions are appropriate for the classroom from a content area and learning perspective, as well as which decisions will actually be implemented in the real day-to-day world of teaching from a practical viewpoint. Simply put, educators are "street level bureaucrats" whose voices cannot be dismissed (Conley, 1991, p. 240).

In their research on parent and teacher voices in standardized testing environments, Mary Alice Barksdale-Ladd and Karen F. Thomas (2000) found that teachers in general tend to voice support and offer solid rationales for the implementation of standards and assessments to improve education. In a collection of interviews with teachers, the researchers found no teachers who downplayed a standards-based curriculum. However, many teachers observed conflicts between district or state standards and their expert knowledge of child development. In other words, teachers recognized that often standards set by state-level officials do not exhibit developmentally appropriate curriculum decisions. Teachers, who generally support the use of standards and recognize the merit of standards-based education, also know how to apply standards in a developmentally appropriate way. As in line professionals, they are equipped to know what content needs to be taught and how to frame standards in a developmentally appropriate way designed to promote the best possible learning and results for students.

TOP-DOWN MODELS ARE INEFFECTIVE

If schools can be conceived as entrepreneurial organizations, or even as businesses of learning, students should be recognized as the clients. States operate as the overarching companies who at their helm sit the chief executive officers or state superintendents. Administrators, districtwide and schoolwide, are the managers, and teachers are the in line professionals who, like equivalent skilled service workers in a company, deliver material and engage with the clients on a day-to-day basis (Conley, 1991). Teachers are key to the success of the organization as a whole, as well as paramount to the successes of the clients the institution serves. Furthermore, in the business world, *in line employee participation* is highly valued and deemed critical in making management decisions. Fear and intimidation, which are archaic business practices embraced through top-down organizational models, result in an unhappy and unproductive workforce. In the best companies, top-down models have been replaced by participative management models, where in line workers are a part of decision making and accountability measures. Workers play valuable roles, and without worker input, businesses wither. Increasing employee ownership increases production, with added evidence of job satisfaction. Happy workers are productive workers in the business world. Giving teachers a voice in the decision-making process embraces participative business models that are proven to be successful on various levels.

Indeed, teachers are the key to the success of the business of learning, and ignoring teachers' expertise in curriculum design and student needs corresponds to an automobile company ignoring trained engineers about the design of their vehicles. Such engineers also share responsibility and account-ability for the success, safety, and reliability of the product; the same is true of teachers. When their voices are added to the decision-making processes at the state level, they become shareholders, officially responsible and accountable for the successful and reliable outcomes of the learners who they teach and know better than anyone else in the school system.

Shared decision-making models are often used in the social service arenas and in the medical field. For example, doctors and patients work *together* using research-based evidence to make decisions about treatments for patients. In the social work area, social workers collaborate with families, doctors, and other professionals and resources to make the best decisions for families and children. The research fruits of these fields also reveal that successful, produc-tive decision making is grounded in shared power and shared leadership among all members of decision-making teams. Shared power and leadership is a concept often ignored by states when designing new standards-based curri-cula. Teachers are rarely involved in the creation of states' curriculum stan-dards and policies. And in cases when teachers are invited to serve on such committees, they report that their participation merely served as token repre-sentative (Barksdale-Ladd & Thomas, 2000).

In a world of education that is increasingly flat, as well as business-driven and politically influenced, teachers must exercise voice in statewide curriculum decisions. There is evidence that top-down models used in decision making in education are not effective nor are those models helpful for teachers (Barksdale-Ladd & Thomas, 2000). Heightened pressure often evoked on teachers by top-down models is often detrimental to both teacher efficacy and students' success. Many contemporary successful business models do not adhere to such top-down approaches; rather collaborative, team-oriented approaches to man-agement and decision making serve as a route to success. The same could be true when decisions are made regarding education curricula at the state level if teachers were more involved.

Like successful business models, the research of Ernest Boyer demonstrates that school leadership frameworks that also highlight collaborative approaches to school management, rather than those of top-down models, are most suc-cessful in regard to student success as well as teacher participation and job sat-isfaction. As well, observations of leadership roles exercised across three school-based, shared decision-making teams, revealed that the team that exhibited characteristics of a top-down model, with one administrator dominating the process and accessing little input from other members of the team, was the most ineffective (Meyers, Meyers & Gelzheiser, 2001). Successful schools operate as democratic community organizations and successful classrooms as democratic environments where all key stakeholders have a voice. If these are the models supported by research at the school and classroom levels, states should closely consider using such models and involve teachers in democratic decision-making processes surrounding curriculum and assessment as well. In a nutshell, by giving teachers a voice in curriculum decisions, states would be aligned with progressive business models that are far ahead of the ones now used by their antiquated public education institutions.

TEACHERS ARE PROFESSIONALS

Teachers have specialized training in subject area knowledge and how to teach it, and they know the qualities, needs, and differences of children more than other stakeholders at the statewide level. They possess substantive knowledge, technical expertise, and firsthand knowledge about student learning. Such vast knowledge positions teachers well to influence the professionalization of schools and negotiate the complex work of instruction across states.

Notable respect for content and practical expertise is awarded to most other professionals in American society. Medical professionals, those in the legal and judicial field, scientists and engineers, to name a few, obtain the utmost respect from the American public. However, those in the field of education, our teachers, do not often share such esteemed respect and value from the general public arena. Perhaps this is because everyone in American society has attended school, at least to some degree. Familiarity with the institution of education may lead American citizens to think that they know how to "do school." Conversely, the content and practical application of knowledge required by other professions is in comparison largely unfamiliar, unknown, or mysterious to the general public, placing such professionals at a higher level on the esteemed profession ladder in American culture.

Whatever the reason, teachers *are* professionals with specific skill sets and practical knowledge and experience. States must acknowledge and use teacher expertise on state-level curriculum committees. In doing so, states concurrently recognize teachers as professionals.

Nonetheless, the perspectives and opinions of elected and appointed officials on decision-making bodies are the ones that have power. Moreover, they often control much of the money for education matters and view their ideas as more valuable than those of teachers. Such actions vividly highlight problems with the system and the perceptions of teachers as professionals.

Licensing boards and committees of many other professions, including those choosing the content of licensing examinations and continuing education requirements, include the representation and the voices of members of the profession. For example, in the medical profession, examination and licensure boards are comprised of medical experts, including those engaged in research, those in administrative positions within higher education institutions, as well as those practicing medicine in clinical settings. Like other professionals, teachers should serve as decisionmakers regarding the curricula that they teach.

ACCOUNTABILITY REQUIRES PARTICIPATION

We live in an era where high-stakes testing is at an all-time high. Accountability serves as a hot topic in education and is directly connected to the issue of teacher voices in curriculum and instruction. There is some debate in regard to which stakeholders should be held accountable for the results of high-stakes testing. Parties deemed responsible for results may include states as a whole, as well as their districts, schools, principals, teachers, and students. Yet, many state or district systems target teachers as the ones accountable for school achievement in either direct or indirect ways. For example, testing results are often disseminated in highly public arenas. Testing results are shared with the general public highlighting statewide pass rates, district-level results throughout individual states, and even individual school teacher-level results via mass media sources. Indirectly, educators are forced out of the teaching profession as a result of such public displays of results. In addition, direct measures of accountability that reveal less than desirable student achievement may lead to threats of or actual cuts in teacher salaries and the loss of their jobs. Such measures hold teachers as responsible parties, as well as targets, placing them on the forefront of school and state accountability issues. If direct or even indirect accountability remedies are to be exercised, teachers as professionals encompass the right to have an active voice in decision making regarding the curricula, the composition of the tests that measure their achievement as well as that of their students, and other conditions for which they are being judged. Allowing a place for teachers' voices around these issues at the state level simply reflects professional courtesy and respect.

It is important to acknowledge that teacher participation is a necessary but not sufficient component in statewide decision making on curriculum and instruction matters. Moreover, while teacher participation alone is not the answer, teacher voices are necessary to provide instructional vision for curriculum design in an effort to improve student learning and performance. Teachers participating in state-level decision making must be knowledgeable and must demonstrate exemplary dedication to the profession and have tangible results to prove it. Further, states must be cautious to *actively engage* teachers on such decision-making committees, rather than having teachers serve as mere place-holders for curriculum and policy that have already been formed at higher levels in the education system.

Using teachers as mere token representatives on decision-making panels would hinder the likelihood that meaningful curricula would be implemented successfully at the classroom level. Statewide decision-making bodies surrounding curriculum decisions must have adequate funding, resources, and reasonable timetables in order to ensure quality (Conley, 1991). Including teachers in statewide decision-making processes regarding curricula recognizes them as professionals, increases the likelihood that standards and assessments are developmentally and content appropriate, and embraces collaborative models for leadership in the business of education. Teacher participation in statewide decision making surrounding curriculum design creates greater teacher accountability. The degree of power held by teachers can indeed, make a positive difference in how well schools and classrooms operate. Change cannot come from outside the education system; it must evolve from within, from those who know the classroom and its students the best—our teachers.

COUNTERPOINT: Stergios G. Botzakis
The University of Tennessee

The question of who should have power in curricular choices is loaded with political implications. This question affects multiple groups of people and leads to controversies such as the adoption of teacher-proof direct instruction materials that undermine the teaching profession, vouchers for private and charter schools that teach more effectively, and what should be considered common knowledge and essential skills to be a citizen. Additionally, "policy entrepreneurs" (Salinger, 2007) may also take advantage of policy changes in order to fund their own initiatives or sell their products and services. Questions of curricular policy, with all of their outcomes, necessitate the inclusion of multiple shareholders in decision making, ranging from students to teachers, parents, administrators, employers, and politicians, but for the sake of argument in the present essay, one party will be removed from consideration: teachers. Although teachers are singled out, it should be emphasized that the position taken in the following pages involves active classroom teachers' role in statewide curriculum decisions. Importantly, building successful organizations requires fostering talent from within (Abrams, 2011), with teachers ideally becoming the administrators and policymakers who have insights into class-room circumstances and the realities of working with students.

There are multiple reasons why teachers should have decision-making powers when it comes to curricula, beginning with such insights that accompany their status as the primary interface with students and parents in schools. Teachers are the de facto enactors of curricula and see how they work on a daily basis, but as noted next, teachers are also limited by their position and may not be able to make connections to larger concerns that may arise across a state regarding the education needs of all of its students. In this essay, first those limitations will be noted and an argument will be made that teachers should not have decision-making powers in designing statewide curricula. That argument is followed by a positive model for educational success based on a framework where teachers do not have a voice in creating curricula but also are not marginalized, having much freedom in designing and presenting instruction.

TEACHERS' LIMITATIONS

Teachers in the United States have myriad responsibilities and concerns in their schools. They have to plan and individualize instruction, teach multiple classes often composed of large numbers of students with great and diverse needs, eat lunch in short order, assess students, work as and with staff members, gather teaching materials, contact parents, counsel students, attend to various school duties, and in the face of all of this organize and manage their time well. Having a voice and role in creating curricula requires much time and energy, and working teachers have precious little of each to spare. In regard to designing curricula, teachers have been limited by an additional factor created by the crush of the school year: slowness to adapt to change.

Multiple education studies on teachers have shown that what most determines how they teach depends on their own experiences in school; briefly put, they teach as they themselves have been taught—often without regard to education research, recommendations, or best practices developed by others. Working from one's experiences is not a fatal flaw, though it does not lend much advantage when working in changing contexts, such as those involving new technology and literacy or working with differing sociocultural groups. The past century was marked with increasingly rapid and dramatic change, both socially and technologically. Diverse students confronted teachers with different learning situations and needs. Pen and paper were replaced by pixels and bytes and differing conceptions of what it means to be literate. Traditional skills such as cursive handwriting became marginalized with the rise of word processing, and the proliferation of information via the Internet transformed how research was conducted and presented.

Combining new technology and literacy demands with traditional curricular demands is a difficult undertaking for many teachers, particularly without the benefit of education research or other resources that might better inform their practice. Synthesizing such information into pedagogy requires time, trial, and error. Additionally, this potentially helpful information may seem at odds with content area knowledge, and the question of relevance comes into play. Teaching agendas that include attention to specific content knowledge may create difficulties in building bridges to students' out-of-school experiences. These different contexts require teachers to think of education from the outside (Alvermann & Eakle, 2007) and move into uncomfortable spaces where they might not be experts. Students tend to be more comfortable with newer types of texts and technologies, and they learn and read differently because of them. Such texts and technologies are rarely taught as central on their own in school, nor are they taught on their own terms. This lack of attention has negative effects for our students as 21st-century literacy skills require knowledge of nonprint texts and an understanding of media in general. Students use visual texts as a matter of course every day, and they are more likely to be comfortable comprehending visual text structures than they are reading print-based works that traditionally are the foci of classroom activities. Many teachers still view such activities as frivolous or undemanding, particularly when high-stakes assessments come into play.

Because of the many demands in their workday, teachers frequently leave their welfare in the hands of unions and professional organizations that they assume have their best interests in mind. These organizations may do much to improve teachers' working conditions, but they have not explicitly addressed curricular issues on a wide scale, a void that in recent years has been filled by research entities, such as the National Reading Panel or the Carnegie Foundation, which conduct and synthesize education studies, as well as by "policy entrepreneurs" (Salinger, 2007), such as textbook and commercial companies that produce texts and teaching materials. The effects of these two policy actors have largely been the creation of recommendations by the former, which are incorporated into education policies, followed by the tailoring of commercial products according to these recommendations—sometimes in name only. The result has been a high value on national standards and programmatic instruction accompanied by the marginalization of teachers to the point of blame for poor school or student performance. This pattern is particularly pronounced regarding elementary education in the United States and disturbingly has produced little or no effect on student outcomes on international student achievement in reading and math as measured by the Programme for International Student Assessment (PISA).

A MODEL THAT WORKS

In contrast to the current state of U.S. schools are those of Finland, a country that ranks high on the PISA. In the 1960s, Finnish schools struggled in the middle of the pack on PISA results, the same situation U.S. schools are currently in. However, Finland began an initiative to improve their education effectiveness by reducing class size, increasing teacher pay, and requiring that all of their teachers complete a rigorous master's program. A national curriculum was created and required of teachers, but they were given the freedom to design their own courses using these standards as a guide, not a series of strict steps. Finnish schools also detached themselves from the standardization movement adopted by many nations, such as the United States, deciding that such tests would be too expensive in terms of instructional time, material cost, and student stress levels. Instead, to measure performance, small yet statistically significant groups of students were assessed in their academic accomplishment periodically. The lack of attention to standardization freed teachers to teach their classes in individualized manners, and the resulting pedagogical diversity prevented adoption of packaged programs that have denigrated teachers' professional status in the United States. In Finland, teachers are well trained and well compensated, and they are given freedom to exercise their professional knowledge in creating and implementing instruction.

That Finland's educational framework relies on standard curricula but does not dictate how those curricula are taught is in sharp contrast to current U.S. education policy where standardized assessment drives instruction to the point where specific texts and programs are approved for schools wishing to accept federal funds. As many education scholars have stated, education is driven—some might say has been hijacked—by assessment, as if constant measuring will foster student achievement. What is more, U.S. teachers are not required to have advanced degrees, are not competitively compensated compared with other professions, and are often limited in terms of what and how they can teach while facing larger class sizes. To make matters worse, standardized assessment seems to be spreading to teacher evaluation, with any blame or praise for student performance correlated and attributed to an individual's teaching ability.

Critics may point to Finland's relatively homogeneous population and small size as contributing factors to their success on PISA measures and conclude that there are no lessons in Finland's education system for U.S. policy and practice. However, when compared with neighboring Norway, Finland's geographic characteristics seem negligible. Norway is similar in size to Finland but follows education policies more akin to those in the United States, with minimal teacher license requirements, relatively low teacher pay, and a standardized testing framework. Class sizes in Norway tend to be higher and resources unevenly distributed among communities. These similarities to the United States lead to the conclusion it is "not necessarily size and homogeneity but, rather, policy choices that lead to a country's educational success" (Abrams, 2011, para. 12). Although teachers are not in charge of creating curricula in Finland, they are afforded considerable compensation, advanced education, and autonomy in creating and delivering classroom instruction. They are not marginalized but trusted as informed professionals.

VOICES FROM OUTSIDE

Though concerns about boosting student achievement while also empowering teachers are important to educational progress, curriculum is a starting point for instruction. Creating effective curricula requires a balance between past, present, and future, and as was previously discussed, teachers sometimes can overly focus on their own education experiences and content areas at the expense of relevance, innovation, and circumspection. This section explores current efforts by education stakeholders to design effective and responsive state curricula to prepare students for current circumstances while also preparing them for future endeavors. These voices come from diverse places but are helpful in transforming pedagogy via an emphasis on concerns of content knowledge, critical thinking, and the changing demands of technological and social flux. Such balanced curricula promote a notion of being informed citizens in relevant and useful manners.

The Common Core State Standards Initiative (CCSSI) is a nationwide project defining standards for English language arts and mathematics for all grade levels. The CCSSI is a state-led effort coordinated by the National Governors Association (NGA) Center for Best Practices and the Council of Chief State School Officers (CCSSO). The standards were developed with input and feedback from teachers, school administrators, and experts, "to provide a clear and consistent framework to prepare our children for college and the workforce" (CCSSI, 2009, para. 1). Although the initiative is not yet a nationally mandated policy, 41 states and the District of Columbia have formally adopted the Common Core framework. Their effects will be widespread as states take them up as their curricular standards.

The aim of these standards, to prepare students for degrees past high school and also emphasize thinking skills that will aid them in future situations, echoes those put forth by professional organizations. The standards present detailed lists of curricular content, with models and suggested readings, but not explicit directions on how to implement instruction. Also, the CCSSI standards address ways that media have developed in the 21st century regarding digital practices and expanded definitions of text. The standards contain gestures toward the inclusion of nonprint texts (e.g., images) and the need for students to analyze meaning and different forms of representation across different modes and technologies. By definition, the standards state the content knowledge and cognitive work teachers and students should engage in and provide a starting point for instruction.

The CCSSI makes overtures toward 21st-century skills but with a heavy emphasis on traditional English and mathematics content. The emphasis on these two areas echoes the unfortunate emphases made in elementary curricula that have severely limited instruction in deference to heavily tested subjects. In contrast, and recognizing the importance of science, engineering, and global concerns in education, the Partnership for 21st Century Skills (P21) (2009) is made up of a 34-member council including educational publishers such as McGraw-Hill; international corporations like Disney, Apple, and Microsoft; educational organizations such as the NEA; and companies such as Crayola and Lego. This organization's stated intentions are to prepare students for the global economy "by weaving 21st century interdisciplinary themes into core subjects" (P21, 2009, p. 2).

While short on curricular content, the P21 provides much-needed vision and practical considerations concerning the need for students to develop creativity, problem solving skills, collaboration, and adaptability over time. The outcomes of schooling are meant to be relevant, useful, adaptable, forward looking, and marketable in terms of producing effective and creative workers. Coupling the curricular demands of the CCSSI with the innovative and broad thinking goals of the P21 provides a balanced framework that teachers can take up and put to use in designing and implementing instruction.

CONCLUSION

Creating and carrying out education policy does not lend itself well to a hypothetical situation where power lies in one sovereign entity. As the title of the recent popular educational documentary noted, Superman is not on the way to save education, and no single group, whether they be students, teachers, administrators, politicians, or national organizations, can fully inform what needs to be done to improve and foster scholastic performance. However, it is also not entirely clear with all the demands that go along with creating and carrying out instruction that teachers' time is best spent on creating large scale curricula, for statewide or national adoption. Teachers' efforts are better spent, at least in part, in giving feedback to such efforts but even more so in designing and carrying out courses that address their students' needs as well as challenge them to academic success.

The lesson taken from Finland is that standards and curriculum are secondary concerns to teacher preparation, attention to class size, and creating a greater cache for the teaching profession. These conditions contribute greatly to a context that promotes student learning, effective teaching, and overall academic success. In this configuration, curriculum is treated as a set of guidelines rather than directives for instruction, and teachers' efforts are better put toward tailoring instruction to their students with an eye to larger curricula as set by state and national entities. Curricula should provide the content of instruction, which includes considerations of content knowledge and the ability to apply thinking to present and future situations, and it falls upon the teachers to configure how that instruction will be delivered. Such license restores dignity and respect to what is otherwise a maligned and marginalized profession and offers the United States its best chance at bolstering the academic achievement of its students.

FURTHER READINGS AND RESOURCES

Abrams, S. E. (2011, January 28). The children must play: What the United States could learn from Finland about education reform. *The New Republic.* Retrieved January 31, 2011, from http://www.tnr.com/print/article/politics/82329/education-reform-Finland-US

Alvermann, D. E., & Eakle, A. J. (2007). Challenging literacy theories and practices from the outside. In J. Lewis & G. Moorman (Eds.), *Adolescent literacy instruction: Policies and promising practices* (pp. 64–81). Newark, DE: International Reading Association.

Barksdale-Ladd, M. A., & Thomas, K. F. (2000). What's at stake in high-stakes testing: Teachers and parents speak out. *Journal of Teacher Education, 51*(5), 384–397.

Common Core State Standards Initiative. (2009). *About the standards.* Retrieved January 31, 2011, from http://www.corestandards.org/about-the-standards

Conley, S. (1991). Review of research in school decision making. *Review of Research in Education, 17,* 225–266.

Darling-Hammond, L., & Wise, A. E. (1985). Beyond standardization: State standards and school improvement. *The Elementary School Journal, 85*(3), 315–336. Retrieved from http://www.jstor.org/stable/1001526?origin=JSTOR-pdf

Dewitz, P. D., Jones, J., & Leahy, S. B. (2009). Comprehension strategy instruction in core reading programs. *Reading Research Quarterly, 44*(2), 102–126.

Gramsci, A. (2005). Some problems with modern pedagogy. In D. Boithman (Ed. & Trans.), *Further selections from the prison notebooks* (pp. 139–160). Minneapolis: University of Minnesota Press.

Meyers, B., Meyers, J., & Gelzheiser, L. (2001). Observing leadership roles in shared decision making: A preliminary analysis of three teams. *Journal of Educational and Psychological Consultation, 12*(4), 277–312.

Partnership for 21st Century Skills. (2009). *About us.* Retrieved January 31, 2011, from http://www.p21.org/index.php?option=com_content&task=view&id=42&Itemid=69

Salinger, T. (2007). Setting the agenda for adolescent literacy. In J. Lewis & G. Moorman (Eds.), *Adolescent literacy instruction: Policies and promising practices* (pp. 3–19). Newark, DE: International Reading Association.

Slavin, R., & Madden, N. (Eds.). (2001). *Success for all: Research and reform in elementary education.* Mahwah, NJ: Erlbaum.

COURT CASES AND STATUTES

Brown v. Board of Education, 347 U.S. 483 (1954).

No Child Left Behind Act of 2001, 20 U.S.C.A. §§ 6301 *et seq.*

3

Does national accreditation of education schools improve teacher and education leadership programs?

POINT: Katharine Rasch, *Maryville University*

COUNTERPOINT: David Reinking and Jamie Colwell, *Clemson University*

OVERVIEW

As detailed in the chapter of this volume on standardized assessments (Chapter 4), standards involve measurement and value. Salient in discussions of standards in U.S. education are concepts of accountability, achievement, teacher quality, and so-called standards-based assessment (SBA) systems. In mainstream media and local conversations, these topics are usually associated with PK–12 public schooling, and although praised by some stakeholders, serious concerns have been expressed by teachers and school administrators that these top-down practices and policies have led to a narrowing of the curriculum and have reduced morale among teachers and other school personnel (Hamilton et al., 2007).

Less known to the general public is that over the past decade matters related to curriculum standards and SBAs have been introduced into higher education under the auspice of national accreditation of teacher education agencies and state departments of education—a focus of the present chapter. More than half of the states partner with national accreditation agencies working in allegiance with domain-specific, specialized professional associations, such as the National Association for the Education of Young Children (NAEYC) and the National Council of Teachers of Mathematics (NCTM), to standardize curriculum, oversee what they deem as teacher education program improvement, and to evaluate the SBAs developed by university and college programs.

With slogans of "no child left behind" and "evidence-based curriculum," a growing "what works clearinghouse of best practices," and so forth, at first blush it might seem there would be little disagreement among education researchers, scholars, and teacher educators about the merits of accreditation and its promises of program improvement. After all, why would any educator not want to employ the best possible teaching practices, improve their certification programs, or allow any child to fall behind other ones academically?

However, accreditation is one of the most contentious topics in many higher education institutions. In part, this contention parallels similar difficulties voiced by PK–12 educators: Professors and other seasoned professionals in higher education are reluctant to relinquish freedom to design and implement curriculum that they believe is important, especially to those who might have agendas that are not aligned with ideas that many education scholars value. Further, the perception of a loss of academic freedom to a top-down bureaucratic system is unsettling for many university and college professors—especially those who take pride in having built expertise in education theory and practice and as a result established internationally acclaimed reputations in education leadership—just as it is troubling for educators in public schools.

Other concerns of educators in teacher preparation and leadership programs mirror those of public school administrators and teachers. Accreditation as it presently stands is perceived as time consuming. Committee work, report preparation, unit-level data collection and comparisons, exhibit production, and site visits by outside overseers are only a few of the matters associated with accreditation that are sometimes perceived as taking time away from traditionally valued practices, such as advising teacher candidates, mentoring doctoral students, and·teaching.

Alongside the time spent on accreditation are the costs associated with it. Faculty time devoted to accreditation translates to costs. Further, in some cases additional faculty and staff need to be hired to guide the departments and the overall unit through accreditation procedures. As well, and especially in larger teacher education institutions, elaborate and costly data collection systems are needed to organize, sift through, and analyze compliance data. In addition, noncompliance or nonparticipation in these procedures can lead to the loss of an institution's accreditation, which, in turn, can affect overall student enrollment in a school and its revenue because potential applicants cannot receive the necessary teaching credentials to be employed in a state's public schools. As with public schools, accreditation is a high-stakes matter that can affect multiple aspects of teacher education programs.

On the other hand, education reformists place some of the blame of failing public schools, high dropout rates, and persisting achievement gaps on teacher preparation programs. Perhaps this perspective is best illustrated by the latest theme of the National Council for Accreditation of Teacher Education (NCATE) (2010), the principal accreditation agency of U.S. schools, which is captured by the opening words of a recently released panel report:

> *The education of teachers in the United States needs to be turned upside down* [italics added]. To prepare effective teachers for 21st century classrooms, teacher education must shift away from a norm which emphasizes academic preparation and course work loosely linked to school-based experiences. (p. ii)

Not surprisingly, the NCATE panel was principally composed of administrators and not university faculty, and it was guided, in part, by entrepreneurs and politicians. In short, the panel passionately argues that radical changes must be made in teacher education that require a shift away from what they believe to be antiquated ivory towers of academe.

The following essays address matters of national accreditation with an eye on whether the significant resources devoted to and the efforts made by state departments and other governmental bodies, accrediting agencies, and education administrators and faculty over the years have improved teacher education and leadership programs.

In the point essay, Katharine Rasch (Maryville University) argues that recent accreditation and education reform efforts have great potential in developing reflective practitioners. Although she does not take the stronger position of accreditation agencies that the teacher education system needs to be entirely "turned upside down," as they suggest it, she recounts how various members of the education system can collaborate to produce stronger and more cohesive programs of study. In part, Rasch argues, this enhancement is because accreditation standards and oversight allow for stronger connections among the content, skills, and dispositions expected of teachers and greater possibilities of bringing these qualities to schools.

In the counterpoint essay, David Reinking and Jamie Colwell (Clemson University) argue that present accreditation processes and requirements may actually have the opposite effect to the stated purposes of accreditation agencies to help improve teacher education programs. In part, they believe that national accreditation can, and often does, create a repressive environment characterized by narrow attitudes that diminish the creative potential that is needed for developing quality teachers and education leaders. Reinking and Colwell conclude the counterpoint essay with a careful analysis wherein they attempt to show that there are no strong reasons to associate program improvement with present accreditation practices.

As shown in the subsequent essays, the direction in which the accreditation of teacher education programs evolves over coming years will certainly have enormous effects on teaching and learning in higher education and beyond.

A. Jonathan Eakle
The Johns Hopkins University

POINT: Katharine Rasch
Maryville University

With the myriad of organizations and individuals who are concerned about who is teaching in America's classrooms and leading America's schools, there has also been an almost constant discussion and analysis about how, and if, teachers and education leaders are making a difference in classrooms and schools. Yet, throughout most of the 20th century, the requirements to license teachers and the programs that have prepared those teachers were quite variable, and, until the late 1970s, largely this licensure was unregulated beyond the academic credentials and programs of typical schools and universities (Darling-Hammond, Pacheco, Nichelli, LePage, & Kammerness, 2005). While national accreditation of teachers began in the early 1950s, it followed the path set by regional accreditation procedures that were used throughout the early and mid-19th centuries. Regional accreditation procedures existed namely to set standards and provide a system of accountability for colleges and universities only in their respective areas.

This manner of accreditation was voluntary and provided self-regulation of institutions through private associations, of which the education institutions were a part, rather than through government regulation. In the case of professional accreditation for teachers, increased scrutiny of PK–12 education and the beginning of the development of curriculum standards in the 1970s began a trend toward more regulatory and externally governed accountability procedures for university-based teacher education programs and a cycle of quality improvement. Criticisms arising from publications such as *A Nation at Risk* and *A Place Called School* focused on the irregularities and problems with teacher performance. These criticisms caused further scrutiny of teacher and educational leadership preparation. Thus, the NCATE began to provide oversight for teacher preparation.

The NCATE process was completely redesigned in the mid-1980s to focus on elements of professional accountability. Emphasis moved away from inputs and focused on curriculum coherence, research-based teacher preparation practices, better connections to the field of education, and adequate resources and responsibility for coherent professional preparation. From 1985 to 2000, state licensure standards, national learned society standards (e.g., National Science Teachers Association, Educational Leadership Constituent Council), and authority for state teacher education program approval for colleges and universities became more intertwined and regulated. In many state university systems, accreditation for teachers and school leaders was no longer voluntary but directly tied to state program approval. A second accrediting organization (Teacher Education Accreditation Council [TEAC], 2010) was established in 1997. "TEAC's entire accreditation process is built around the program's case that it prepares competent, caring, and qualified professional educators. TEAC requires the program to have evidence to support its case, and the accreditation process examines and verifies the evidence" (TEAC, 2010).

In 2000, the NCATE standards were further amended to be more focused on the outcomes of teacher and educational leader performance as a result of the programs and the use of performance data for systematic program improvement. Like institutional accreditation, the specialized accreditation of programs for teachers and educational leaders provides both oversight and incredible opportunities for institutions to study and challenge the status quo, to respond to the public, and to examine the results of programs in which candidates are prepared.

OPPORTUNITIES

The current accreditation and teacher program approval processes have provided an extraordinary opportunity for each school, college, and department of education to focus on its programs, its assumptions, its expectations and outcomes for its candidates, and its obligations to the professional community. As Linda Darling-Hammond et al. (2005) and others have reported, several important elements have made a difference in the design of teacher education programs: content learning process and learning context.

In *Educating School Leaders,* Arthur Levine (2005) likewise suggested the importance of purpose, curricular coherence, curricular balance, and assessment in his study and criticism of educational leadership programs. He also emphasized the importance of faculty composition and research. The accreditation process requires institutions to scrutinize and examine each of these in the process of self-study and program development and improvement. This process has improved teacher education and educational leadership programs in the following ways: Accreditation has required each institution to carefully consider the institutional context in which programs are offered as well as the important research and wisdom of practice that guide the institution. In this process, groups of faculty must engage in substantive dialog and collectively endorse the mission, vision, and outcomes of the programs.

The explicit review of the conceptual and research literature in teacher education assists faculty in examining current leaders in their field and the areas where research most carefully inform the outcomes established for each program. This is in stark contrast to the vague and inferential connections of perceived purposes of individual faculty member's work and has altered the direction of many programs. In this process, consideration of national, state, and institutional standards must provide explicit program outcomes related to this examination. They must also systematically promote opportunities to engage practitioners in the analysis and endorsement of the institution's outcomes and provide further context for outcomes and standards to which the institution will be held. Over the continuous accreditation process, the outcomes for institutions have become increasingly explicit and transparent to the candidates in the programs.

The process of faculty deliberation and consensus around context and focus of programs has required institutions to reaffirm the commitment to teacher education on campus. Collaborative ventures with faculty in arts and sciences have been enhanced through the emphasis on program assessment. While not all faculty members have participated willingly initially, programs emerge from the process with a stronger sense of identity and assurance that candidates who are becoming teachers and school leaders will participate in programs that have been reexamined, refocused, and carefully assessed. Faculty ownership of these programs has increased; responsibility for the accountability for candidate performance is shared more broadly through the processes of accreditation.

RESULTS OF EMPHASIS ON ASSESSMENT

Assessment drives the accreditation process and has produced extensive improvement in program approval in two important ways. Faculty members have collectively worked to ensure that assessments actually measure candidate performance on the specific program outcomes. The process necessitates faculty involvement and ownership in ways that older, input-driven processes did not require. The move from attention to objectives and curriculum alignment to assessment of candidates' professional knowledge and skills has been difficult; institutions continue to refine assessments, but the discussion and self-study has shifted dramatically.

In addition, the entire faculty must come to consensus and common expectations for candidates in collective, deliberative, and extensive assessment. This emphasis on assessment has provided new assurance for candidates that expectations are clearly outlined throughout the programs and tied to their individual performance. The process of outlining key assessments throughout the program has also resulted in more cohesive and sequential programs. As assessments are used at key transition points throughout the program, candidates must provide evidence of their knowledge and skills not just in courses but in the matriculation through the program. Institutions have had to outline explicitly the formative and summative points at which candidates are held responsible for demonstration of program outcomes. This process also ensures that each candidate is responsible to demonstrate knowledge and skills throughout the program in much more explicit ways.

The second result of the emphasis on assessment is that it has improved teacher education and educational leadership programs through the ways in which assessment data are tightly controlled, analyzed, and used for program improvement. Accreditation has assisted units in emphasizing how data are used in increasingly systematic and sophisticated ways. Schools, colleges, and departments of education not only are examining assessment data for individual candidates but also are aggregating data over time to examine their own integrity of assessments and assurances of quality control in programs. This process has ensured that program and unit faculty members are responsive to the data presented and committed to the improvement of the quality of instrumentation. As each program delineates transition points from admission to program exit, faculty are also better able to evaluate the effectiveness of key experiences and assessments.

There is emerging professional consensus that the clinical aspects of preparation for both teachers and educational leaders are extremely important not just in quantity but in quality and focus (Boyle-Base & McIntyre, 2008; Darling-Hammond et al., 2005). Accreditation has suggested very careful structure and expectations of knowledge and skills necessary for both teachers and educational leaders. Accreditation standards have assisted faculty in delineating a sequence of experiences that is explicit and, in most cases, closely tied to coursework in teaching methods and educational leadership responsibilities. Current standards for both TEAC and NCATE, as well as the program standards for educational leadership, rely heavily on the evidence presented by departments of education with regard to candidate performance in the field. These standards (as part of the overall assessment system) have enhanced and accentuated the importance of attention to the authentic performance, veracity of assessment, and responsibility for the growth and development of PK–12 students during the field/clinical experiences. For teacher candidates, the range of professional responsibilities that are demonstrated include attention to the diverse needs of learners, support for families, and outreach to the broader community. School leaders must focus on every aspect of instructional leadership and the use of data for school improvement. Schools, colleges, and departments of education have had to collaborate with PK–12 partners with very specific criteria, rather than the assumptions that time in the field will automatically imply a certain set of skills for each candidate.

The accreditation process requires institutions to focus on the importance of preparing candidates to serve diverse groups of PK–12 students. This emphasis must be explicit; it must be pervasive in the curriculum and the assessments used by the institution. While there remains great variability in the extent to which institutions embrace diversity as a strength of program candidates, every institution has had to attend directly to helping candidates prepare themselves and enhance their skills working with students of different ethnicities, English language learners, and students with exceptionalities.

There have been long-held assumptions that teacher education would include rich preparation in content and a certain set of pedagogical skills that would be gleaned through coursework and some field experience. There is also a perception by the public that conformity to the public education system and commitment to the ideals of public education are necessary for a competent, caring professional. The current accreditation processes require that the broader professional community collaborate in the design and development of curricula, field experiences, and assessments. This has required that schools, colleges, and departments of education find more explicit structures for outreach. In addition, through this process, the schools, colleges, and departments of education assume responsibility for oversight of their programs in relationship to the needs of the community. Education schools have been widely criticized for being out of touch and removed from the public schools. The accreditation process has provided structure and standards to address what has been a valid criticism for some institutions.

POLICY QUESTIONS

There are critical policy questions being raised with regard to teacher reward systems and tenure as the consequences of No Child Left Behind (NCLB) (2001) reach more school districts and require reconstitution of schools. Experiments with charter schools and schools of emphasis are butting up against traditions of tenure and job seniority for teachers and principals. In the process, salary structures that reward teachers based on advanced degrees and years of service are being scrutinized and criticized. NCATE processes require state departments of education to provide evidence of the enhanced skills of teachers pursuing master's degrees and doctoral programs leading to additional licensure. These programs have received little attention in the past and did not necessarily focus on demonstration of knowledge and skills directly related to practice. Current standards have made expectations for these programs more explicit and delineate a higher set of skills for these professionals.

Throughout this process, leaders in individual states have played a critical role in setting policy and dictating the relationship between national accreditation and state program approval. In some cases, state policymakers and officials regulating program approval have endorsed advances in accreditation and provided support for institutions to look carefully at the success of programs. In other instances, competing agendas and regulations have encumbered institutions and made the processes more bureaucratic or conflicted. This dichotomy has led to confounding and confusing situations, especially given how variable the state regulations and processes are.

While reflecting on the improvement of teacher education and educational leadership throughout the accreditation processes in the past 20 years, this does not intend to imply that their processes are perfected. Ongoing research and development are critical, as the nation's teachers and leaders continue to struggle with the challenges of providing excellent and equitable education for all students. The accreditation agencies' work has suggested that there are many more questions and issues to be examined. Critics of accreditation continue to question the relative emphasis on content knowledge, pedagogy, and clinical competence.

CONCLUSION

It is clear that the institutional foci on accreditation range from begrudging compliance to rapt attention to continuous improvement. The scope and effectiveness of program responsibility varies based on the attitudes of leadership and faculty members who engage, or not, in the accreditation process. The tension between regulation and accreditation is ongoing in the professional teacher education community. In the ongoing discussions and merger of TEAC and NCATE to form the Council for the Accreditation of Educator Preparation (CAEP), the discussion of the adequacy of evidence and attention to accountability will continue to change. Nonetheless, teacher education has undergone intense internal scrutiny that has required reexamination of programs and serious study of the effectiveness of current practices.

COUNTERPOINT: David Reinking and Jamie Colwell
Clemson University

This essay takes the position that national accreditation, as currently conceived and implemented, does not contribute to improving teacher education and leadership programs. In fact, this essay argues that accreditation today can, and often does, inspire superficial responses that are sometimes detrimental to programs. Such responses are derived from a posture of compliance that can stifle innovation and a genuine commitment to programmatic improvement. Further, this essay takes the stance that whatever accreditation may contribute to programmatic improvement may be offset by potentially negative outcomes that rarely enter discussions about accreditation. Finally, this essay argues there are no strong warrants that accreditation leads to improvements in education programs.

BACKGROUND

Accreditation was not originally framed as a means to directly improve education programs. Prior to the late 1990s, accreditation of education programs, like accreditation of programs in law and medicine, were conceptualized and implemented primarily to assure the public that programs met a minimal threshold of professional legitimacy. The focus was on dimensions such as adequate resources, qualifications of faculty, and the reasonableness of a program's curriculum. As in other fields, the role of education accreditation in promoting improvement was typically a by-product attained by weeding out weak programs or by leveraging additional resources needed to bolster programs with marginal capacity.

In the late 1990s, the NCATE took a distinctly different approach. Although not deserting entirely the goal of warranting that programs have adequate capacity, the predominant focus became more transformational, basing accreditation on evidence that programs were actively and explicitly engaged in meeting standards as evidenced by measurable indicators of performance. In short, accreditation was conceptualized and implemented as an engine for education reform by standardizing professional preparation one program at a time, with the implicit goal of enhancing the relatively poor public image of education as a profession.

Nevertheless, the transformative intent of accreditation to reinforce professionalism through standards and accountability is fraught with challenges, difficulties, and ambiguity. For example, the appearance of the TEAC as an alternative accreditation organization was due at least in part to dissatisfaction with NCATE's prescriptive stance and inflexible requirements and the belief among institutions and influential educators that NCATE was counter to authentic improvement. Or the TEAC alternative suggested that any possible benefits of NCATE accreditation were outweighed by costs in time, energy, and resources or by negative byproducts of participation. The appearance of TEAC at least tacitly suggests that the dominant NCATE approach to accreditation has not been widely accepted as a clear force for program improvement.

In our view, although TEAC mitigates some concerns by permitting more conceptual and logistical flexibility and by being less prescriptive than NCATE, many other problems remain. Like NCATE, for example, TEAC also views accreditation as an active means to implement education reform through professionalization by insisting that programs address broad consensual standards and quality principles, all of which must be documented by ongoing, rigorous collection of valid and reliable (i.e., measurable) outcomes from multiple sources. Thus, we believe that both accrediting organizations are, to varying extents, subject to the fundamental limitations that we discuss subsequently in the present essay. That TEAC and NCATE share similar goals, albeit with somewhat different approaches, was validated by the merger of the two organizations as we wrote the present essay.

FUNDAMENTAL LIMITATIONS OF ACCREDITATION

Accreditation has been criticized for its potential negative effects on professional programs when compared to alternatives such as free market approaches used elsewhere in the world, where respected programs thrive and weaker programs wither. Further, accreditation has been criticized as "'dumbing down' teacher education through a narrow emphasis upon technical pedagogical knowledge and performance outcomes" (Carlson, 2008, p. 97). Certainly, the current focus of accreditation privileges easily quantifiable aspects of future teachers' performance and thus encourages education programs, for better or worse, to be driven mainly by quantifiable data. In fact, NCATE has had to back away from its original inclusion of teacher candidates' dispositions in their accreditation standards, in part because those dimensions were difficult to measure. Thus, accreditation standards and requirements do relatively little to inspire programmatic innovation or excellence aimed at promoting difficult-to-measure abilities and dispositions and may actually inhibit such efforts by moving energies and resources toward more mundane, though quantifiable, aspects of teaching.

Another relevant dimension of the current accreditation climate is highlighted in Patricia Graham, Richard Lyman, and Martin Trow's (1995) argument that education accreditation is fundamentally flawed because it attempts to address two inherently conflicting goals: (a) ongoing assessment and evaluation aimed at positive transformation and (b) certifying to the public that a program meets minimal standards. In commenting on those conflicting goals, Frank B. Murray (2001) stated the following:

> The second function invariably overwhelms the first because the incentives favor the production of a public relations document that magnifies the institution's strengths and hides its weaknesses. This is precisely the opposite of what is needed if the first function is to be served. (p. 50)

In fact, he later reported "despite TEAC's repeated assurance that only unaddressed weaknesses, not weaknesses themselves, were problematic, [programs] decided to bury . . . perceived shortcomings and not speak to them at all" (Murray, 2009, p. 64). That statement is particularly poignant because Murray was TEAC's president at the time it was written.

Accreditation in education today also leaves little time for thought, reflection, or innovation outside the boundaries defined by the accreditation process. That is, accreditation is no longer a relatively straightforward, concentrated effort every few years to document a reasonable and coherent program that has adequate capacity. Instead, it is an ongoing, all-encompassing, labor- and resource-intensive effort requiring every accredited program to document continuously that it is engaged in gathering and reflecting on evidence of increasing improvement toward achieving accreditation standards.

Engaging in ongoing accreditation activities creates tremendous challenges for individual programs to meet an ambitious agenda for improvement, standardization, and legitimacy in the eyes of accreditation organizations. Notably, it demands incredible time and resources including the direct, ongoing participation of almost all education faculty as well as administrative coordination and staff support. For example, to maintain accreditation, programs must continuously collect and analyze prodigious data verifying, even at the level of individual courses, that preservice teachers are being explicitly exposed to and evaluated on the content and experiences dictated by accreditation standards. In at least some cases, the demands of providing the ongoing data and documentation for accreditation become de facto the education program, again suggesting the importance of knowing whether that condition is an improvement or a liability.

Accreditation in teacher education also faces a unique challenge when compared to other professions. Education programs typically depend to some extent on the involvement and cooperation of faculty in other disciplines located in other administrative units such as departments of mathematics and science. It is difficult to insist that such outside faculty submit to the demands of accreditation in another field. Further, it can create friction between academic units and individual faculty that is not conducive to positive mutual efforts to discuss and implement constructive improvements in programs (Huang & Barrea-Marlys, 2008).

This dynamic of university life, especially when coupled with the ongoing, resource-intensive, and difficult demands of accreditation, invite superficial, sometimes subversive, responses for the sake of giving the impression that accreditation requirements are being met. Such a response is particularly likely when the stakes for accreditation are high, such as when the loss of national accreditation also means, for example, the loss of state accreditation. Gamesmanship, either programmatically or individually, is not uncommon to minimize intrusions, to maintain public appearances, or to accommodate the differing philosophical positions and multiple agendas of individual faculty without jeopardizing the more standardizing forces of accreditation.

More importantly, innovative ideas that do not mesh well with accreditation frameworks may be dismissed outright because they complicate or are at odds with the demands of templates for accreditation. An example of the former is Bullough, Clark, and Patterson's (2003) account of how a rigorous, theory-grounded internal process of programmatic improvement created serious threats to accreditation because it did not fit NCATE's templates and technocratic approach to evaluation. The latter is illustrated by the first author's (David Reinking) experience of when a program's faculty ultimately rejected an initially well-received suggestion for a programmatic change when someone pointed out that it did not fit into the NCATE conceptual framework. Likewise, the second author, Jamie Colwell, was required to include several assignments in a course she was teaching simply for the sake of satisfying NCATE requirements, although the assignments were ill suited to the course goals and the students who were taking it.

As these examples illustrate, accreditation can encroach on academic freedom. Indeed, one supporter of accreditation lamented that program auditors have found that systemic efforts at quality control were undermined by faculty members' idiosyncratic preferences and styles (Murray, 2009). Faculty can be formally or informally pressured administratively to adapt the content and structure of their programs or courses to accommodate the vicissitudes of accreditation. Even relatively innocuous and historically sacrosanct expressions of a faculty member's expert interpretations of a course, such as a syllabus, are now accreditation artifacts that must follow prescribed frameworks. The prescriptive stance of education accreditation today feeds faculty members' irritation, annoyance, and even subversion hidden beneath a veneer of compliance. To our knowledge, such issues have not been acknowledged or addressed directly by accreditation organizations or within the literature on accreditation. In our experience, they are also often ignored by institutional administrative leadership and individuals invested in public relations who are not willing, or qualified, to look beneath the surface to assess the full range of accreditation's consequences.

Further, accreditation organizations do not explicitly acknowledge or accommodate cultural differences created by the respective missions of distinctly different institutions, such as large research-oriented universities and smaller, local, or regional institutions. For example, NCATE requires programs to establish and describe a unifying conceptual framework that undergirds all aspects of all programs. Because of the various expert perspectives found in large schools of education, such a singular view is, from our experiences, not likely or even advisable. Thus, in the end, the framework that is developed is simply a way to satisfy accreditation requirements and not an authentic artifact aimed at providing substantive guidance for programmatic improvement.

That problem is exacerbated by the common practice of putting individuals who work at smaller institutions in charge of evaluating how programs at large universities have—or have not—addressed accreditation requirements (see Bullough, 2002). The influence of a conceptual framework is also substantially mitigated when many of the education programs at the largest research institutions are arguably regarded as among the best programs by virtue of the quality of their students and faculty. We argue that authentic improvement is less likely when such differences in academic culture are not acknowledged and accommodated, as currently they are not.

Finally, the effects of the current approach to national accreditation on programmatic improvement are inherently limited by the fact that accreditation in education plays a more limited role than in other professions. For example, to practice law, an individual must pass the bar exam, and one cannot stand for the bar exam without having a degree from at least a provisionally accredited institution. On the other hand, to become a certified teacher in many states, it is not necessary to have a degree from an institution that is accredited. Ironically, often the same individuals arguing for tighter control of the traditional professional preparation of teachers also argue for shortcuts to certification, for example, by allowing people in business or the military to enter the education profession without meeting the same standards. Further, of the approximately 1,300 programs preparing teachers and education leaders, only slightly more than half have sought accreditation. In fact, several of the largest and most highly regarded education programs such as the University of Wisconsin and Harvard University have disregarded accreditation and presumably find it unnecessary, irrelevant, or ineffectual in fostering programmatic quality. Such cases highlight not only that the opportunities for programmatic improvement through accreditation are limited nationally but also underscore the fundamental ambivalence in the field of education to the benefits of accreditation as it is currently conceptualized and implemented.

WEAK WARRANTS FOR PROGRAMMATIC IMPROVEMENT

The activist and often prescriptive role of accreditation today, its extensive, ongoing demands on education programs, and the potentially negative effects of those demands suggest that strong warrants are necessary to support any claims of programmatic improvement. We find no such warrants and believe those invested in current approaches to accreditation should be held accountable for offering such evidence. In this section, we address possible warrants that, at present, are unsatisfactorily weak or unachieved, and we suggest some stronger warrants that might be considered.

The benefits of national accreditation for program improvement are self-evident. This warrant is represented by the TEAC president's statement: "No one has ever doubted that TEAC's system would benefit a program. Having solid evidence for claims, verified by an audit, is simply good in and of itself" (Murray, 2005, p. 314). In light of the numerous potential limitations we have cited earlier in the present essay, we find such a position to be disingenuous and an unconvincing non sequitur. It assumes that simply holding a program accountable, leveraged by accreditation, will inevitably lead to genuine improvement. That warrant is also curiously inconsistent with accrediting organizations' demands on programs for valid and reliable evidence to support adherence to standards or other claims. Is it equally plausible to argue that the high quality of some programs is self-evident?

The data gathered during accreditation demonstrates that programs are improving. This warrant is clearly a self-fulfilling prophecy and can immediately be discounted. The data demanded to support compliance cannot logically be used as evidence of improvement. Further, it privileges quantitative data over the deeper qualitative analyses that may be necessary to reveal negative, collateral, offsetting effects, or only superficial compliance rather than genuine improvement. High-stakes assessments also have inherently weaker validity (Nichols & Berliner, 2007).

Some programs improve as a result of accreditation. Some programs certainly improve. However, such improvement would be expected under virtually any reasonable model of accreditation, including a simpler, less intrusive model focused mainly on capacity and inputs.

Most programs on average improve when they are accredited. There have been relatively few systematic attempts to substantiate this warrant, and the results are decidedly equivocal or difficult to interpret precisely. For example, using in-depth qualitative methods, Jingzi Huang and Mirta Barrea-Marlys (2008) reported some benefits as well as detrimental effects from one institution's experience with accreditation. An analysis sponsored by Educational Testing Service (ETS) (Wenglinsky, 2001) explored the link between program characteristics and scores on teacher licensing exams. Accreditation was not among the five factors related to those scores, and the study concluded that teacher preparation programs are typically not uniformly successful or unsuccessful. One study (Gitomer, Latham, & Ziomek, 1999) did show that graduates of NCATE institutions were more likely to pass licensing exams, but a stronger, more valid comparison would be between programs that were granted accreditation and those who sought accreditation but failed or were given provisional accreditation. Even if data supporting this warrant existed, it could not be assumed that the widespread benefits were achieved at acceptable costs or could not have been accomplished more efficiently.

Accreditation fosters improvement by ensuring that a program is explicitly addressing consensual standards of the field. This warrant might have merit if there was clear consensus in the field of education about what overall standards are foundational and if there was strong evidence that conformance to those standards was a critical component of effective programs. There is neither, especially at the programmatic level. For example, TEAC claims that its approach to standards is more valid than that of NCATE because its standards are generated by leaders of the field independent of the agendas of NCATE's constituent professional organizations. Unlike NCATE, TEAC also does not impose state or specialty area standards on its members, because it believes that there is too much variance in these standards, and there is little evidence that the standards are valid, or that strict adherence to standards leads to improvement. Neither do accreditation organizations lay claim to any evidence to support that adherence to standards is a key ingredient to improving programs. For example, NCATE's executive director recently stated that there needs to be a stronger scientific knowledge base about effective programs.

Much stronger warrants would be necessary to support claims that accreditation produces programmatic improvement. Interestingly, stronger warrants would be available if accreditation organizations were held to requirements that parallel their expectations of education programs. For example, what conceptual framework guides the belief that accreditation leads to programmatic improvement? From what theoretical or empirical base would such a conceptual framework originate (e.g., theories and evidence related to institutional change)? What is the value added by accreditation? What exactly is programmatic improvement, and what would be valid and reliable evidence of it? What standards represent a professionally grounded and legitimate process of accreditation (e.g., do no harm; implement accreditation that is sensitive to the realities of those who work on the frontlines of teacher education)?

CONCLUSION

Enhancing the quality of teacher education and leadership programs, as well as bolstering public confidence in teaching as a profession, can occur on multiple fronts and through many means. National accreditation may play a role in addressing both goals, but we do not believe that there are convincing arguments, let alone evidence, that it directly contributes to programmatic improvement. In fact, there are many reasons to worry that education accreditation may be having a detrimental effect on program improvement, while consuming an inordinate amount of time, energy, and resources. It has, in our opinion, unrealistically and unreasonably far overreached its potential influence on programmatic improvement, and it has produced too many instances of undermining innovative, meaningful, and authentic improvements in programs of teacher education and leadership. A productive future direction, we believe, would be to seek a more effective and realistic balance between the external accountability and leverage of accreditation and more authentic internal processes associated with meaningful reform. That alignment will be achieved, we argue, only when it is acknowledged that genuine programmatic improvement cannot be legislated or dictated by externally imposed technocratic approaches to accreditation such as those currently in place.

FURTHER READINGS AND RESOURCES

Alstete, J. W. (2004). Accreditation matters: Achieving academic recognition and renewal. *ASHE-ERIC higher education report* (Vol. 30, No. 4). Hoboken, NJ: Wiley.

Boyle-Base, M., & McIntyre, D. J. (2008). What kinds of experience? Preparing teachers in PDS or community settings. In M. Cochran-Smith, S. Feiman-Nemser, D. J. McIntyre, & K. E. Demers (Eds.), *Handbook of research on teacher education: Enduring questions in changing contexts* (3rd ed., pp. 307–330). New York: Routledge, Taylor and Francis Group.

Bullough, R. V., Jr. (2002). Thoughts on teacher education in the USA. *Journal of Education for Teaching, 28*(3), 233–237.

Bullough, R. V., Jr., Clark, D. C., & Patterson, R. S. (2003). Getting in step: Accountability, accreditation and the standardization of teacher education in the United States. *Journal of Education for Teaching, 29*(1), 35–51.

Carlson, D. (2008). Conflict of the faculties: Democratic progressivisim in the age of "No Child Left Behind." *Educational Studies, 43,* 94–113.

Darling-Hammond, L., Pacheco, A., Nichelli, N., LePage, P., & Kammerness, K. (with Youngs, P.). (2005). Implementing curriculum renewal in teacher education: Managing organizational and policy change. In L. Darling-Hammond & J. Bransford (Eds.), *Preparing teachers for a changing world: What teachers should learn and be able to do.* San Francisco: Jossey-Bass.

Gitomer, D., Latham, A., & Ziomek, R. (1999). *The academic quality of prospective teachers: The impact of admissions and licensure testing* (Research Report Number RR-03-35). Princeton, NJ: Educational Testing Service.

Graham, P., Lyman, R., & Trow, M. (1995). *Accountability of colleges and universities: An essay.* New York: Columbia University Press.

Hamilton, L. S., Stecher, B. M., Marsh, J., McCombs, J. S., Robyn, A., Russell, J., et al. (2007). *Implementing standards-based accountability under No Child Left Behind: Responses of superintendents, principals, and teachers in three states.* Santa Monica, CA: RAND Corporation.

Huang, J., & Barrea-Marlys, M. (2008). Gains and challenges in the national accreditation process: A case study. *The International Journal of Learning, 15*(8), 57–63.

Levine, A. (2005). *Educating school leaders.* New York: The Education Schools Project.

McKnight, D. (2004). An inquiry of NCATE's move into virtue ethics by way of dispositions (Is this what Aristotle meant?). *Educational Studies, 35*(3), 212–230.

Murray, F. B. (2001). From consensus standards to evidence of claims: Assessment and accreditation in the case of teacher education. *New Directions for Higher Education, 113,* 49–66.

Murray, F. B. (2005). On building a unified system of accreditation in teacher education. *Journal of Teacher Education, 56*(4), 307–317.

Murray, F. B. (2009). An accreditation dilemma: The tension between program accountability and program improvement in programmatic accreditation. *New Directions for Higher Education, 145,* 59–68.

The National Council for Accreditation of Teacher Education. (2010). *Transforming teacher education through clinical practice: A national strategy to prepare effective teachers.* Retrieved February 20, 2011, from http://www.ncate.org/Public/ResearchReports/NCATEInitiatives/BlueRibbonPanel/tabid/715/Default.aspx

Nichols, S. L., & Berliner, D. (2007). *Collateral damage: How high-stakes testing corrupts America's schools.* Cambridge, MA: Harvard University Press.

O'Brien, P. M. (Ed.). (2009, Spring). *Accreditation: Assuring and enhancing quality* (New Directions for Higher Education No. 145). San Francisco: Jossey-Bass.

Teacher Education Accreditation Council. (2010). *About TEAC.* Retrieved from http://www.teac.org/about/about-us

Wenglinsky, H. (2001). *Teaching the teachers: Different settings, different results. Policy information report.* Princeton, NJ: Educational Testing Service. Retrieved August 17, 2010, from http://eric.ed.gov/ERICWebPortal/search/detailmini.jsp?_nfpb=true&_&ERICExtSearch_SearchValue_0=ED446138&ERICExtSearch_SearchType_0=no&accno=ED446138

COURT CASES AND STATUTES

No Child Left Behind Act of 2001, 20 U.S.C.A. §§ 6301 *et seq.*

Should standardized student assessments guide curriculum and instruction in schools?

POINT: Marc L. Stein, *The Johns Hopkins University*

COUNTERPOINT: Christopher Knaus,
California State University, East Bay

OVERVIEW

Without a doubt, the evaluation of products completed by various workers such as those in the manufacturing industry and students has been a critical part of cultures since antiquity. During modern times, many products became increasingly governed by laws and standards. A standard is part and parcel of two related dimensions: value and measurement. In the past, for example, the U.S. economy was set to a gold standard and commodities and exchanges were measured against the value of that metal. Further, standard scientific measurements allow comparisons, or assessments, to be made between aspects of subjects and objects, such as their height, mass, and volume. For instance, the value of an ounce of gold can be assessed in comparison to an ounce of lead. Since at least as early as the cognitive scientific revolution of the 1980s, standards of value and measurement have also been a prevailing, often debated, and polarizing education topic.

On one side of the debate, advocates of the standardization of curriculum and instruction have loosely amalgamated to form what has come to be known as the standards movement, which over the past two decades has touched nearly every corner of curriculum and instruction in the United States. In part, this recent movement was a reaction to progressive notions in education that emerged in the context of countercultural shifts caused by political and social events such as resistance to U.S. involvement in the Vietnam War and the

Watergate scandal. During that period, transparency and openness became more saliently valued social commodities, and progressive education practices such as "open education" and "whole language" gained popularity wherein children were, in theory, free to naturally explore and learn without rigid boundaries and strict guidelines.

By the mid-1970s, the political and social pendulum began to swing away from progressive notions toward more traditional ideas and structures. Education policies and practices also began to change. Due to concerns over global competitiveness and economic crises, such as rampant inflation and crude oil shortages, U.S. education institutions began to be closely scrutinized by policymakers, politicians, and the wider public. In this atmosphere, the Reagan administration's National Commission on Excellence in Education was formed and charged with examining the overall quality of education in the United States. The establishment and work of the commission coincided with Reagan's desire and efforts to rein in government spending and, in particular, the federal funding of education. In fact, during that time and in years that followed, a notion advanced by the Republican Party was to entirely eliminate the U.S. Department of Education (ED).

The National Commission on Excellence in Education's (1983) work culminated with the seminal publication of *A Nation at Risk*. That report, framed as an open letter to the public, began with passionate remarks related to other ones of the Reagan era, such as follows:

> If an unfriendly foreign power had attempted to impose on America the mediocre educational performance that exists today, we might well have viewed it as an act of war. . . . We have even squandered the gains in student achievement made in the wake of the Sputnik challenge. . . . We have, in effect, been committing an act of unthinking, unilateral educational disarmament. (p. 1)

To address what it identified as education mediocrity, Reagan's commission made recommendations under five categories: (1) Standards and Expectations, (2) Content, (3) Teaching, (4) Leadership and Fiscal Support, and (5) Time, meaning school attendance and hours spent on homework assignments. To be sure, *A Nation at Risk* and its recommendations set the stage for other politically charged education reform efforts that followed it, such as the No Child Left Behind (NCLB) Act (2001), which was signed into law by George W. Bush in 2002.

Although extending the work and concepts of Reagan's education commission, at the core of the NCLB are the same components found in the five *A Nation at Risk* categories. Leading the NCLB list of directives are annual administrations of tests aligned with state standards and periodic reporting of student achievement and school progress. Further, as of late, policymakers and educators have worked across states to develop a set of common core curriculum standards, which will purportedly afford a single reference point for subject area knowledge, teaching, and learning in the United States. In this vein, to align with these commonly shared curriculum standards, there are ongoing discussions about the development of nationwide assessments. These dimensions of standards and assessments have had and will continue to have multiple and far-reaching effects on U.S. education, which are well beyond the scope of a single chapter (for more details of these effects, see the Standards and Accountability volume of this book series).

In the following essays, the question to what extent, if any, should standardized student assessments that have come out of the *Nation at Risk*/NCLB legacy guide curriculum and instruction in schools is debated. First, from a reformist position, Marc L. Stein (The Johns Hopkins University) provides additional details about how standardized assessment and curriculum have become visible in U.S. education, especially during the past decade. Then, he uses that foundation to argue that curriculum, instruction, and assessment are interrelated, and he presents a conceptual framework, drawing from Andrew Porter and colleague's work, consisting of three general and related concepts—(a) *intended curriculum,* (b) *enacted curriculum,* and (c) *assessed curriculum*—to support his case. Stein's essay concludes with an argument for how and why assessments might help guide educators in designing and implementing meaningful curriculum and instruction.

Taking the counterpoint position, Christopher Knaus (California State University, East Bay) argues that standardized assessment and curriculum have contributed to continued inequities in the United States. Beginning with colonial practices, imperialism, and the history of education, he attempts to show that dominant social groups maintain power through crafting what counts as education, deciding on what academic content is valued or not, and determining who is considered to be educated. In short, the design of standard curriculum and assessments aligns with what is known and valued by dominant groups who control governments, labor, and capital. Relating Knaus's position to Stein's threefold framework of curriculum, Knaus argues that it is not the "what" or the "how" of schooling that is the principal question of education in the United States but who is served or excluded by the present state of education policy and practice and the resulting allocation of capital resources to schools and beyond.

A. Jonathan Eakle
The Johns Hopkins University

POINT: Marc L. Stein
The Johns Hopkins University

A s the noted educational historian Diane Ravitch (2010) stated, "Testing is not a substitute for curriculum and instruction" (p. 111). Virtually all policymakers, academics, teachers, and parents would agree with this statement. However, this does not mean that testing has no place in education and the educational system. Rather, testing is an important tool for both education policymakers and classroom teachers to improve student learning. The debate over the role of assessments and the influence that those should have on instruction is not new nor did it begin with the implementation of the reauthorization of the Elementary and Secondary Education Act (ESEA) commonly referred to as NCLB. However, given the impending reauthorization of ESEA, this debate will certainly remain salient and deserves revisiting.

The following essay begins with a brief overview of standards-based reform that has been a cornerstone of most federal and state education policy in the United States during recent decades and serves as a useful beginning point for understanding the issues involved with the question under consideration. Second, a conceptual framework from the work of Andrew Porter is presented that demonstrates the interrelated nature of assessments, curriculum, and instruction. This is followed by an argument for how and why assessments can and should help guide teachers, schools, and districts in their decisions about the curriculum and instruction that they provide to their students.

STANDARDS-BASED REFORM

Standards-based reform as a focus of education policy has come to particular prominence with the implementation of NCLB (2001). While standards-based reform has not meant the same thing in all instances of its use, there are several common characteristics that are germane to the issue of why standardized assessments should guide curriculum and instruction in schools. Laura Hamilton, Brian Stecher, and Kun Yuan (2008) provided a thorough and helpful guide in understanding standards-based reform that I briefly summarize here.

A central component of standards-based reform is the creation by states and school districts of specific policy statements or expectations about what they believe students should know and be able to do across the range of academic subject matter and grade levels. These policies and statements take the form of curriculum and content standards, instructional frameworks, and pacing guidelines. This has been termed the intended curriculum. The intended curriculum sets the targets for the desired student skills and knowledge across the range of subjects and domains. In order to be certain that students are adequately prepared for advanced academic work and beyond, it is of critical importance that these targets are of high quality.

A second important component of standards-based reform is the concept of alignment among all aspects of the educational system. Teachers are the ultimate point at which students interact with curriculum. Therefore, a useful definition of alignment is the degree to which the content of particular classroom instruction overlaps with the expectations found in standards documents. A teacher whose instruction is improperly aligned with the intentions of the standards documents might cover fewer topics (or perhaps even topics not found in the standards) or might cover topics at a different level of cognitive demand than intended for a specific grade level and so forth. Alignment is not only limited to descriptions of classroom instruction but this concept can also be applied to curricular materials such as textbooks as well as to standardized assessments of student achievement, described subsequently. It is believed that an educational system that exhibits a high degree of alignment or coherence across its policies, curriculum, and instruction will be better able to provide a high quality education to its students.

Standardized assessments are the third important component of standards-based reform. A standardized assessment is one that asks test takers to perform the same or similar tasks, under the same conditions, and is uniformly scored. The goal of standardization is to allow for the comparison of the performance of each student to the performance of all other students, independent of other extraneous or irrelevant factors to the domain or construct being tested. Standardization provides the grounds whereby individual characteristics, other than those related to the construct or domain of interest being assessed, have no appreciable effect on the scoring and interpretation of those scores (Koretz, 2008).

Information generated by assessments provides a mechanism to monitor the level and progress of student performance. This information is useful at all levels of the educational system but is especially relevant in providing evidence of effective or ineffective instruction. Information generated from assessments is feedback into the system and is expected to engender changes that lead to better student performance. W. James Popham (1987) terms this concept "measurement-driven instruction," meaning that assessments should influence teachers in their decisions about what is taught in their classroom. It is important to remember that assessment is a fundamental instructional tool used by classroom teachers. Information on student performance gained from classroom assessments at the end of units and lessons are used by teachers to identify areas where individual students or the whole class performed well or poorly and then to make decisions for future instruction based on these data. Likewise, results from larger scale standardized assessments can be used in the same purposeful manner when the testing results are reported back to teachers and school administrators in sufficient detail to be constructive.

A CONCEPTUAL FRAMEWORK OF CURRICULUM

It is important to realize that subject area content, instruction, and assessments are all aspects of a larger concept of curriculum design and as such, are not truly separate entities. They are interconnected and are all statements about what we believe students should know and be able to do as a result of their educational experiences. The work of Andrew Porter and colleagues provides a helpful framework for thinking about curriculum (Porter & Smithson, 2001; Porter, Smithson, Blank, & Zeidner, 2007). One might think of the curriculum of a given subject in a given grade as put forth by state and local standards documents as the intended curriculum, teachers' classroom instruction or implementation of that curriculum as the enacted curriculum, and the standardized assessment used to gauge student learning of the intended curriculum as the assessed curriculum.

The three components of content, instruction, and assessment that make up curriculum are related to one another in a simplified form of feedback loop whereby each component influences the other two. For example, the intended curriculum—whether based on state and district standards documents or based on textbooks or other academic materials used by a teacher (which are often based on state standards)—can and should influence what teachers teach in their classrooms. In short, the intended curriculum is the resources that teachers use when creating their classroom instruction. Similarly, the assessed curriculum, whether large scale standardized assessments or teacher-generated classroom assessments, can and should be based on the intended curriculum. Just as in the previous example, the content and topics represented by the individual items on a given assessment should originate from intended and enacted curriculum.

Why is this conceptual framework important in understanding why assessments should guide instruction and curricular decisions? First, it reminds us that arguments about whether assessments should drive instruction or whether instruction should drive assessments are missing the fundamental interconnectedness of instruction, content, and assessments; all three elements work together as parts of a complete system. The framework also allows for the assessment of the degree of alignment between the constituent components. In

fact, research has shown a significant relationship between the level of alignment of a teacher's instruction and the intended and assessed curriculum and
higher student achievement (Gamoran, Porter, Smithson, & White, 1997). On
its face, this finding makes sense; students who are exposed to instruction that
is in tight alignment with curricular standards tend to do better on assessments
based on those same standards than peers in classrooms that are less aligned.
Logically, a caveat is that instructional alignment is most desirable when the
standards that are the focus of the alignment are of the highest quality.

IMPACT OF ASSESSMENT ON CURRICULUM AND INSTRUCTION

On their own, neither assessments nor standards targets have much leverage in
guiding and improving classroom instruction. Simply posting new standards
and benchmarks on state websites or providing a one-shot in-service professional development (PD) session for teachers does not stand much chance of
guiding teachers' instruction into alignment with the instructional goals set
out in those standards and benchmarks.

Assessment and Curriculum Content Standards

Nonetheless, there are several key characteristics necessary for assessments to
be able to influence what is taught by teachers in classrooms in positive ways.
First, the intended curriculum that assessments are based on should be of the
highest quality and should reflect the core knowledge and skills for a given
subject as determined by content area experts, teachers, and other policy stakeholders. Further, these curricular targets should be limited to a number that is
manageable for classroom teachers. Lengthy and copious lists of standards and
expectations present an unreasonable expectation for instruction and can be
counterproductive. When confronted by such an extensive list of requirements,
teachers are likely to selectively choose only those standards that they believe
can be covered given time restraints.

In addition, many large scale state assessments neglect to measure all standards put forth in their curricular documents, and many tests tend to focus on
standards components that are more readily assessed and are of lower cognitive
demand on typical students. When combined with high-stakes accountability
regulations, this creates perverse consequences such as overuse of instructional
time to teach test taking strategies and instruction that is geared toward the
specifics of a given test versus the standards and academic expectations that
underlie them.

Many have noted that the range of quality in the curricular content standards and benchmarks developed by states under NCLB is vast. States such as California, Indiana, and Massachusetts have generally been considered to have high quality standards that are rigorous in content and marked by their clarity and specificity in academic expectations. At the other end of the spectrum are states that have curriculum standards so vague in their expectations for educators and students that the standards are essentially meaningless as guidance for teachers in designing and implementing their instruction.

Common Core State Standards

A proposed solution to the problem of 51 sets of standards from 50 states and the District of Columbia has come through the recent Common Core State Standards Initiative (CCSSI) led by the National Governors Association (NGA) and the Council of Chief State School Officers (CCSSO). Their work has produced standards for mathematics and English language arts. As of this writing, 40 states and the District of Columbia have voluntarily adopted these standards. While it is too soon to know the consequences of adoption of the Common Core State Standards, there are several near-term outcomes that are potentially likely and positive. First, with a large number of states using the same standards, the conversation about what students should know and be able to do expands to a much larger group of educators, policymakers, and other society members. In the age of globalization, it is important that all American students, regardless of the state in which they are educated, receive a common education based on high, widely agreed on standards that will prepare them for their work lives beyond secondary school. This is preferable to our current system of individual state standards that can be of varying quality and at times intensely parochial, such as the 2010 U.S. history standards of Texas.

In addition, the adoption of common standards across states will expectantly free up capacity at state departments of education from the work of creating standards and will enable them to address other areas of need in their schools and districts. Cross state common standards are also likely to lead to the creation of common assessments. By pooling resources among states, it is much more likely that these new assessments will be designed to avoid many of the undesirable aspects of current state assessments, such as focusing on lower-level learning dimensions, as suggested earlier in the present essay.

Professional Development

Further, savings in time and effort afforded by common standards and assessments could be applied to a more robust system of sustained PD for educators to learn how to meaningfully integrate the intended curriculum into classroom instruction. These PD experiences should be of high quality and provide teachers with the opportunity to work individually and in groups to both understand the intent and details of the curricular standards and how to best integrate the standards into their daily classroom instruction. PD should also be targeted to best inform teachers in how to use data generated from standardized assessments to inform their instructional practices. Simply providing teachers with the proportions of students at advanced, proficient, and basic levels of performance (which has often been the case) is not particularly useful in identifying specific subject area knowledge and instructional practices that need to be strengthened.

Evaluating Instructional Practices

Teachers also need ways to link their instruction to the results from standardized assessments in a way that is actionable. In order to be actionable, standardized assessments need to be reported to teachers at the topic level such that teachers can see the topic areas where students performed exceptionally or poorly. Secondly, teachers need a similar picture of their instruction in relation to the same set of standards and topics. With such a picture, teachers can gauge their instructional practices to be able to know how those practices affect their students' achievement and then make adjustments to their instruction to address student deficiencies. Over time, teachers would also be able to investigate whether the changes to instruction had the intended effect on student performance. A potential tool that could be used to accomplish this are the Surveys of the Enacted Curriculum (SEC) developed at the Wisconsin Center for Educational Reform, which are used to collect and report data on teachers' instructional practices. The same surveys can also be applied to standards documents and assessments. The resulting data provide an objective method for teachers and administrators to assess the degree of alignment among instruction, standards, and assessments. When used as a PD tool, the SEC has been shown to be effective in promoting positive changes in instructional practices (Porter et al., 2007).

Data on student performance—individually and collectively—should guide instructional and curricular decision making of individual teachers, schools, and districts. By using data from standardized assessments, teachers and school communities can identify problems that need attention and propose solutions to those problems. Further, data from assessments are an important source of information that can help in evaluating if valued academic goals are being met. When these goals are not being met, assessment data can help inform efforts to modify policies and instruction as part of a system of continuous improvement. In order for our educational system to make progress in providing an effective and world-class education to all students, educators must use every available tool at their disposal. Standardized assessments are one such tool.

COUNTERPOINT: Christopher Knaus
California State University, East Bay

Insofar as the purpose of education is not agreed on in the United States, a uniform system framed by standardized student assessments should not guide curriculum and instruction in schools. In theory, standardizing curriculum and instruction so that students might be, in turn, compared in how well they learn seems like a good idea. Yet, in practice, such standardization results in one-size-fits-all approaches unable to educate a wide range of students in a wide range of ways.

Underlying this one-size-fits-all approach to schooling is an assumption that objective assessments can measure students in terms of academic performance and intelligence, as if the context in which students go to school (and subsequently work) is irrelevant. Yet, perhaps the most devastating challenge to standardized student assessments is that the majority of Americans have not agreed on what schools should do in the first place. In essence, standardized assessments measure a narrowly tailored set of relatively irrelevant school outcomes without asking American citizens what ideas and practices should be assessed. Indeed, local communities care about what their children learn and in fact may be much more attuned to what they need to learn to be successful in their localities. Thus, those communities should be allowed to develop local education goals that foster democratic participation in all of their children. Then, they should be supported in developing authentic curriculum, instruction, and assessment strategies needed to reach such goals. In short, in a democracy a distant authority should not be dictating what counts as education in a community.

After presenting a brief overview of the purpose of schools in the United States, this counterpoint essay clarifies how a one-size-fits-all approach standardizes the lowest common denominator in public schools. Further, this provides for inauthentic assessments, ignores if students have adequate opportunities to learn, prioritizes competition over cooperation, deprofessionalizes teachers, and ignores local contexts and needs.

STANDARDIZING INEQUALITY BY DESIGN

Schools in the United States began, in part, to ensure proper etiquette among the children of white upper-class landowners. Schools were soon expanded in efforts to "civilize" displaced indigenous children, many of whom were forcibly removed from their families. In contrast, black children, initially enslaved and later disenfranchised by exclusive racial policies, were violently punished if they were caught reading texts or writing. This historical foundation helped ensure that many communities of color distrusted school systems because schools had been designed to silence their discourse—the way their children thought, talked, worshipped, dressed, moved, and so forth. Any attempts at resisting such "education" practices were met with school or state-sponsored violence.

Out of this history of colonization and imperialism came a progressive movement to cast schools as a way to better society, and, in the latter part of the 20th century, equal opportunity was eventually granted by law to all children regardless of race, ethnicity, language, gender, and disability. Through continued protests, additional legal interventions, and so on, public schools slowly began to teach all children, giving rise to a structural problem: How do you define academic success in a diverse America? As soon as school attendance became a requirement for all children, definitions of academic success and the purpose of schooling became battleground issues for control over what should be taught, how it is taught, and who should be invited into such conversations. As described subsequently, standardized assessments are, and continue to be, a primary way through which dominant social groups have attempted to prioritize their own interests, maintain control, and not equalize opportunity among all children.

The Stanford–Binet IQ test was the first standardized test designed to be developed and marketed specifically to segregate society (Garrison, 2009). Those who scored well were scientifically determined to be more intelligent, deemed meritorious by virtue of their access to test content, and received access to the best resourced schools. Those who scored low were branded uneducable and provided limited educational opportunities because, the test makers argued, they were destined for life as factory workers. The eugenics movement, most popular during the first half of the 20th century, also used these tests as scientific justification for racial and class-based exclusion, advocating sterilization of those who scored low (those groups included not only people of color but also gays, lesbians, and people with disabilities). Over the decades, such tests continue to be tinkered with in ways to ensure that wealthier and socially dominant populations score higher. Civil rights groups maintain that such tests are culturally biased, and research has long documented the disparate impact of standardized assessments based on race, class, gender, language, and disability (Kohn, 1999).

Despite this knowledge of bias, during the past few decades there has been a rise in standardized student assessments that guide curriculum and instruction, allowing educational testing and curriculum development corporations to determine what is taught in schools and who has access to the best resources. Yet educators could choose from numerous other standards. In addition to abundant assessments used to limit access to higher education exemplified by the SAT, ACT, MCAT, LSAT, GRE, and GMAT, K–12 schools use standards developed by content-based experts such as the National Writing Project and the National Council of Teachers of Mathematics (NCTM), research and scholarly organizations including the American Educational Research Association and National Association for Multicultural Education, teacher professional organizations such as the National Education Association (NEA) and state teachers associations, as well as local school boards and state certification boards. All of these interests advocate the importance of their standards, but teachers carry the burden of implementing these often disjointed, contradictory standards that come and go with new superintendents, new secretaries of education, and new textbook adoption policies. Thus, at the policy level, enforcing standardized assessments and the resulting curriculum and instruction does not address the needs of local students or teachers but instead what those outside of the everyday operation of schools and communities believe is needed to support a global capitalist economy.

ONE-SIZE-FITS-ALL: THE LEAST COMMON DENOMINATOR

At the school level, standardized curriculum and instruction categorize students in the same biased way as do more global institutions, even though the purpose of schooling vastly differs by geography, wealth, family, culture, and individual student. Standardized assessments make limited accommodation for special education students, recent immigrants, relocated out-of-state students, English language learners, the homeless, or students living amidst violence. Standardizing curriculum and instruction also treats students as if they all need to know the same things regardless of where they live, what they want to do with their lives, and what their families want, need, and value. Nonetheless, authentically assessing student knowledge entirely depends on what students and local communities need from schools, thus measurement tools must be developed to respond directly to a range of cultural perspectives and different ways of thinking. In addition, standardized assessments presume one way of thinking, forcing students into believing in one correct answer, when in reality, there are often many options. Standardized student assessments instead measure the lowest common denominator of academic skills in order to standardize multiple-choice tests, which are administered under the guise of efficiency.

In this vein, the following yearlong scene is all too familiar in many high school urban classrooms: At the beginning of their senior year, students who have not yet dropped out of school or passed the state's high school exit exam (which may be 50% to 60% of the students of color left at the school) are placed into remedial mathematics and English test preparation courses. Such students no longer are given the option of drama, visual arts, biology, social studies, or economics. Along the course of the year, perhaps a third of the students of color will drop out, frustrated by a school day filled by test prep courses in math and English. A month before the first round of tests, several classrooms are created for students who are designated as the lowest achieving amongst the lowest achieving. For these students, their entire six-course day might be filled with rote-and-drill math and reading activities. Many of these students will drop out; others will tune out. Even if they pass the test, students may not have enough credits in other core subjects to graduate, and they will be years away from being academically ready for college. These are the students ignored by standardized curriculum, treated as if they are less intelligent and capable and who ultimately are labeled as dropouts, which holds them in continued disparate circumstances.

One-Size-Fits-All Provides Inauthentic Assessments

Insofar as standardized assessments do not provide for authentic evaluations, teachers guided by standardized curriculum and instruction have fewer tools available from which to respond to students. Standardized assessments measure the impact of school in narrowly defined, often multiple-choice generated ways, ignoring the complexity of children, teachers, schools, and the learning process. Rather than assess critical thinking, perseverance or capacity to be creative in the face of barriers, standardized assessments typically measure standardized English language proficiency, base level content recollection, and timed test taking skills. Rather than assess student capacity to tell an engaging story, standardized assessments evaluate punctuation and vocabulary definitions of rarely used words that are more common in privileged households. Further, measuring how well students are able to translate information bits into multiple-choice tests has limited practical application. Such information is not useful to teachers developing balanced students who not only know how to write using Standard English conventions but also have something powerful to say in other ways. In addition, standardized assessments provide no actual data on how smart students really are, how well they know the curriculum content, or how effective their teachers are, and these assessments are typically too infrequent to meaningfully guide classroom instruction.

One-Size-Fits-All Ignores Student Opportunities to Learn

Students are also set up to fail when a curriculum based on standardized assessments does not take into consideration whether students have adequate opportunities to learn. Many urban students of color attend run-down schools; are taught by a revolving door of young teachers not familiar with their local community or students, let alone good teaching practices; and have outdated curricular materials, limited computer access, and poorly stocked or no libraries. These school conditions do not compare to more affluent schools, and one should not expect similar results from inadequate facilities, outdated curricular materials, and less qualified teachers with less district support than their affluent counterparts, particularly when teacher capacity to creatively address student need is limited by standardized curriculum.

In addition to unequal school conditions, low income students also tend to have less at-home support, because often their parents, who often did not successfully navigate K–12 or college, have to work multiple low-paying jobs. In addition, urban communities continue to react to the violence that affects their neighborhoods, resulting in youth and adults who grow up facing violence, emotional trauma, and barriers to good health care. Standardized assessments do not take into consideration the context in which students grow up, much less what students need in order to engage in a classroom or complete homework that teaches disconnected information. Moreover, standardized curriculum, by definition, ignores issues that impact students at home. Instead, standardized scores report what is already well known: School inequality continues, and aligning curriculum and instruction to such measures does not equalize student opportunities to learn.

One-Size-Fits-All Prioritizes Individual Competition Over Cooperation

By standardizing assessments, educators measure a watered-down notion of achievement that fosters needless competition amongst unequally supported students and educators. This competition, reflected in the battle for higher grades and higher test scores, encourages busy work for students, as they strive for percentages and not meaningful knowledge and life skills. This competitive framing ignores that different students learn differently and also that cooperation might actually bring out the best in students. Rather than have students develop skills to collaborate on assignments and address issues facing their communities, standardized assessments prioritize students doing better than their peers and better than other communities.

Educators are also forced to outperform each other despite obvious inequalities in school resources. The competition is not equal: Affluent families and schools have additional resources to ensure their children excel on tests that are already culturally biased toward their children. Yet teachers and principals are still evaluated for how well students do on standardized assessments in comparison to other schools. Teachers and principals are evaluated regardless of the resource level of the school, community, and district. This added pressure limits schools from offering engaging courses that will not directly increase test scores but also reinforces competition over scores that do not mean very much. Because of the focus on competition for resources (and to maintain one's job), the threat of failure on standardized assessments encourages schools and boards to push potentially low scoring students out of their schools. Thus the achievement gap actually is a gap in wealth hidden by standardized assessments, and it results in a competitive atmosphere that limits student access to a well-rounded curriculum in favor of higher test scores.

One-Size-Fits-All Deprofessionalizes Teachers

Standardizing curriculum and teaching, while not addressing school inequalities, further deprofessionalizes teachers. Under such an approach, teachers are forced to comply with standards-justified mandates that contradict research in child development, curriculum design, special education, language acquisition, multicultural education, and critical pedagogy. Indeed, many teachers read aloud from prepackaged scripts while walking around classrooms, unable to observe or respond to students. Teachers regularly report that they do not receive useful PD to help them deepen their teaching strategies and are frustrated by standardized curricula with limited room to respond to student need. This frustration is exacerbated when teachers are labeled as failures because of their commitment to working in hard-to-staff schools. Dictating how teachers can interact with students ensures that teachers who are creative, caring, and passionate might either leave the profession or stop being engaging. That is exactly the type of teacher most children want and need, yet it is precisely that kind of educator who is limited by standardized instruction.

One-Size-Fits-All Ignores Local Community Concerns

Standardized assessments guiding the curriculum also limit local input. Most standardized curricula ignore local histories and perspectives while promoting mainstream ways of thinking. What is assessed for in history standards, for example, typically reflects the perspective of European colonizers, not the Iroquois, Ohlone, or Navajo. Assessing student insight into a perspective students may not agree with might tell a teacher something about how well they are teaching multiple perspectives, but standardized assessments do not focus on local histories and minority perspectives. Thus, from the teacher and student perspective, standards simply do not reflect the range of academic skill sets or needed knowledge and diminish the value of local histories. These local concerns are reflected in pathways toward local employment; there are many pathways beyond graduation for students, and standardized curricula often ignore what is needed to successfully navigate the local communities students live in. And yet at a minimum, the purpose of schools for local communities should be about being successful locally. Standardizing education simply does not value local perspectives in ways that allow local control over what matters.

CONCLUSION

The real question is not whether standardized student assessments should guide curriculum and instruction, because they already do. Measurement of disconnected tidbits of information students can translate onto timed multiple-choice tests already determines which students graduate, what teachers remain in the classroom, and which schools are closed. Despite what is known about how such standardized assessments do not adequately measure students of color, English language learners, students with disabilities, and low income students, their use in schools is pervasive.

Rather than prescribe general solutions to widespread school failure, the ever persistent achievement gap, and the revolving door of teachers that leave the profession within their first 3 years, the use of standardized student assessments to guide curriculum and instruction prescribes a one-size-fits-all solution to dozens of interrelated, complicated sets of problems that impact student academic engagement. Instead of focusing on measurement, national interests should work with school officials to devise local goals and then help develop ways to measure progress toward those goals.

FURTHER READINGS AND RESOURCES

Gamoran, A., Porter, A. C., Smithson, J., & White, P. A. (1997, Winter). Upgrading high school mathematics instruction: Improving learning opportunities for low-achieving, low-income youth. *Educational Evaluation and Policy Analysis, 19*(4), 325–338.

Garrison, M. J. (2009). *A measure of failure: The political origins of standardized testing.* New York: SUNY Press.

Hamilton, L., Stecher, B., & Yuan, K. (2008). *Standards-based reform in the United States: History, research, and future directions.* Santa Monica, CA: RAND Corporation.

Kohn, A. (1999). *The schools our children deserve.* New York: Houghton Mifflin.

Koretz, D. (2008). *Measuring up: What educational testing can really tell us.* Cambridge, MA: Harvard University Press.

National Commission on Excellence in Education. (1983). *A nation at risk: The imperative for educational reform.* Retrieved February 20, 2011, from http://www2 .ed.gov/pubs/NatAtRisk/index.html

Popham, W. J. (1987). The merits of measurement-driven instruction. *Phi Delta Kappan, 68*(9), 679–682.

Porter, A. C., & Smithson, J. L. (2001). *Defining, developing, and using curriculum indicators* (Consortium for Policy Research in Education Research Report Series, RR-048). Philadelphia: Consortium for Policy Research in Education Research.

Porter, A., Smithson, J., Blank, R., & Zeidner, T. (2007). Alignment as a teacher variable. *Applied Measurement in Education, 20*(1), 27–51.

Ravitch, D. (2010). *The life and death of the great American school system.* New York: Basic Books.

Sleeter, C. E. (2007). *Facing accountability in education: Democracy and equity at risk.* New York: Teachers College Press.

COURT CASES AND STATUTES

Elementary and Secondary Education Act of 1965, 20 U.S.C. §§ 6301 *et seq.*

Larry P. v. Riles, 495 F. Supp. 926 (N.D. Cal. 1979), aff'd in part, 793 F.2d 969 (9th Cir. 1984) (striking tests down).

No Child Left Behind Act of 2001, 20 U.S.C.A. §§ 6301 *et seq.*

5

Should the focus of literacy education be on "reading to learn" or "learning to read"?

POINT: P. David Pearson, *University of California, Berkeley,* and Gina Cervetti, *University of Michigan*

COUNTERPOINT: Marcia Invernizzi and Latisha Hayes, *University of Virginia*

OVERVIEW

The sounds of "reading to learn" and "learning to read" easily slide from the tongues of many educators—especially in reference to elementary school curriculum and instruction in the United States. While these phrases are often spoken by educators the distinction between them is not always clear. The purpose of this chapter is to unpack what these phrases actually mean and how the phrases have become a seemingly central axiom in much reading education practice.

The phrase has old roots in a great divide of reading education that is marked off between word recognition and text comprehension processes and methods. In the late 19th century, much of the research on reading was simply about the sounds and markings associated with written words. Gradually, some studies gave way to the relations among oral and written language and thinking processes. For example, in the first half of the 20th century educational psychologists such as Edward Thorndike became interested in topics of how memory, whether it is working memory or latent memories, might influence the comprehension of a text. However, the continued focus during that time on word recognition in beginning reading research and instruction is evidenced by the highly popular McGuffey primer and first readers' texts with their controlled sentenced length and vocabulary and repetitive patterns, such as "The fat cat sat on a mat." As the skills of children sharpened, they advanced to higher level texts with more complex vocabulary and ideas, and as they reached the later elementary grades, students read increasingly sophisticated texts, including American classics. The McGuffey series illustrates one of the first examples of graded readers. This has evolved into what today is frequently referred to as "reading levels," which attempt to match the concepts, words, and grammatical level of a text to the developmental level of typical children at a particular time such as fourth grade.

By the 1970s, meaning-based reading research and its application reached a zenith, partially as a result of Ken and Yetta Goodman's seminal research on the analyses of miscues, which, grossly put, are the errors that children voice while reading printed texts aloud. Whether the meaning of the text is altered by a miscue is an example they drew upon. For instance, consistently substituting "Jan" for "Jane" will likely not change the meaning of a given text; whereas, replacing "Job" for "Jane" would. The Goodman's research helped to spawn the whole language movement, which emphasized reading as a meaning-making process. Further, insofar as text meanings and interpretations can greatly vary, whole language methods were as much about thoughtful teaching as about reading comprehension. As a result, whole language approaches were viewed as cornerstones for teacher empowerment.

Related to the meaning-based notions of whole language is another one that has been a bulwark of reading research and instruction during the past half century: schema theory. In reading research, this perspective emphasizes the role that past memories and experiences can have on organizing meaning while reading texts, how much attention needs to be devoted to familiar and unfamiliar texts, and so on. In a related way and during the same time, meaning-based instruction and learning via the work of David Ausbel, Jerome Bruner, Jean Piaget, and others enabled teachers and researchers to draw on concepts of metacognition, which, simply put, is "thinking about thinking." Skilled readers, for example, are well aware of when they can breeze through a passage without great effort and when they need to pause to use "fix up" strategies, such as rereading a sentence or seeking out the meaning of an unfamiliar word. To be sure, the 1970s and 1980s could well be considered the golden age of cognitive psychological research and instruction about reading comprehension, and many of the ideas of whole language, schema, and metacognitive theories influence what is taught in much of teacher education today. However, these approaches, although reaching beyond those of the rote memorization, behaviorism, and so forth of a previous time, are slowly but surely giving way to even more expansive notions of reading texts that encompass not only the printed type but a variety of communication modes and expressions, none the least of which are multimedia ones, such as those of digital formats, cinema, three-dimensional objects, and spaces.

Nonetheless, as the 20th century began to close, the wave of meaning-making approaches to reading education curriculum and instruction was challenged—in part, because it led to open-ended explorations that sometimes did not foster academic achievement for some children. Gaps persisted among vulnerable student populations, and direct instruction of the basics of letter sounds, memorization exercises, and controlled texts came back into fashion in some corners of education. This was fueled by a growing body of research that highlighted the utility of phonics, or "sounding out" words; how the early awareness of discrete units of sounds in language or phonemes predicted the later academic success of readers; and so forth. Consequently, for several years there raged what is known by educators as the "great debate" of reading education, which pitted whole language advocates against those of direct instruction of basic processes, which included, among other things, phonics. Championing direct instruction was Jeanne Chall, whose developmental stages of reading texts was misapplied as showing a neat divide between what she referred to as "learning to read" and "reading to learn," which became a slogan in the ongoing polemics of liberal and conservative education policy and practice.

Today, many literacy education researchers and practitioners do not adhere to a rigid cut between "reading to learn" and "learning to read." The great debate between the phonics and whole language camps was settled more than a decade ago with truce-like logic supporting "blended approaches" to instructing and learning from texts. Nevertheless, the divide continues in education policy and practice and in the design of curriculum programs that are pitched to one side of the previous divide or the other.

The following essays are written by eminent reading education scholars who present arguments regarding the debate over "reading to learn" and "learning to read." The point essay in this chapter is written by P. David Pearson of the University of California, Berkeley, and coauthor Gina Cervetti of the University of Michigan, whose seminal work in meaning-based reading education, including the relation of schema theory to text reading, has spanned the decades between the golden age of reading comprehension research and the present. Taking the counterpoint side of the issue, Marcia Invernizzi and Latisha Hayes of the University of Virginia describe the rich word study tradition that comes out of the University of Virginia's McGuffey Reading Center. This tradition has laid a foundation in constructivist processes about the relations of spelling, word recognition, and reading in context.

A. Jonathan Eakle
The Johns Hopkins University

POINT: P. David Pearson
University of California, Berkeley

Gina Cervetti
University of Michigan

A persistent homily about reading instruction is that children first must learn to read and only then can they read to learn. In other words, once children have acquired "the basics"—sight words, decoding skills, literal comprehension of text, and a few vocabulary skills like inferring word meanings from context—they can read to learn from text. Advocates of the traditional learning-to-read model commonly offer one of the following arguments in defense of content-light early reading materials:

- reading materials in the primary grades should focus on simple versions of everyday experiences, so that the unfamiliar process of acquiring the "code" or the cipher that maps written language to oral language can be the focus,

- when students are offered meaningful materials, they use the available context to determine the pronunciations of words, thus deflecting them from the critical early reading task of figuring out the letter-sound match they must acquire, or

- the motivation to master the code is so compelling that content matters little, so even the seemingly meaningless content of decodable texts such as "Dan can fan Nan" can sustain students' interest.

What these three rationales share is the underlying assumption that learning more about the world around them is not something that can or should matter to beginning readers.

We take issue with this traditional perspective on the trajectory of reading instruction and acquisition and instead propose that reading to learn should be a central focus from children's very first encounters with texts. Specifically, we suggest the following:

- There should not be a time when meaningful texts should be withheld from students.

- There is no stage of reading development at which readers are not also learning to read.

- There is no stage of reading development when the goal should simply be getting words off a page.

- We should regard knowledge acquisition as inseparable from reading development.

To develop these four points, three constructs—authenticity, motivation, and learning—are developed in subsequent portions of the essay.

AUTHENTICITY

Authenticity has two faces—(a) text and (b) task. An authentic text is one written for one or more purposes—to communicate, to inform, to persuade, to engage, or to entertain. By contrast, an inauthentic text is one created for a special, usually pedagogical, purpose—to teach, practice, or test some sort of skill such as decoding words in the *at* word family, such as cat, mat, and fat. In short, inauthentic texts would never be written if we had not "invented" the instructional apparatus that defines schooling. Some people dub these special texts instructional ones; however, our favorite label "textoids" better conveys the notion that these types of texts lack a connection to purposeful reading.

Unlike textoids, authentic texts require students to orchestrate a range of skills in order to make meaning from them; inauthentic texts are often constructed in a way that focuses practice on a single skill or strategy. One might infer from this distinction that it would be easier to read single purpose, inauthentic texts, but that is not necessarily true, because while textoids present fewer challenges and reduced cognitive load, they also offer fewer cues about how to make meaning in response to them.

Tasks can also range along a continuum of authenticity. Authentic reading tasks are the kinds of reading that we do as adults and always involve putting reading to work in the service of a goal. We read to gather insight, gain information, establish communicative relationships, and so forth. What makes a task more or less authentic is whether it entails one or more of the real-world purposes and thus invites the processes that readers use when they are engaged in reading for a reason other than simply practice.

Some advocates of traditional learning-to-read perspectives suggest that the consequences of failing to teach precursor skills are too grave to risk in favor of a meaning-driven approach. They point to research suggesting that students who are not equipped early with skills, such as sight word recognition, often experience reading problems later. For these educators, authenticity represents a luxury that they believe struggling readers cannot afford. We suggest that there is no reason that these skills cannot be acquired by students concurrently in the context of meaningful reading; it may even be true that it is an essential support for basic reading acquisition.

Even mature readers encounter stumbling blocks along the way and draw on particular skills and strategies to get around those blocks. But skills and strategies are leveraged at precisely those moments when needed, not during a special lesson about them. Inasmuch, strategy instruction is much more effective when situated in reading to learn, because strategies make more sense when students have a purpose for using them—for doing things like attacking unknown words. In other words, meaningful reading offers situations where readers realize that they do not understand and need to do something different. This makes sense when the goal of reading is learning but little sense when texts do not resemble those that readers would typically read for understanding such as a newspaper article, instruction manual, or academic article. As Julianne Turner and Scott G. Paris (1995) pointed out, students who have few opportunities to use reading strategies for the purpose of supporting authentic reading might doubt the usefulness of strategies.

In reading meaningful texts for meaningful purposes, the need to invoke a wide array of reading strategies—from decoding to comprehension to critique—will arise naturally because reading to learn is rich with opportunities to encounter the kinds of struggles that invite the use of strategies. And these are precisely the struggles that readers do, can, could, and should engage in because reading is a meaning-making process. Another advantage of meaningful materials is that they encourage readers to use context to monitor their reading output to ensure that it "makes sense," a practice that is virtually impossible with specially designed early texts—and absolutely essential for reading to learn.

Unfortunately, strategy instruction—in the ways in which it has been put into practice as reflected through basal series and kits—is in need of reform. In these cases, strategies are taught as content-free routines that can be applied to any text. Instead, strategies should be taught as tools that help readers unlock the meanings of texts (McKeown, Beck, & Blake, 2009). Otherwise it can breed an excessive reliance on abstract, content-free, metacognitive introspection about strategy use (Pearson & Fielding, 1991). The same could be said of phonics instruction—phonics rules are only a means to an end, which is for understanding and gaining new knowledge.

This is not an admonition against the direct instruction of strategies. Pedagogically, a teacher might pull a strategy, such as decoding a particular pattern or finding a main idea or inferring the motive for a character's action, out of context to conduct an explicit lesson on it—to deal with the strategy as an object of instruction. But then, she should put that strategy in a meaningful context and guide students in learning how it can be applied to overcome a hurdle with a text in the interest of making meaning of it. Moreover, good strategy instruction can sometimes be provided on the fly at the point of contact at which a hurdle is encountered—and always on the way to meaning making. So all other things being equal, the more strategy instruction can be contextualized and in the moment, the sooner we are likely to convince novice readers that these tools really do help them to derive meaning from texts.

MOTIVATION

Motivation is critically important for learning to read. Curiosity and individual interests through reading are powerful factors in sustained engagement with texts (Wigfield & Guthrie, 1997). Meaningful reading invites students to associate reading with their lives off the page in ways that make reading relevant. These factors influence students' willingness to exert the effort required to persist through challenging aspects of the texts that they select, and as a result, they take more ownership and personal responsibility in relation to their work. It is this very willingness to exert the effort that allows readers to marshal *all* of their cognitive resources, including attention and discrimination required for accurate decoding on the road to making meaning.

Additionally, involvement in purposeful reading activities supports both positive attitudes toward reading and reading achievement. Using reading to learn something about the world nurtures a sense of personal mastery. This is not only inherently desirable but it is also a foundation for students to come to understand the purposes of reading, and it seems to play a role in students' decisions about whether to engage in reading in the future. It is not surprising, then, that the simple act of giving students reasons to read and write—reading to learn or investigate or writing to record and communicate—supports their literacy development.

Advocates of the traditional model of beginning reading often suggest that meaning is less important in the early stages of instruction because children are caught up in the joy of making words come alive and mapping printed words onto their oral language. They suggest that involvement in text is enough to sustain children even if the texts are not inherently meaningful. While it may be true that decoding words is exciting for some children, there is little evidence to suggest that this form of involvement is sustaining. In fact, tasks that emphasize practice in applying discrete reading skills may be associated with a decreased motivation for students to learn. On the other hand, when reading is associated with learning meaningful content and involves personal interests and sensible purposes, students (especially those who struggle) can come to see reading as a way of seeking information, insight, and enjoyment.

LEARNING

While advocates of the traditional learning-to-read perspective point to the gap in reading achievement that exists between the educational haves and have-nots as justification for an early focus on emergent literacy skills, equally harmful and enduring gaps may develop as a result of an exclusive focus on those skills. In fact, the gap in useful content knowledge may be as perilous and persistent as the reading achievement gap. Susan Neuman (2006) called the failure to address differences among children in content knowledge a "critical oversight." Moving beyond the basics, students can learn much from text, including the following:

- Understandings about and investigations of phenomena in the natural world

- The human condition, including the insights that literature can offer about interpersonal relationships, the relationship of humans to the world around them, and the social and internal lives of people living in different cultural and historical contexts

- Disciplinary ways of knowing and investigating the world, such as how a biologist thinks about ecology or how an historian understands conflicts among nations

- The nature of text and of language, including understandings about form–function relationships across different text genres

- Their identities, as when readers see themselves such as their gender, ethnicity, or familial situation reflected in a story

- Metacognitive and metalinguistic knowledge of how language works

Further, learning, operationalized as the acquisition of knowledge, is more than a convenient by-product of reading; it is fuel for reading comprehension (Anderson & Pearson, 1984). Today's new knowledge is, quite literally, tomorrow's prior knowledge. And learning is more than only fuel of comprehension; it is also an agent of motivation, aptitude, positive attitudes, and even the development/refinement of specific skills and strategies. There is much to learn from research that focuses on reading and writing as tools for acquiring knowledge. It appears that situating reading as a tool for learning supports students' motivation to read, as the feedback young readers receive from the thrill of acquiring knowledge goes a long way to sustain them in further reading and learning activities. It also appears that learning goals support students' progress on a range of reading aptitudes—from word recognition to comprehension.

Reading to learn also situates academic assessment in just the right position and in context. When the focus on learning to read is associated with assessments that break the task of reading into a series of discrete skills, such as rapidly naming letters and manipulating phonemes, these benchmarks can be easily mistaken for good reading (Pearson, 2006). Rather, the consequences of participating in valid assessments that put the emphasis on orchestrating a range of enabling skills in the quest for new learning are that students are encouraged to use reading for meaningful, self-selected purposes; those purposes should be the target we are always moving toward in assessment and instruction.

WHAT WE ARE NOT SUGGESTING

Suggesting that students should read meaningful texts for the purposes of learning is not an argument against the explicit instruction of reading strategies. We are not arguing that teachers should simply bathe kids in high quality text and watch instruction take care of itself. To the contrary, sharing the secrets of one's success as a reader is the essence of good instruction, especially when students are not privy to those secrets and when students find themselves in situations where it is not obvious what strategy to use or how to use it. However, teaching in an explicit and highly intentional manner can and should still be embedded in the broader goal of attempting to acquire knowledge.

What we are arguing against is a steady diet of generic, decontextualized strategy instruction for any aspect of reading pedagogy—comprehension, vocabulary, or decoding. We should maintain vigilant awareness that explicit instruction, as helpful as it can be in particular situations, is always irrelevant until it is *applied*. It is only when we see that students can apply strategies to the real reading of authentic texts—where acquiring knowledge and insight is the purpose—that we can be sure that they have truly acquired those strategies and integrated them as useful tools in their academic repertoire. It may be helpful to think of strategies and skills as analogous to a legal precedent; in law, principles are anchored by cases that give specificity and meaning—and teeth—to the principles. In a similar way, we can imagine abstract routines, but we will always situate those principles/routines in specific attempts to understand specific texts for specific purposes.

We are committed to high quality strategy instruction that demonstrates the purpose and utility of strategies at every step along the way. To do that, kids must receive immediate feedback demonstrating to them that strategies are useful—that pulling out just the right tool to help you over a hurdle at just the right moment makes you a smarter, more effective and more strategic reader. In a sense, strategies are just like phonics rules—only a means to an end. It is when either a phonics rule or a strategy routine becomes an end unto itself that bad things happen. In these cases, there is mock compliance from students but no real uptake. Instead, they keep the strategies tucked away in a special "school talk" box that is hauled out only when the assignment requires it and then put back into that box well out of reach of everyday reading. The only way to block such mock compliance is for educators to provide guided apprenticeships that help students learn how, when, and why to apply strategies so that they can see their transparent benefit to the broader goals of making meaning and acquiring knowledge from texts.

CLOSING

We end with the same argument we used to begin this essay—that the commonly voiced learning to read/reading to learn dichotomy is false. First, learning to read could, should, and does entail goals of meaning making and acquiring knowledge at every step along the developmental continuum. Second, there is never a step in that continuum of becoming a more skilled reader when we are not "learning to read"; skilled readers who read to learn are also learning to read better—and to solve new problems they encounter as they read. Third, the contrast between explicit teaching and authentic activity is as spurious as the dichotomy between learning to read and reading to learn is false. Explicit teaching should be used to support authentic activity, and explicit teaching of strategies should always begin and end in an authentic application. Fourth, when educators lead students with the goal of knowledge acquisition, the skill and strategy acquisition face of reading is rendered more sensible, important, and transparent. It is clearer to students why the acquisition of a particular skill set is important when they see the immediate payoff in their learning.

The crux of our argument is simple: We are always reading to learn, and we are always learning to read. The one supports the other at every step along the way. The sooner we accept that premise, the sooner we discard counterproductive instructional programs and meaningless texts and in their stead develop maximally effective curricula that encourage students to learn more about how their world works as they become more facile readers.

COUNTERPOINT: Marcia Invernizzi and Latisha Hayes
University of Virginia

S hould the focus of literacy education be about "reading to learn" or "learning to read"? This oft-repeated phrase is an example of a broad-based summary statement of developmental shifts in the growth of literacy misapplied. Coming from Jeanne Chall's (1983) description of the developmental stages through which most students progress in their journey toward mature reading, learning to read and reading to learn aptly describes a relative shift in emphasis, not a dichotomous "either-or." Unfortunately, well into the 21st century, the field of literacy education is still prone to polarization, and learning to read versus reading to learn has become yet another sound bite in the polemical politics of literacy education.

It's too bad. Scholars who study the process of learning to read have never denied the paramount importance of reading for a good purpose, whether that purpose is to learn what vegetable will be put on top of the pizza on the next page, to learn where butterflies go at night, or to learn if Biscuit will find a friend. At the same time, scholars who study the process and context of reading to learn have never denied the importance of access to the printed word. No one can learn to read without a reason to do so, and no one can read to learn if they can't read printed text.

The phrase *learning to read* is typically associated with the "code," the printed words we look at when we read printed text. In this context, learning to read is about cracking that code, decoding the orthography or spelling, reading the words, irrespective of their meaning. In contrast, the phrase *reading to learn* is typically associated with reading for meaning, reading to learn new ideas, and so forth. This viewpoint assumes that the reader is already facile with decoding and word recognition and there is nothing further to learn about written words. In this essay, the argument is advanced that learning to read includes learning to read for meaning and information and that reading to learn includes learning more about words.

READING STAGES

The phrases *learning to read* versus *reading to learn* hearken back to Chall's theory of reading development in which students progress from an acquisition phase to more advanced reading processes. The purported shift from learning to read to reading to learn typically occurs at around the fourth grade when the elementary curriculum shifts to content area learning. Chall (1983) described a parallel shift in how most readers approach text at about this time, moving from an emphasis on bottom-up processes concerned with word recognition and decoding, to an emphasis on top-down processes concerned with "getting the message" (p. 34). For typically achieving students, this shift occurs at about the same grade level such as fourth grade, but according to Chall's reading-stage theory, the processes readers adopt as they approach text depend more on stage of development than grade.

According to Chall's (1996) theory, emergent readers in Stage 0 use top-down processes such as prediction, picture context, and memory to fit the "message to the medium" because they lack the alphabetic knowledge needed to decipher print media without prior knowledge of the story or information. In contrast, Chall's Stage 1 learners become preoccupied with printed media, as they apply their newly learned decoding skills to access the message; they use a predominantly bottom-up process in reading text, a process that continues into Stage 2 with "increasing backup of a top-down process" when the difficulty of the medium outstrips the word-level skills of the reader (p. 34). Readers especially rely on top-down processes when the going gets tough, either because the orthographic makeup of the word exceeds their ability to decode it or because the word's meaning is unknown to them even after decoding. This interaction between the medium and the message continues across the stages, though the top-down approach receives more emphasis in Stage 3, *reading to learn new ideas.* Typically achieving students reach Stage 3 by Grade 4 but remain in this stage throughout the intermediate and middle school years where reading is used to learn new information, word meanings, and concepts.

Chall's reading stages continue on through college and adulthood. Stage 4 readers, typically found in Grades 9 through 12, mostly rely on top-down processes and use bottom-up processes when encountering unfamiliar vocabulary. These readers read from a range of genres and perspectives and learn to consider ideas from multiple viewpoints. If you are reading this essay, you are a Stage 5 reader, according to Chall's theory, and you read for your own personal and professional purposes. Although your facility with orthography is quite efficient, you too might use some bottom-up processes in reading an extremely complex text about an unfamiliar topic.

Chall's (1983) description of reading development provided a powerful model for teachers to guide the content of their literacy instruction, emphasizing phonics and decoding in the first grade (Stage 1), fluency in the second and third grades (Stage 2), and cognitive strategies to increase comprehension and vocabulary in third grade through eighth grade when students are learning to read new material (Stage 3). High school teachers and college instructors would concentrate on teaching students how to deal with multiple points of view (Stage 4) and to construct and reconstruct their own understandings through critical thinking strategies entailing analysis, synthesis, and judgment (Stage 5).

On the surface, the shift in instructional emphasis that moves gradually from decoding to comprehension appears to equate learning to read with decoding in Stages 1 and 2, and reading to learn with comprehension in Stages 3 through 5. However, Chall (1983) was clear that "the process of comprehension is practiced in all of the stages, from the earliest to the most advanced" (p. xxiv). Further, though her stage theory called for the explicit teaching of phonics and decoding only in Stages 1 and 2, she also called for the "systematic study of words" in Stages 3 and 4 (p. 86). Nevertheless, a cursory reading of Chall's stage theory often results in the erroneous belief that decoding and comprehension are mutually exclusive and that phonics and spelling instruction are not necessary beyond the third grade except for struggling readers who are below grade level in their achievement. We would argue that there are no stages of reading development in which written word knowledge, from either a top-down or bottom-up perspective, is not essential.

WRITTEN WORD KNOWLEDGE

Written words are both the medium and the message. Written words have sound or phonological attributes and meaning or semantic attributes. In addition, written words carry concepts within their word parts or morphological attributes communicating relationships among ideas. These attributes are germane to the argument for the central role written word knowledge plays in both learning to read and reading to learn. Attributes of written words are melded together through their orthography; thus, understanding the spelling system is essential in acquiring vocabulary knowledge integral to learning.

Written word knowledge is at the crux of the learning to read versus reading to learn debate for several reasons. First, knowledge of written words is acquired gradually across the grades; the process of learning about them doesn't stop with the mastery of phonics. While it is true that an important prerequisite for learning to read includes cracking the alphabetic code and learning phonics, the orthographic makeup of words goes well beyond letter-sound correspondences. Written words are composed of larger letter patterns, which are related to both sounds such as *wind*-noun and *wind*-verb, meaning such as *pale–pail*, syllables such as *in-ter-est-ing,* and morphemes such as *in-tract-able*—all of which require instruction beyond the phonics traditionally associated with learning to read. Word study must continue beyond phonics if students are to progress in their written word knowledge and learn from text. Second, capitalizing on spelling-meaning connections across derivationally related words such as *modern* and *modernize* is an underused approach to expanding the word knowledge that is the foundation of reading to learn. Third, and perhaps most compelling, written word knowledge is acquired in a stagelike progression that marches in accord with overall literacy development.

While there is a correlation between stages of written word knowledge and grade levels, there can be a disparity between students' stage of development and their grade-level placement. If the developmental word knowledge of students is ignored for the sake of curriculum coverage or grade-level standards, existing student gaps in written word knowledge simply widen. A literal interpretation of learning to read followed later by reading to learn can result in negligent education practices by excluding the important role of reading for meaning and information in the early stages of reading and the critical role of written word knowledge in the latter stages. There is no stage at which written knowledge and reading for meaning are not essential.

WRITTEN WORD KNOWLEDGE DEVELOPS GRADUALLY

The average high school student can read over 40,000 words, but they did not learn them overnight (Templeton, Bear, Invernizzi, & Johnston, 2010). Written word knowledge develops gradually over time in stagelike progressions spurred by instruction and practice. In all stages, students read to learn and learn to read progressively more difficult words by discovering how spelling relates to sound, pattern, and meaning.

Developmental stages of written word knowledge correspond to the hierarchical tiers of English orthography that developed throughout history: alphabet, pattern, and meaning. Written English is alphabetic at its Anglo-Saxon base, so the first stage is about acquiring the *alphabetic principle,* or the letters and combinations of letters used to represent the speech sounds of English. Learning the systematic and predictable relationships between written letters and individual speech sounds is a necessary first step toward acquiring a beginning reading vocabulary—words that are in the spoken language of most beginning readers (Henderson, 1990). This bottom-up process is helped along by top-down scaffolding by supportive teachers sensitive to the importance of reading for meaningful purposes. Nevertheless, beginning readers must negotiate the alphabetic tier of written English if they are to move toward greater ease in accessing information off the page and constructing their own knowledge base.

The pattern tier of English orthography was acquired during the French occupation of England after the Norman invasion and accounts for the multitudinous spellings associated with a single phoneme, such as the long *a* vowel sound in English such as *late, eight, steak,* and *plain.* Fortunately, these patterns fall into predicable, often rhyming, categories and are easily taught through systematic word study of high frequency spelling patterns in conjunction with wide reading in trade books and readers. While the reading vocabulary in easy chapter books typically read during this second stage are still within the oral vocabulary of most students, newer reading vocabulary is added to the familiar base and the increase in sheer volume of word recognition fuels the possibility of silent reading. Top-down processes interact with the bottom-up process of decoding and results in greater fluency and more self-directed and increasingly silent reading as students acquire patterns within words.

While words have meaning in every tier, an explosion of meaning units, or morphemes, was layered on top of the pattern tier of written English during the Renaissance. The proliferation of new scientific knowledge, concepts about government, art, and culture necessitated the need for new vocabulary to express these ideas. A sophisticated Latinate and Greco vocabulary was added to the existing corpus of written English, which added to the language layers of meaning units or morphemes including Latin and Greek affixes, stems, and roots. Students who have already acquired knowledge of the alphabetic and pattern tiers of written English are well poised to benefit from the study of these multisyllabic words and their word parts. The generative potential of word study in this tier is exponential because of the many spelling-meaning connections within derivationally related word groups such as *recite, recital,* and *recitation.*

Acquiring the specific word features characteristic of each tier of English orthography takes the average student approximately 16 years or longer. Though Chall (1983) recommended "systematic word study" across her reading stages, she didn't specify the content of such word study beyond the first two. An understanding of the more advanced stages of written word knowledge and their correspondence to Chall's later reading stages can help fill this void. Systematic word study that builds on principles of sound, pattern, and meaning can advance students' reading vocabulary and simultaneously enhance comprehension. Further, understanding the developmental nature of written word knowledge can help teachers design the content and pacing of their instruction to match their students' needs as they learn to read and learn to read to learn across the grades and stages.

SPELLING-MEANING CONNECTIONS BUILD VOCABULARY

Chall (1996) argued that the vocabulary load in children's texts shifts at about the fourth-grade level, moving from familiar, high frequency words that exist in most children's oral vocabulary to more abstract, lower frequency academic and conceptually complex word meanings tied to domain-specific information. She conjectured that lower socioeconomic status children fall behind in their reading achievement around this point because of their lack of exposure to information and the corresponding academic vocabulary. Without the requisite background knowledge and vocabulary, top-down processes become of limited use. Chall referred to this phenomenon as the "fourth-grade slump."

One often overlooked solution to the fourth-grade slump lies in the generative power of vocabulary instruction that builds on spelling-meaning connections in multisyllabic words. Words that share similar meanings often share similar spellings even if the pronunciation changes across derivational forms (Bear, Templeton, Invernizzi, & Johnston, 2008). Spelling-meaning connections can be seen in word pairs such as *reside–residential* and *confide–confidential.* In these word pairs, the *i* is retained in the adjectival form to signal the meaning relationship to the base word, the verb form. The spelling remains the same even though the sound of the *i* changes from a long vowel sound in *reside* and *confide,* to a *schwa* sound in *residential* and *confidential.* Morphophonemic aspects of derivational relations like this can generalize to thousands of words that work the same way. The combinatorial aspect of prefixes, suffixes, and Greek and Latin roots also adds generative power to the study of spelling-meaning relationships. Insofar as over 60% of English vocabulary and over 90% of the vocabulary of the sciences is created through a combination of Latin and Greek roots, prefixes, and suffixes, knowing how these Latin and Greek roots and morphemes combine to make new and related words can significantly increase vocabulary knowledge and impact reading comprehension through high school. Instead of teaching vocabulary one word at a time, educators can teach the meaning *system* inherent in English orthography by grouping words that share the same root. For instance, words related to time (*chron*), such as *chronic, chronology, chronicle,* and *synchronize,* can be grouped and compared to words with another root. When this kind of word study is connected to ideas and themes in texts students read, the result can be an exponential growth in subject area vocabulary. Word study that capitalizes on the spelling-meaning connections empowers students to learn to read longer, harder words and to learn more about the ideas words represent. An exploration of spelling-meaning connections has the potential to reduce the fourth-grade slump.

DIVERGENCE OF STAGES AND GRADE LEVELS

Some students in the upper elementary grades and beyond are still unable to spell or decode words accurately and fluently, and this shortcoming has a crippling effect on learning across the curriculum, destroying student motivation and a sense of self-efficacy in their ability to learn. Teachers are often caught in a dilemma between what they are required to teach, referring to the curriculum and what they know their students need such as reading instruction. Students are required to read to learn content information, but many have not yet learned to read or write well enough to do so.

Struggling readers are by no means a homogeneous group. Their background knowledge of content-specific information varies as much as their literacy skills. Yet, a commonality among them is their lack of written word knowledge. Readers may be in the sixth or eighth grade, but their word knowledge may be in stages of development associated with word patterns, or worse, alphabetics. If the educational assumption for students past a certain grade level is that students no longer require instruction associated with learning to read, these students are placed in double jeopardy; they neither receive the literacy instruction they need to move forward in development, nor access the content in their textbooks. Until attention is paid to students' developmental word knowledge, regardless of their grade placement, achievement gaps will continue.

Stage theories of reading development are valuable because they provide a framework for the timing and pacing of instruction that match the precise needs of children. Unfortunately, stage theory is often misinterpreted and misused in terms of learning to read and reading to learn. One major misinterpretation is that word-level instruction is only for the primary grades and unnecessary in later grades. A second misinterpretation is that encouraging and teaching students how to read to learn is reserved for the upper grades. An overemphasis on word-level skills in the early grades to the exclusion of learning information and concepts can be as detrimental to vocabulary and knowledge development as the exclusion of word study in the upper grades. What some early stage theorists failed to articulate was how progressively deeper levels of written word knowledge related to meaning or morphology can increase vocabulary knowledge. Shane Templeton and colleagues (2010) described a process of parallel vocabulary instruction in which teachers build awareness of high frequency morphemes in content area study, even in the early grades, through explorations of simple affixes and roots.

CONCLUSION

Stage theory is present in schools to assist in planning curricula, and it is also valuable in teacher education. Students follow a predictable route of development, and teachers must understand this continuum. Appropriate instruction depends upon what reading procedures should be taught at particular points in time. Linnea Ehri (2005) explained that developmental theories not only describe the processes and skills that "emerge, change, and develop" but they also identify causes of movement from one stage to the next. A teacher's job is to help students move from those stages where reading to learn is limited by bottom-up approaches to more advanced stages where reading processes become increasingly more interactive and top-down. At no point is reading just about decoding or simply getting words off the page, and at all points reading for self-determined purposes is paramount. The commonality across the purported *shift* from learning to read to reading to learn is the written word knowledge central to both. Instead of dichotomizing learning to read and reading to learn, the field of literacy education would benefit from a new refrain: "learning to read and learn."

FURTHER READINGS AND RESOURCES

Anderson, R. C., & Pearson, P. D. (1984). A schema-theoretic view of basic processes in reading comprehension. In P. D. Pearson (Ed.), *Handbook of reading research* (pp. 255–291). New York: Longman.

Bear, D., Templeton, S., Invernizzi, M., & Johnston, F. (2008). *Words their way: Word study for phonics, vocabulary, and spelling instruction* (4th ed.). Upper Saddle River, NJ: Pearson.

Chall, J. S. (1983). *Stages of reading development* (1st ed.). Fort Worth, TX: Harcourt Brace College.

Chall, J. S. (1996). *Learning to read: The great debate* (3rd ed.). Fort Worth, TX: Harcourt Brace College.

Ehri, L. (2005). Development of sight word reading: Phases and findings. In M. J. Snowling & C. Hulme (Eds.), *The science of reading: A handbook* (pp. 135–154). Malden, MA: Blackwell.

Henderson, E. (1990). *Teaching spelling* (2nd ed.). Boston: Houghton Mifflin.

McKeown, M. G., Beck, I. L., & Blake, R. G. K. (2009). Rethinking comprehension instruction: Comparing strategies and content instructional approaches. *Reading Research Quarterly, 44*(3), 218–253.

Neuman, S. (2006). How we neglect knowledge—and why. *American Educator, 30,* 24–27.

Pearson, P. D. (2006). Foreword. In K. Goodman (Ed.), *The truth about DIBELS* (pp. v–xix). Portsmouth, NH: Heinemann.

Pearson, P. D., & Fielding, L. (1991). Comprehension instruction. In R. Barr, M. L. Kamil, P. B. Mosenthal, & P. D. Pearson (Eds.), *Handbook of reading research* (Vol. 2, pp. 815–860). New York: Longman.

Templeton, S., Bear, D. R., Invernizzi, M., & Johnston, F. (2010). *Vocabulary their way: Word study with middle and secondary students.* Boston: Pearson.

Turner, J., & Paris, S. G. (1995). How literacy tasks influence children's motivation for literacy. *The Reading Teacher, 48*(8), 662–673.

Wigfield, A., & Guthrie, J. T. (1997). Relations of children's motivation for reading to the amount and breadth of their reading. *Journal of Educational Psychology, 89,* 420–432.

6

The Race to the Top program: Should America be the global leader in math, science, engineering, and technology education?

POINT: Mark A. Templin, *University of Toledo*
COUNTERPOINT: George G. Hruby, *University of Kentucky*

OVERVIEW

The purpose of the present chapter is to touch on two themes of education in the United States: (a) competition among its states for federal funding and (b) the perceived need that the country's public schools should better prepare students to contribute to innovations in science, technology, engineering, and math (STEM) to be competitive in the global marketplace. As detailed in the subsequent two essays, in 2009, the U.S. Congress passed the American Recovery and Reinvestment Act (ARRA) authorizing billions of dollars for improving education through state-based initiatives.

This multibillion-dollar program was labeled Race to the Top (RTT), and to compete for federal funding, the states were awarded points for their plans to meet particular goals, such as enhancing the curriculum standards and assessments of their schools and instruction, to improve their data collection and analyses of student and teacher performance, and so forth. Further, the state competitors needed to demonstrate how they might increase teacher effectiveness and achieve greater equity in their school communities. Perhaps most significant to many wider community members, educators, and policy-makers was that the states needed to provide blueprints of how they might transform their failing schools to successful ones. Many states joined in the RTT competition and after two rounds of awards, 12 states earned sizable funding from the federal government.

Some states did not compete for RTT monies for various reasons; a salient point brought up before the race began was that the competition favored densely and highly populated states. Further, some states complained that the criteria set forth by the competition would diminish rather than improve their education systems. For some states it did not seem feasible to advance alternative schooling options, such as charter schools, in small districts that were sometimes challenged to support a single school. Indeed, in the end, much of the RTT funding ended up in densely populated states such as New York, Maryland, and Massachusetts. In many cases, those who received federal funding are traditionally Democratic Party strongholds, such as Hawaii, or swing-vote states in recent national elections, such as Florida, Ohio, and North Carolina. As a result, some people perceived that the race was more or less fixed from the start and was driven by political motives.

As noted in the following essays, competition is tightly woven in the capital fabric of the United States. There have been many other significant races that have captured the national spirit and many of its human and material resources, such as the ones that came out of Manifest Destiny and the Cold War era—the race westward, the nuclear arms race, the race to be the first nation to put a person on the moon. And in this vein, the backdrop of many of the country's schools is their competitive sports programs, which some people claim set the stage for being successful on Wall Street as well as Main Street. Yet this stance is not without criticism, especially in education contexts with notions such as school equity and "no child left behind," and among those who deem collaboration and cooperation as more valued dimensions of society than individual accomplishment.

In some respects, notions of collaboration and cooperative networks that extend beyond national borders have been promoted by the scientific community. Often this is seemingly out of necessity because challenges such as the threat of pandemic disease and global pollution know no national boundaries. In another respect, a few U.S.-sponsored science projects have been fueled by ideas that by pooling wider resources, knowledge can be advanced more rapidly, such as shown through collaborative space exploration endeavors (e.g., those that came out of and include the Apollo-Soyuz Test Project) and the more or less international inclusion effort to successfully map the human genome.

Nonetheless, an aspect of the RTT competition was centered on science education—alongside related domains of technology, engineering, and math—which has been deemed as a national priority because of perceptions that the United States is losing its cutting edge in these areas to other countries. Thus, alongside the four major categories of school reform efforts mentioned earlier in the present overview, state competitors for RTT awards could earn additional points toward their final score by submitting a proposal that addressed all of the dimensions of the STEM priority, which are to (a) offer a rigorous course of study in mathematics, the sciences, technology, and engineering; (b) cooperate with industry experts, museums, universities, research centers . . . to prepare and assist teachers in integrating STEM content across grades and disciplines, in promoting effective and relevant instruction, and in offering applied learning opportunities for students; and (c) prepare more students for advanced study and careers in the sciences, technology, engineering, and mathematics, including by addressing the needs of underrepresented groups and of women and girls in the areas of science, technology, engineering, and mathematics (U.S. Department of Education [ED], 2010, p. 8).

In the following essays, these and other dimensions of the RTT program are taken up. In the point essay, Mark A. Templin of the University of Toledo defends the goals of the national program. Nonetheless, although conventional science and related disciplines operate with notions such as replication, verifiability, reliability, constants, and so on, he argues that the current state of education is under a powerful specter of false testing—not so much testing toward a scientific truth but rather that the test functions as a political object. Templin suggests this object actually separates educators and their students from the possibilities to freely explore and inquire—hallmarks of science that is practiced in its best sense. Even so, Templin advocates that the United States should strive to be the global leader in STEM education.

George G. Hruby of the University of Kentucky unpacks RTT policy in the counterpoint essay and uncovers how seemingly dissimilar concepts drive questions such as the one that guides this chapter, conflating state grant competitions with social goals that suggest a global education race similar to the arms race of the last century. From this stance, any national race is disingenuous, and to suggest that there is a race between nations when national borders are increasingly perforated by multinational entities is a tenuous proposition. Laced throughout Hruby's essay are political, social, and economic dimensions of education initiatives in the United States and how RTT, No Child Left Behind (NCLB) (2001), the common core curriculum movement, and so forth, all carry a common capital brand.

A. Jonathan Eakle
The Johns Hopkins University

POINT: Mark A. Templin
University of Toledo

The United States should strive to be the global leader in STEM education. Two main arguments support this assertion. First, the White House argues that STEM-related careers are essential to helping the United States meet the challenges of thriving in a 21st-century global economy; thus, leadership in STEM education is essential for shaping our nation's future economic vitality. Second, U.S. Secretary of Education Arne Duncan argues that the educational system must address the issue of unequal access to STEM education. As the American Association for the Advancement of Science points out, equal access to STEM education is essential to help all Americans make informed choices when participating in democratic decision-making processes. Hence, America's position as leader or follower in STEM education has profound economic, moral, and political dimensions that will impact the nation's future.

Global leadership in STEM education requires that teachers and students participate within complex teaching and learning environments. Such environments must focus on developing inquiry and problem solving "habits of mind" and deep understanding of key STEM-related concepts. This goal must take precedence over the mere memorization of facts. In other words, the classroom must help students learn to think, judge, and act like scientists, mathematicians, and engineers and not simply acquire some of the official knowledge from those respective fields. This change in curriculum and instruction represents nothing less than a cultural shift of the U.S. classroom.

Traditional curriculum orientations view students as largely "ignorant until taught"—that is, as having little or no prior knowledge of the topic at hand. An inquiry or problem solving curriculum orientation, in contrast, views the student as having some degree of knowledge prior to instruction even though that knowledge may be different to the knowledge commonly accepted by experts in STEM fields. This pedagogical difference in how students are viewed as learners has substantial implications for classroom instruction. If students can be thought of as having no prior knowledge, then readings and lectures about a topic, followed by recitations and repetitive drills, might make sense. If, on the other hand, each student already knows something about the topic or problem at hand, then the teacher and students need to first discover what that knowledge is and then work collaboratively to interrogate its utility, meaning, and power. This latter process favors small group instruction with each group working on unique aspects of the topic or problem.

The RTT initiative attempts to tackle the problems of improving STEM education by encouraging states to vie for federal education dollars through a competitive grant process. In order to make real classroom change, state initiatives will no doubt need to tackle the problem of changing classroom curriculum culture. But these reformers will be confronted with a dilemma because RTT, as with other education initiatives such as NCLB (2001), focuses its leading points on test-based educational accountability (TBEA), a form of accountability that values high-stakes, large-scale, standardized tests. In fact, RTT extends this form of accountability to not only measure student performance but also the performance of educators.

TBEA might not be the right set of climbing tools to the "top" if teaching and learning involves freedom and action—ideas elaborated subsequently. Although considerable attention has been paid to RTT, two questions concerning its relation to TBEA have not been asked: (a) What kind of political object is a test or a test score? (b) How does TBEA change teaching as a human activity? In addressing these questions subsequent portions of the present essay also touch on STEM education and freedom.

TESTS AS POLITICAL OBJECTS

Hannah Arendt (1958) identified five categories of political objects: (a) necessities; (b) use objects; (c) exchange objects; (d) art works; and (e) speech, deeds, and actors. Speech, deeds, and actors are merged into one category because the speech and deeds of particular actors cannot be separated from them. Within this conceptual frame, tests are very similar to cubist artworks. Cubism has several general characteristics. First, it is a form of representation that reduces nature to simplified geometries and monochromes. Second, rather than from a single point of view, cubism attempts to simultaneously capture multiple perspectives. In doing so, objects and the spaces objects occupy fragment and contours blur. Third, as a result of these methods of representation, the structural arrangement of cubist art may appear to lose reference to what is typically considered realistic. Nonetheless, the structure of cubist artwork is rigorously organized (see, for instance, Picasso's 1907 landmark painting *Les Demoiselles d'Avignon*).

Tests and test scores used within TBEA share similarities with cubism. For example, test scores are reductive, boiling down complex constructs to a single number with mathematics as the vehicle of expression. In addition, like cubism, test elements such as subscale scores, percentile ranks, stanines, z-scores, and so forth each simultaneously convey different interpretive points of view. In short, test specifications redefine the contours and fragments of curriculum and instruction. Like cubism, tests are made self-sufficient by the rigorous architecture of standards and specifications used to construct, support, and justify the test. Thus, tests are artfully crafted, mathematically based entities that can take on a reality of their own. However, the real successes of education, such as helping a student become involved in school activities like a science fair project rather than in less productive rote behaviors, are not part of the TBEA picture. Within the testing picture frame, such education actions are merely anecdotes—easily dismissed and cancelled by the effects of the "artful" test object. In short, when policymakers rely on tests to make judgments about curriculum and instruction, they are drawing on a cubistlike snapshot image that distorts and diminishes the actual dimensions of teaching and learning. Moreover, under TBEA, the political distances between policymaker and teacher leave little room for actual human accountability—the ability to tell one's own story. In this respect, teachers are losing their political voices to an abstraction made possible by a set of mathematical scores.

The creation of political distance and the insufficiency of educators' political voices give rise to issues of inscrutability. In other words, there is a disconnection between what educators value and what policymakers who control resources, such as material and staff support, value. Similarly, the use of an abstract and enigmatic scoring system in the competition for RTT funds seems to have politically distanced some state governors from federal policymakers just like the distancing experienced by teachers and principals under TBEA. And state officials seem to have reacted similarly:

> When the winners [of RTT funding] were announced, some state governors expressed concern and disappointment at what has been identified as an "*inscrutable process*" [italics added], leaving them to wonder whether it would be worth participating in future rounds of the competition. (Peterson & Rothstein, 2010, p. 1)

The result is that, like these governors, educators are restricted by TBEA, and they may be forced to conform to requirements and engage in activities that have little to do with what they deem to be most important for the students that they serve to learn. Progressive educators, for example, want their students to be able to think and act creatively, which involves freedom—a position that frames the following section of the present essay.

STEM TEACHING AS A HUMAN ACTIVITY INVOLVING FREEDOM

Teaching in its best sense involves freedom (Templin, 2008). Indeed, the word *education* is derived from the Greek *educare* and involves freely bringing forth that which is within the individual. From this view, education is ultimately a liberating act of bringing out the best in students. Certainly, such freedom can be a goal of teaching in any subject area, such as those of STEM.

Teaching for freedom in science inevitably involves inquiry—the freedom to (a) ask scientifically oriented questions, (b) seek evidence, (c) formulate and communicate explanations, and (d) evaluate alternative explanations. Inquiry is not so much a choice of teaching methods but rather a classroom culture that a teacher fosters and encourages. Classroom scientific inquiry is rarely hard scientific inquiry, but it allows the teacher and students to legitimately participate at the periphery of science. Joseph Krajcik and Charlene Czerniak offer project-based science (PBS) as a coherent model for what a classroom scientific inquiry environment could look like. PBS has five key features: (a) relevant to students' lives, (b) students engage in inquiry and perform investigations to answer their questions, (c) students, teachers, and members of society collaborate on the question or problem, (d) students use learning technologies to investigate, develop artifacts or products, collaborate, and access information, and (e) results in a series of artifacts or products that address the question or problem. A PBS teaching unit may feature either a scientific investigation or a design project. Thus, PBS is conducive to teaching engineering and technology as well, because problems in these fields often involve the creation or modification of a design according to at least one constraint. Mathematics can be taught using either an investigation or a design project. Scenarios for science and technology are provided as examples of teaching consistent with PBS. These same scenarios could be recast as mathematics units that foreground mathematical and engineering problem solving situations.

SCIENCE: AN INVESTIGATION SCENARIO

Science in classrooms is often structured around a scenario with particular scientific problems to solve. The following scenario begins with a middle grades science teacher who is interested in helping students to better understand ecological relationships. Rather than beginning the unit with a lecture or whole-class reading from the textbook, the teacher decides to take the class out to the schoolyard and ask the students questions, for instance, "How many individual living things do you suppose are in this yard, and how many different types of living things are in this yard?" In response, students begin to call out guesses— "a thousand . . . a million . . . over a billion!" The teacher then asks, "Suppose the number of living things was close to one million, would we be able to count the organisms and get an exact number?" Some students respond yes and others say no. Once the class goes back inside the school, the teacher encourages the students to think about how this could be done. Eventually, the students decide that arriving at an exact number is not practical, but they could make an estimate that would be fairly close to the exact number. The teacher then forms small student groups and asks each group to develop a method estimating the number of living things in the schoolyard. During subsequent days, the students are encouraged to talk with peers of other groups to refine their ideas; then each group presents their method to the class.

Based on their own group's thinking and after hearing from all of the other groups, each group decides on a final method to try out in the schoolyard to estimate the number of living things in it. Students collect the materials they will need and then the class goes outside to set up their estimation methods and collect data. Some groups finish a little sooner than others. The teacher asks those who finish early to go over their data and decide if they are satisfied with their final result—"Think. Does the number you estimated make sense?" she asks them. Finally, she has each group develop a computerized slide presentation to describe what they did and to present their findings to the class. Following the presentations, she invites a local ecologist to the class who talks with the students about how scientists actually sample populations in the environment. The sharing between the scientist and the students is a two-way conversation as the students share what they did and as the scientist explains how, with more sophisticated concepts and tools, students could possibly refine their estimates.

TECHNOLOGY: A DESIGN PROJECT SCENARIO

The following scenario illustrates a middle grades teacher of technology's goal in helping his students understand how new technologies can change how we live (for better or worse) and to gain experience by designing an artifact around one constraint. The teacher begins by pointing out that technology is all around us. He asks the students, "How many different technologies are there in this room?" Immediately, students respond that the computer on his desk is a technology. "What else?" he asks. Students identify various items—"the projector, the whiteboard, my pen"—and eventually one student says, "The floor." Some students look puzzled; how could the floor be a technology? The teacher asks the class to think about that—"How could we think of a floor as a technology?" After discussing this for a while, students reason that it must be a technology because the floors in old buildings look like they are made out of different materials than the floors in newer buildings. Another student says that the ceiling and the walls are technologies, too. The teacher concludes this discussion by encouraging the students to stop and look around periodically to observe how much technology surrounds and affects them as they go from place to place.

The following day, the teacher asks the students to report what they observed, and then he introduces the idea that most technologies are developed around one or more constraints. To do this he asks, "How big do you think an oceangoing ship can be?" Most students say that there is no limit. Then, the teacher shows the class Internet images of ocean liners and battleships passing through the Panama Canal. When the students see the pictures of a battleship they are amazed—"It barely fits!" "There are only nine inches of clearance," the teacher reports. Then he informs the class that they will be testing how many pennies a boat made of aluminum foil can hold if the boat can be no wider than 50 mm, and invites them to form small groups to sketch a design based on these criteria. In writing journals, students record their thinking while addressing a guiding question "Why do you think your design will hold a lot of pennies?" As students advance their designs, they perform experiments on their boats, make changes, and record what they have found. In the end, students share their final designs with one another. As they engage in their inquiries and experiments, the teacher assesses students' understanding of the concept of buoyancy expressed through their journal entries, other artifacts they explore and develop, and the boat design products.

CONCLUSION

TBEA systems, as currently conceived, seem ill suited for measuring or producing the active spaces that could educate and liberate students in ways consistent with the goals of RTT and as illustrated by the scenarios presented earlier in this point essay for several reasons. First, TBEA tends to view teaching as a labor rather than an action. In doing so, TBEA foregrounds issues of cadence, forcing compliance to a rigid timetable through artifacts and procedures such as pacing guides and short cycle assessments. A rigid time schedule is detrimental to the inquiry represented in the scenarios, because freedom of thought means that student learning cannot be forced into regular intervals. Second, TBEA tends to ignore context in an effort to make the commodity of education available to all. In contrast, the two scenario inquiries that were previously shared depend on context. For example, if there is no schoolyard that is safe or available, the teacher must modify the inquiry so that it fits the context of the particular classroom or school. Thought is not a commodity but rather a faculty, and faculties are learned through active use in context. Third, for inquiry to be successful, teachers must be actors, not laborers. Actors are personally invested in both the processes and the outcomes of their actions. Hence, they must retain their individual voices with regard to their actions. Actors are the ones "to make public use of one's reason at every point" (Kant, cited by Arendt, 1982, p. 39). Laborers, in contrast, need only be concerned with their pace in the depersonalized issue of production—they arguably need no voice; they need only to listen.

In the scenarios presented earlier in this essay, the teaching is complex and the teacher must assume a personal stake in teaching and learning. They, as actors and not laborers, must have the freedom to be continually inquisitive about how the students are thinking and have a public voice in shaping education. Teaching speech acts and teaching deeds cannot be separated from individual teachers; otherwise teachers are no longer actors capable of participating in a project involving freedom. At best, current TBEA environments measure "labor" aspects of schooling. Changing this situation would require teachers, test developers, policymakers, and other stakeholders to work in dynamic dialogue. The work of Randy Elliot Bennett and Drew H. Gitomer (2008) moves accountability thought a step in this direction by honoring the complexity of teaching required under RTT and by acknowledging that professional support is integral to accountability. Future accountability thought must also recognize that accountability processes themselves must become spaces of action that prompt teachers to tell, interpret, and be responsible for their individual professional stories and retain their voices in and through their teaching.

COUNTERPOINT: George G. Hruby
University of Kentucky

The question debated in this chapter includes three elements that are only distally related. Thus, each of the question's elements will be discussed separately, only briefly suggesting a topic around which they unite: the conflation of psychometric and sociometric data and its interpretation. This counterpoint essay asserts that faux crises, international threats, and other politically vibrant distractions should be distinguished from the real reasons and likely bases for coherent educational reform.

RACE TO THE TOP

The U.S. Congress passed the ARRA in 2009, authorizing $5 billion for improving education through state-based initiatives. Of that, $4 billion was devoted to RTT to (a) help states enhance educational standards and assessments, (b) improve the collection and use of data in educational decision making, (c) increase teacher effectiveness and advance equity in teacher distribution, and (d) demonstrate effective ways to turn around struggling schools (ARRA, 2009, sec. 14005, & 14006).

RTT was promoted as President Barack Obama's answer to President George W. Bush's NCLB (although the former did not displace the latter, formally known as the Elementary and Secondary Education Act [ESEA]; NCLB simply failed to win congressional reauthorization). As a result of the contrasting metaphors in the names of the two programs, it is easy to confuse the race in RTT as a race between students (some of whom would, in fact, be left behind if potential winners were to win a race). Actually, however, the race in question is between states competing for the initiative's limited federal education funding; it is not between students.

The RTT funding cycle went through three phases. Most, but not all, states competed. Delaware and Tennessee won awards in the first phase; Massachusetts, New York, Hawaii, Florida, Rhode Island, the District of Columbia, Georgia, North Carolina, and Ohio (in order of points scored) won smaller awards in the second. As of this writing (June 2011), a third round has been announced to provide yet another chance for states that failed to get funding in the earlier rounds. However, the amount of money available to those states will be much less than was received by the earlier winners.

The fine print in the funding applications and the various advisories and FAQs issued by the White House and the U.S. Department of Education (ED) made it clear that, beyond the general goals of the act previously mentioned, politically popular specifics merited additional points toward the award calculations. Pertinent to the question here addressed, states that bolstered STEM education in their application plans were awarded extra points—but so, too, were states that expanded opportunities and funding for charter schools, aligned their state curricula with the Common Core State Standards Initiative (CCSSI), garnered support for their plans from teacher unions and professional organizations, or passed legislation to improve and implement teacher evaluation systems to more easily replace less effective school personnel.

EDUCATIONAL MEASURES OF INTERNATIONAL LEADERSHIP

I assume that the reference to global leadership in the question posed in the chapter title presumes reliable forms of international assessment for comparison purposes. Arguably, we lack these. In any case, the RTT initiative details no specifics on this topic. As with the confusion about students being the contestants in the RTT competition, so with nations as competitors, there is no formal inclusion of international standards or comparisons in the RTT funding initiative guidelines. (To be blunt, it is difficult to winningly critique aspects of RTT that are not, in fact, formal elements of RTT.) Still, to be *the*—rather than merely *a*—global leader means having some valid and reliable yardstick by which to measure such leadership; thus, this is the crux of this otherwise nebulous element.

That American school children should be the best in the world in their academic achievements is an understandably desired point of pride, and there are very good reasons to be concerned about the lack of academic rigor and student engagement in some of our schools. But most international comparisons are conceptually flawed, and even the best are shaky. To begin with, the putative declining status of the United States in the global arenas of diplomacy, industry, finance, and innovation are not due to the scholastic abilities of our 8- or 15-year-olds. Our standing is due to the competence, or lack thereof, of our current leadership—mostly white, mostly Ivy League men (a few women) in their 40s through 70s. If, on the basis of indicators from the past decade or so, our ship appears to be sinking, it is *they* who are to blame—not the kids, not the teachers.

But let us pretend that raising alarms over American scholastic achievement is not a cheap ploy to divert attention from the failings of the leadership elite. When making comparisons, it is important that like be compared to like, that one compares apples to apples and not to kiwis or passion fruit. If we want to evaluate our schools, we need to compare them to one another or to previous measures per school over time. It does not make sense to compare a country as large and diverse, not to mention as economically powerful, as the United States with nations like Korea, New Zealand, or Finland and wring our hands over the result. We are in no way, as a nation, in danger of being conquered or subordinated by any of these smaller countries. And the use of national averages occludes more than it illuminates.

It might make more sense to compare individual states within the United States to other nations as economic competitors. It turns out that if we do so in meaningful ways, we find ourselves well ahead of the pack (Salzman & Lowell, 2008). But the logic of a global economy (not to mention our own federalist government) reminds us that *alliances* with smaller nations featuring specialized economies (and culturally distinct school systems) make the most sense for our collective advancement. This is the logic of globalization, after all, for which we are said to be in need of preparation. Clearly we are off to a poor start in preparing for globalization if we do not accurately conceptualize the logic of globalization.

Flawed International Comparisons

Representation of the data is curiously skewed in reports of international educational advantage. For instance, the 2009 U.S. ranking of 14th in reading on the Programme for International Student Assessment (PISA) comparisons conducted by the Organisation for Economic Co-operation and Development (OECD) does not reflect the fact that the seven nations just ahead of the United States all have statistically similar scores. It makes no sense to rank order nations on the basis of test scores that indicate no statistically significant difference. On the basis of a normal distribution of the nations included in the comparison, the United States lands about in the middle, or average tier, of nations. But, then, altruistically, the United States is the only nation of the group that offers a mandatory, comprehensive K–12 public education system for all children and teens, regardless of their background or proclivity for academic success.

Because tests like PISA, or Trends in International Mathematics and Science Study (TIMSS), etc., are based on sampling data, it is crucial that the samples be comparable but at the same time represent the distinct expectations and achievement of each nation. These two goals can conflict and necessary trade-offs need to be negotiated carefully; it is not clear that the current international comparisons do so. In addition to this validity concern, variable correlations between scores on the various international comparisons suggest possible reliability issues with the tests as well.

Cultural differences are a difficult issue to parse in such comparisons. It is well known, for instance, that poverty levels correlate strongly with school performance. The United States has more poverty than any other PISA nation reporting its poverty level (21%), and its economic disparities are far greater. PISA does not control for this. Moreover, American poverty is inequitably distributed geographically, too, festering and metastasizing in urban ghettos and rural wastelands. As a result, the United States not only has students of poverty but it has schools of poverty and school districts of poverty: Such environments compound the poverty effect on individual student performance. This is a national scandal, but PISA results underscore precisely why it matters for interpreting comparative educational outcomes.

Take the PISA data on reading, for instance (roughly similar scores in math and science suggest the following points are true for those subjects as well, and science and math education websites have shared the reading data as significant [e.g., Admin., 2011; Hassard, 2011]). For U.S. schools where free-and-reduced-lunch (FRL) students make up less than 10% of the student body, the average PISA reading score is 551; for schools with 25% to 50% FRL students, the average score is 502; for schools with 75% or more FRL students, the average score is 446 (McCabe,

2010; Riddile, 2010). Clearly, the inverse correlation between a school's performance on the PISA reading literacy measure and its poverty level is profound.

The overall average PISA score for the United States in reading is 500, placing the United States, as noted, at 14th in the PISA pack. But if U.S. schools are disaggregated by percentage of FRL students and matched only to nation-states with similar levels of student poverty, America's ranking rises to the top. Comparing U.S. schools with 10% or less FRL students to nations where the poverty level is under 10%, the United States ranks #1 in reading at 551 (well ahead of #2 Finland at 536). When U.S. schools of 10% to 25% FRL students are compared to nations with similar poverty levels, again, the United States is #1 in reading at 527 (just ahead of #2 Canada at 524).

Comparing schools with more than 25% FRL students is not possible because none of the PISA nations that report their poverty level have a level that high. However, our poorest schools (with FRL students of 75% or more, and an average score of 446) do only slightly worse than Austria (471), the worst performing PISA nation reporting a poverty level of only 13.3%. That's not so bad, if you think about it. Equally telling, Mexico is one of the few PISA nations with a poverty level that probably exceeds 25%, but few of Mexico's 15-year-olds of poverty attend middle or high school, so no meaningful comparison to U.S. schools with similar poverty rates is possible (still, U.S. FRL students > 75% = 446; Mexico's overall average = 425).

This raises the issue of whether it makes sense to focus on population averages in international comparisons, since it is the performance of the top tier of students that will probably matter most for a nation's future, particularly in highly complex domains such as those addressed by STEM education (Salzman & Lowell, 2008). If we are going to get worked up about average performance, then clearly we need to address student poverty as a national education issue. But if this is a political impossibility, we might as well ignore population averages and attend instead to the scores of top tier students. It is not as if our future scientists, engineers, technicians, and mathematicians are going to hail from the bottom half of our nation's classrooms. Granted, in focusing on our best and brightest, we further accelerate our nation's presumed and deeply ironic bet that pampered elites can save American democracy. But this is an unconscionable waste of human capital. Nonetheless, the United States seems committed to this course for now.

LEADING OR LEADERS IN STEM EDUCATION?

Student scores aside, what else might indicate being the global leader in STEM education? Might it mean producing more STEM graduates than other nations? Should we be doing everything we can to increase the number of students majoring in STEM fields at the expense of those preparing for other fields? I'd suggest not. Just because STEM fields are important for the advances that increase our nation's financial, industrial, and cultural productivity, it may not be the case that we need more STEM students to do this better. The success of the new technologies, after all, is not due to the number of users with advanced technological knowledge. Rather, the productivity of the new technologies comes largely from designs that are intuitive and easily learned, even by former humanities majors like myself. Potentially, the new technologies could make it possible to require *fewer* STEM students without endangering future success. In any case, the number of students attracted to STEM ought to be determined, as always in America, by market fundamentals. If we truly need more STEM graduates, we'll pay for them, and if we do so, we'll get them. If we don't, then we won't. There is no such thing as a free lunch (outside of the public schools).

More is not necessarily better; better is better. Producing more STEM students, at least as a national percentage, is a pointless quest by itself. A factoid currently circulating widely on the Internet suggests that there are more Chinese students in the top quintile of their class than we have students in school, full stop. If producing more than other nations is the key to success, then we're doomed. But if producing better students is the key—students with higher-order comprehension and analysis skills, higher-order creative and conceptual ability—then we arguably might maintain our advantage in spite of our smaller population.

But if this were the case, why would we want to confine these objectives to STEM curricula alone? Indeed, it might be dangerous to silo science away with math, engineering, and technology in K–12 education. Although math is important for science at the postsecondary level, it is scant in the K–12 science curriculum until the secondary grades and then is found mostly in physics and, to a lesser extent, chemistry. By contrast, science education texts and materials, from information-based elementary readers to high school biology textbooks, present students with demanding *literacy* challenges: specifically, the specialized vocabularies, semantics, and discourses of science's diverse fields of inquiry (including technology and engineering).

Studies of readability and text difficulty in secondary grade texts across school subjects demonstrate that only textbooks in science continually challenge students' reading ability year over year. The other content areas tend to plateau at an eighth- or ninth-grade reading level (Adams, 2009). This literacy-science connection may explain why, per state, National Assessment of Educational Progress (NAEP) scores for fourth- and eighth-grade science correlate with

NAEP reading scores but not with NAEP math scores (states with above average science scores have high reading scores but not necessarily high math scores). Worth noting in this regard, the CCSSI emphasizes literacy standards not only for English/language arts but also history/social studies, science, and technical subjects. The math standards are not related, except in one illustration, to science at all. The value of sequestering science with math and shop classes is therefore questionable, but that is precisely what is being underwritten by the current RTT funding initiative.

RACE TO THE TOP, GLOBAL COMPETITIONS, AND STEM EDUCATION

As noted, each of the three elements packed into the previous question are interesting to consider separately, but evaluating how they relate is not so clear. STEM education is not one of RTT's four main objectives, and it is arguably not even the most noteworthy secondary element of the initiative. Although STEM education is favored by the RTT scoring rubric for state awards, so are many other innovations (e.g., charter schools, the Common Core Standards). At the same time, although global competitiveness is a loose rationale for supporting the improvement of American public education it is not a formal element in the RTT award calculations.

Granting that improving public education across the nation is a goal with positive implications for the nation's future, we might rather ask ourselves how we could improve public education most effectively. Would it be through emphasizing STEM education over other subject areas? I do not see that the point position on this question has made a compelling argument in this regard. Would being better than other nations in STEM or any other subject area improve public education? That statement seems to get the causal relationship backward.

One reasonable measure of educational quality is how well schools do in terms of student achievement from year to year. Better achievement over time suggests improving schools, baring ceiling effects. To foster an improvement of that measure, we might do well to look at the most powerful co-variables to educational achievement. In school, that would be the effectiveness of the teacher. Out of school, that would be the socioeconomic status of the student. So addressing teacher quality and student poverty would be the two most important elements in any programmatic approach to improving public education on behalf of international competitiveness or anything else.

RTT turns a blind eye toward—really races away from—the topic of student poverty. But it takes seriously the issue of teacher effectiveness. Thus, RTT is off to a good start, if only on one leg, in its ostensible race to improve America's public education systems. What that has to do with STEM education and international comparisons is obscure, as I've repeatedly noted in this counterpoint essay, but I would encourage anyone worried about an undue emphasis on STEM education in American schools to ponder the data that underscore America's sublimely blissful ignorance of science concepts and the scientific method (e.g., Mooney & Kirshenbaum, 2009).

FURTHER READINGS AND RESOURCES

Adams, M. J. (2009). The challenge of advanced texts: The interdependence of reading and learning. In E. H. Hiebert (Ed.), *Reading more, reading better* (pp. 163–189). New York: Guilford.

Admin. (2011, January 6). PISA: It's poverty not stupid. *Mathematically sane.* Retrieved from http://mathematicallysane.com/pisa-its-poverty-not-stupid

Arendt, H. (1958). *The human condition.* Chicago: University of Chicago Press.

Arendt, H. (1982). *Lectures on Kant's political philosophy* (R. Beiner, Ed.). Chicago: University of Chicago Press.

Bennett, R. E., & Gitomer, D. H. (2008). *Transforming K–12 assessment: Integrating account-ability, testing, formative assessment, and professional support* (Educational Testing Service, Research Memorandum [ETS RM-08-13]). Retrieved July 20, 2010, from http://www.ets.org/s/commonassessments/pdf/CBAL_TransformingK12 Assessment.pdf

Hassard, J. (2011, January 5). PISA test results through the lens of poverty. *The art and teaching of science.* Retrieved from http://www.artofteachingscience.org/?p=3233

McCabe, C. (2010, December 9). The economics behind international education rankings. *NEA Today.* Retrieved from http://neatoday.org/2010/12/09/a-look-at-the-economic-numbers-on-international-education-rankings

Mooney, C., & Kirshenbaum, S. (2009). *Unscientific America: How scientific illiteracy threatens our future.* New York: Basic Books.

Peterson, W., & Rothstein, R. (2010). Let's do the numbers: Department of Education's "Race to the Top" program offers only a muddled path to the finish line. *EPI Briefing Paper.* Washington, DC: Economic Policy Institute. Retrieved April 27, 2010, from http://www.epi.org

Riddile, M. (2010, December 15). PISA: It's poverty not stupid. *NASSP: The principal difference.* Retrieved from http://nasspblogs.org/principaldifference/2010/12/pisa_its_poverty_not_stupid_1.html

Salzman, H., & Lowell, L. (2008). Making the grade. *Nature, 453,* 28–30.

Templin, M. (2008). Making problematic standardized assessment for teacher account-ability: Using political theory to guide science teacher education research. *Journal of Science Teacher Education, 19*(5), 413–416.

U.S. Department of Education. (2010). *Race to the Top guidance and frequently asked questions.* Retrieved May 26, 2011, from http://www2.ed.gov/programs/racetothetop/faq.pdf

U.S. Department of Education. (2011). *Race to the Top fund.* Retrieved from http://www2.ed.gov/programs/racetothetop/index.html

White House. (n.d.). *Fact sheet: Race to the Top.* Retrieved from http://www.whitehouse.gov/the-press-office/fact-sheet-race-top

COURT CASES AND STATUTES

American Recovery and Reinvestment Act, P.L. 111–5, 123 Stat. 115 (2009).

No Child Left Behind Act of 2001, 20 U.S.C.A. §§ 6301 *et seq.*

Should "English-Only" curriculum be eliminated or expanded?

POINT: Elizabeth B. Bernhardt, *Stanford University*
COUNTERPOINT: Jeanne Gilliam Fain, *Middle Tennessee State University*

OVERVIEW

Multiple cultures are coming into contact in areas of the United States that before the last few years have been comparatively homogenous. Like some of the melting pots of typical urban areas such as the ones of the port cities of New York and San Francisco, national regions including those of the Southeast and Mid-Atlantic have become home to many immigrants. In part, this has been the result of easier methods of transcontinental passage than were available in previous years, as well as expanding global communication media that have made the option of cross-national migration seem more reasonable. As well, global messages circulate rapidly among peoples, informing them that resources are obtainable in the United States that might not be available in other parts of the world. These messages are amplified by the enticing commodities and promises targeted to citizens of consumer cultures.

As peoples migrate to different territories, even in the same country, they bring along with them cultural capital (Bourdieu, 1986). Cultural capital includes not only material assets such as the clothes on the backs of people but also the traditions and practices that enable them to be successful whether, for example, methods of barter and/or ethical values. Perhaps the most valuable commodity people carry with them is their language. Indeed, many language scholars, such as Sonia Nieto (1999), have argued that language is the most intimate part of one's culture. As migratory flows of people accelerate, so too does access to various aspects found in the cultural capital of different languages, which are especially salient in public places such as U.S. public schools.

Indeed, there are regions of the United States where large numbers of students speak a common language that is not English. Significantly, these are not always immigrant children who have crossed a national border. For example, many of the border regions where Spanish is commonly spoken, such as Arizona and Texas, were regions that in the not so distant past were predominantly occupied by Spanish-speaking peoples. It was only in the 19th century and following the Mexican-American War that these vast border areas came under the rule of an English-speaking government and its agents.

Common to colonial practices are ways to diminish or erase the cultural capital of subjugated populations. Sometimes this has been accomplished by replacing religious practices and ceremonial centers with the ones of the colonialists, such as how cathedrals were literally built upon the foundations of Aztec temples. At other times, native books were burned and replaced by colonial texts, and indigenous oral languages were outlawed. It can be argued that the expansion of "English-Only" curriculum and instruction in U.S. schools is actuality rooted in centuries of the expansion of empires—in this case, the present empire and its British antecedent.

English-Only proponents contend that the mastery of the dominant local language will enable students to be more competitive in the marketplace. This argument is not new and is at the crux of the related and sometimes fierce Ebonics (African American Vernacular English) debates that have been evident for decades (Labov, 2010). In fact, many, if not most, parents whose first language is not Standard English very much want their children to acquire advanced English speaking, reading, and writing skills—which is a point often made by advocates of English-Only curriculum and instruction. Yet, in English-Only school environments, acquisition of these skills sometimes may be at the expense of children losing their abilities to use the cultural capital of their heritage and in some instances, to fully and intimately communicate with their families.

A solution to language/cultural loss has been bilingual education, which is taken up in detail by Elizabeth B. Bernhardt (Stanford University) in the point essay of the present chapter. In some environments where a second language is paradoxically a dominant one, such as in parts of Texas and California, it may well make sense to teach both the first and second languages concurrently. Alongside the perceived capital value of multiculturalism, there is research that suggests that knowing multiple languages adds to a child's cognitive ability. For instance, bilingual children are able to think "metalinguistically" about how languages work, and they learn to be nimble in their thinking as they switch between the different codes of unlike and similar languages and language parts such as cognates, word roots, and derivatives.

Nonetheless, some areas of the United States are not clearly marked in language zones of black and white, or, in other words: two predominant languages. For example, in the nation's capital—known for its transcontinental diplomatic relations—less than 20% of the city's population speaks a primary language other than English. Of that portion, there are reportedly over 100 languages in the public schools—such as Russian, Yoruba, Persian, Polish, and Chinese—that make up a lion's share. This plurality of languages leads some English-Only advocates to argue the merits of a single, common language, even if Spanish is overwhelmingly the prevailing second language in Washington schools and others. Or, more broadly, these advocates argue that schools should teach only English because it is the current international lingua franca—the language most often used for international commerce, science publications, and so forth. As Jeanne Gilliam Fain (Middle Tennessee State University) points out in the counterpoint essay, these apparently pragmatic notions—along with monolingual laws and regulations, limited community and school resources, cultural and language biases, and research that suggests the advantages of multilingualism—are ones that many teachers of diverse language classrooms confront every day. As the United States becomes increasingly globalized, it is clear that these issues will not disappear, at least in the short term.

In the point essay that follows, Bernhardt advocates the position that English-Only curriculum and instruction should be eliminated. To support her position, Bernhardt cites research on reading comprehension in a second language that shows that readers must have an arsenal of knowledge, ranging from how literacy works, vocabulary and structure, background on topic, and cultural appropriateness. Jeanne Gilliam Fain, in the counterpoint essay, contends that English-Only curriculum and instruction is likely here to stay, and in a country that is populated by students who speak many languages, its use should be expanded.

A. Jonathan Eakle
The Johns Hopkins University

POINT: Elizabeth B. Bernhardt
Stanford University

The question that frames this essay, like many issues in the United States, is not one focused on educational quality but rather on ideology. It targets the political side of cultural diversity with its subtext of the vision of a common language embodied in the American melting pot symbol. This particular subtext enflames the passions of the counterpoint essay perspective of a unified culture—the view that each culture in the melting pot should be valued and, consequently, visible. Unfortunately, the question of the efficacy of an English-Only curriculum in its many guises fails to address the only matter that is really important: whether children learn to comprehend content material with the concomitant ability to think about it critically and how to help them achieve this. Any other formulation of the subject is by and large cultural politics.

This essay takes the "eliminated" side of the question. This said, it is important to state up front that it is hard to argue for the elimination of a model that may not be implemented as it has been defined. English-Only may exist only in the minds of those who want to believe that there can be and should be one common language in the United States. However, in reality some teachers in classrooms labeled "English-Only" report that when they close the doors to their classrooms, they use whatever tools they have available to assist children. And if that means providing a translation or any other assistance with which to understand the structure, vocabulary, and culture of the child's language they will do so. Even teachers who have absolutely no knowledge of a child's first language will report that they seek assistance from native informants in order to support the children they are working with. Teachers do not make classroom decisions based in cultural politics; they make instructional decisions in terms of individual children. The reality that English-Only is not being implemented as it is generally defined is in and of itself an argument that it should be eliminated.

English-Only may exist when a state's department of education curriculum monitor enters a classroom but may fade away when the monitor leaves. This state of affairs reflects the common experience outside of the classroom. Languages other than English have been used in North America over the centuries for all sorts of purposes and continue to be used. Who has not attended a market, gone into an ethnic grocery store or restaurant, or tried to sell a house or a car and not tried to use another language? Why is there the public clamor for foreign language in the elementary schools if it is not about the realization that positive results come about when individuals interact on common and respectful terms? Truly, public cultural politics plays well on talk radio and in TV commentaries, but it gets in the way of personal experience and private rationality.

ENGLISH-ONLY RESEARCH

Over the past 20 years, the question of the English-Only curriculum has been a subject of research—research being the ostensibly neutral approach to answering the question. This research distanced itself slightly, although not entirely, from the politics of the question of the efficacy of instruction exclusively in one language. The findings have been mixed. Research-based answers have been that English-Only is good for learners. This conclusion is represented, for example, in the meta-analysis from Christine H. Rossell and Keith Baker (1996). Another meta-analysis concludes that English-Only is not especially good, noting that "children with limited English proficiency who are taught using at least some of their native language perform significantly better on standardized tests than similar children who are taught only in English" (Greene, 1998, p. 1). Most recently, Robert Slavin and colleagues (Slavin, Madden, Calderón, Chamerberlain, & Hennessy, 2010) have examined the two types of curricular models at the core of the question—Structured English Immersion (SEI) and Transitional Bilingual Education. The researchers controlled for the variable of materials by using the program developed by the authors, *Success for All*, and examining several cohorts of children from kindergarten through fourth grade over a 5-year period.

To overstate the conclusions, over the years, children in one curricular model outperform children in the other and vice versa, but any superiority washes out in the fourth grade. Ultimately, the study indicates no superiority of one curricular model over the other. Children tended to end up in the same place regardless of the curricular model they were in. In other words, they could be taught to read in Spanish initially and transition to English or they could be taught only in English and by entering fourth grade each group reads comparably in both English and Spanish. Ultimately, the researchers argue for "the quality of instruction" not the "language of instruction" (p. 17) as key. This might seem like a happy ending to the cultural politics dimension of the controversy. No one wins; no one loses.

Of course, all of this research should be problematized. In the context of the studies on this topic, it is important to consider the overlap between Spanish and English in terms of orthography, word shape, and cognate load. Without being disrespectful of either language, it is critical to understand that researchers may have found few differences, because in actuality there *are* few differences in Spanish and English at the level the children were learning and in the world that these children encounter on a daily basis. Particularly in the early grades, when children are learning to read and when reading materials directly relate to their life experiences, there may be few differences in what they must process and know.

It is critical to understand that on entering the fourth grade they may be at the same level and that, until the fourth grade, the process has been indeed "learning to read." It is the *reading to learn* phase of reading that is much more crucial (see Pearson and Cervetti, Chapter 5 of this volume). Further, while in each study a measure of language dominance is taken, there is rarely any analysis of literacy use in the home. Understanding the presence or absence of literacy as well as parental literacy level and attitude toward literacy in either Spanish or English is a key feature for all studies to explore. Yet these features of the real lives of children tend to be masked by statistical analyses.

A final dimension that needs to be explored is the singular focus on Spanish. True enough, most nonnative speakers of English in American classrooms are Spanish speakers. Yet there are many thousands of other children who do not come to school speaking either Spanish or English but rather other immigrant languages such as Haitian Creole, Arabic, Vietnamese, and so on and so forth. Making claims about a curriculum as important as that in the early grades without sensitivity to crosslingual and cross-literacy dimensions is to oversimplify the problem and to trivialize the triple jeopardy that these children and their teachers are in. These children must, first, learn the language of schooling; second, learn to read; and third, read in the language of schooling so that they can learn content area material. If research is not respectful of these complex factors, it makes a slanted contribution toward what we understand as an immersion or a bilingual curricular setup. Failing to recognize these complexities keeps a focus on English and demeans the child's dominant language rather than recognizing it as the child's principal cognitive tool.

Again, speculation abounds in this arena and can quickly devolve into a set of cultural politics not substantially different from the cultural politics referred to earlier in this essay. Crucially, none of this addresses the question that is actually the one at hand. So what of the question of how best to help children who do not come to school speaking English achieve the ability to read content area material with comprehension and to think about it critically? In order to get some insight into this question, it is important to consider the research about reading comprehension in a second language. This body of research has rarely, if ever, entered the conversation for three reasons. First, it does not easily fit into one of the dominant ideologies because of its multilingual character. In this research, all languages are perceived to be of equal value and prestige and while English holds the dominant position in the database it is not the exclusive one. Second, the research in the field of second-language reading is by and large conducted with subjects who are in the *reading to learn* phase and in the sixth grade or beyond. A third reason is that most of the database focuses on adult readers with relatively high status. In other words, it often fails to meet the cultural politics standard because it portrays language as a tool, not as a political cudgel. Within the context of these criticisms and concerns, it is crucial to develop a conceptual understanding of what readers, who have by and large achieved the target such as the ability to comprehend and to read critically, actually do and what resources they have or must acquire in order to do it. If we can understand the skills that experts must have in order to read in a language they do not speak natively, then we have an alternative approach to investigating the question of helping learners to strive toward the expert level in schooling.

SECOND-LANGUAGE RESEARCH

What does this body of research, generated across languages, on learners who have achieved a certain degree of expertise, actually demonstrate? First of all, 20% of the second-language reading process is attributable to first-language literacy. The finding implies that second-language readers cannot be expected to do more in their second language than in their first. It also substantiates the notion of transfer from first to second language. Further buttressing this finding, additional studies indicate that one of the most frequent strategies that readers use in reading second languages is mental translation.

Second, research also indicates that 30% of the second-language reading process is attributable to language knowledge, principally vocabulary. This finding means, again to state the obvious, that language knowledge is important. It implies that readers will have reading fluency difficulties without a full arsenal of grammatical and vocabulary knowledge. Yet, to state the less obvious, this finding indicates that grammatical knowledge is necessary yet insufficient. Hence, adding endless worksheets that focus on forms may fail to enhance comprehension abilities. The finding also provides insight into the special case of Spanish. Many Spanish speakers have a large vocabulary for reading in English already—their *cognate* vocabulary. In fact, scientific words used most often for content material, such as *metamorphosis, memory,* and *mercantile* in the fourth grade and beyond are most often cognate words, in contrast to everyday words such as *ball, pencil,* and *blackboard* that are much like the words measured on many early-grade vocabulary tests.

Third, readers use the knowledge they possess to decide what a text is about. Early parts of a text lay the framework. When later parts of a text do not fit the framework, readers continue reconstructing to fit their framework. They do not start over. They use the knowledge sources they have (appropriate or not) sometimes to overcome areas in which they have inappropriate or insufficient knowledge. They also do the reverse—they fail to use appropriate knowledge sources that they possess in relevant contexts. We have not yet uncovered the factors that predict this behavior. This finding underlines the importance of understanding the nature of the knowledge that children bring to school and how it is at play, though invisible, in learners' comprehension processes.

Fourth, readers understand concepts in texts that are culturally compatible and ignore or misconstrue features that are culturally incompatible no matter how much language knowledge they have. This finding implies that cultural patterns, beliefs, and concepts about the world are incredibly powerful—in fact, often more powerful than words on the page. Finally, if learners are permitted to reveal their understanding in the language in which they feel most comfortable, they generate a much higher comprehension score. This implies that confounding comprehension with the ability to produce the language suppresses what researchers try to find out in comprehension assessment. It means that when learners are forced to stay in the language being learned and are assessed in that language, the assessment turns into another grammar or composition examination.

SUPPORTING LEARNING

What do these general findings about expert knowledge in second-language reading tell us about supporting children in their learning of comprehension and critical thinking and about preparing teachers to assist in that process? First, students should be encouraged to read books. As obvious as this might seem to be, they should be encouraged to read in whichever languages they know. Students should be given the opportunity and encouraged to read in their native language, and no language should be privileged above another. Books in relevant languages, by and large Spanish, should be available in their classroom libraries as well as in school libraries. Teachers need to acknowledge that *any* reading is good and not push English-Only. This process will help children capitalize on the 20% support cited previously from native literacy.

Second, given that grammatical knowledge and vocabulary development are critical, learners need to understand how grammatical structure and discourse features aid in understanding. Most importantly, they need to understand word structure and how to recognize cognates in order to fully exploit the 30% of the second-language reading process related to language knowledge.

Third, learners need to be encouraged to develop content expertise. If their interest area is animals or dancing or fishing, they should be encouraged to develop a strong content knowledge in that area. Content knowledge helps learners deepen their vocabulary and learn to think critically such as to be able to make judgments about the accuracy of the content material they are reading.

Fourth, when readers fail to comprehend, they need to have teachers who are sensitive to cultural complexity in texts and who can explain cultural differences. This is particularly critical when second-language readers are reading stories or other kinds of narrative text. Narratives often carry hidden cultural dimensions, and teachers must be able to unlock those for learners.

Finally, readers should be permitted to reveal their understanding of complex material in the language in which they feel most comfortable. Particularly when content area material becomes especially complex, such as in biology or social studies, learners should be given the opportunity to explain processes in the language in which they are most comfortable. Consultants or older learners might need to be brought into the assessment process. The important point is that learners be given the chance to reveal their content knowledge and understanding in a manner that does not conflate understanding with imperfect grammar and pronunciation.

None of these recommendations should be considered in isolation. Reading for learners whose native language is not the language of the classroom is not an additive process whereby readers learn one feature of second-language literacy and then another and then another on top of that. Recent theory (Bernhardt, 2010) points us in the direction of interactive compensatory processing for second-language readers. This means that readers must have an arsenal of knowledge, ranging from knowledge about how literacy works, through vocabulary and structure, through background on topic, as well as to cultural appropriateness. These features do not seem to be employed additively but rather in a back and forth multidimensional manner that assists comprehension—that is, one knowledge dimension can buttress another when something is lacking. The obvious implication here is that the larger or more powerful each dimension is, the higher the probability of enhancing and strengthening comprehension abilities.

COUNTERPOINT: Jeanne Gilliam Fain
Middle Tennessee State University

According to the U.S. Census Bureau, the past three decades have represented a steady increase of multilingualism, especially in metropolitan areas such as New York, Los Angeles, and Chicago that have experienced an increase in the use of additional languages other than English. In addition to English, four major language groups have established a solid presence in the United States: (a) Spanish-based ones such as Spanish-Creole and Latino; (b) Indo-European languages; (c) Asian and Pacific-Island languages exemplified by Vietnamese, Chinese, and Korean; and (d) languages including Uralic languages and indigenous languages of Central and South America. These are only part of the 460 different languages that are spoken at home in the United States. In fact, according to the U.S. Census Bureau, 1 of 5 people in the United States speaks a language other than English. Nonetheless, English remains as the dominant language among all of the languages spoken in the United States.

Not surprisingly, the plurality of languages present in the nation's general population is also evident in its public school systems. The U.S. Department of Education (ED) reports that 1 in 9 children in kindergarten through 12th grade speaks a language other than English while 1 in 4 students in schools will speak another language in addition to English by 2026. To be sure, the country's public schools are becoming increasingly diverse in terms of the languages that students speak. Even so, it is evident that two major languages—Spanish and English—are the ones that will be spoken in the United States into the foreseeable future. Should English-Only be a part of curriculum and instruction in school? For better or worse and simply put, it is—and with little doubt—will continue to be part of U.S. schooling policy and practice.

A thornier issue is whether English-Only curriculum and instruction should be expanded in U.S. public education settings. If across the nation most schools are increasingly populated by students who speak a vast plurality of languages, then the answer is an undeniable yes, which is the ground for the main argument that follows. Nonetheless, it is important to note there are individuals and governments who advocate English-Only schooling in regions that are less diverse; the most common example is in regions, as mentioned earlier in the present essay, where Spanish and English are the two predominant languages spoken. In some areas, depending how one cuts up those areas, Spanish is, in fact, the dominant language. Take, for instance, what has been known as the Spanish Harlem of northeast New York City. Although gentrification has caused recent shifts of its inhabitants and the languages spoken there, it remains the most concentrated area of Spanish-speaking Latinos in the city. These language zones are present elsewhere, such as in San Francisco's Chinatown.

Even in these language zones where languages other than English are spoken, there are groups such as ProEnglish (2011a) who advocate for English as the official language. Their stated action agenda is as follows:

> Adopting laws or constitutional amendments declaring English the official language of the United States, and of individual states; Defending the right of individual states to make English the official language of government operations; Ending bilingual education (e.g. foreign language immersion) programs in public schools; Repealing federal mandates for the translation of government documents and voting ballots into languages other than English; Opposing the admission of territories as states unless they have adopted English as their official language.

Such extreme views have been at the root of many passionate political and social debates. For example, on one hand, pro-English advocates list advantages of learning English for immigrants to be economically successful in the United States. On the other hand, the conditions set forth in such logic imply a language bias, which carries with that bias practices that separate people rather than unify them (e.g., racial and ethnic stereotyping). This has been one of the pressing arguments made against "official English" policies by groups such as the American Civil Liberties Union. Interestingly, a ProEnglish (2011b) "official English map" (where official English has been legislated), reads in large part like a presidential election map—with lines chiefly, but not always, drawn between so-called liberal and conservative states.

MULTIPLE LANGUAGES IN THE CLASSROOM

Setting aside the political controversies, at present it simply is not reasonable or possible to teach seemingly countless languages in a school. For example, imagine an international hub such as New York or Washington where there could easily be six or more different first languages spoken in a classroom. To offer full education services to these students in their first language would require that each grade level have teachers who were fluent in each represented language. Further, textbooks and other material resources associated with language used in schools, such as computer programs, teacher manuals, staff memos, daily announcements, school signage, correspondences with parents, and so on, would need to be available in all represented languages. This type of multifaceted language environment cannot be sustained with the human and material resources presently available to U.S. public schools.

Terrence G. Wiley and Gerda deKlerk (2010) argued that for many people conventional wisdom, in lieu of research evidence, substantiates the claim that children in today's classrooms are not learning to speak English well. As a result of this conventional wisdom, politicians, interest groups, community members, and educators have supported English-Only curriculum and instruction with the idea that immigrant students need to immediately learn English within classrooms. If they do not, they will be at a disadvantage in navigating the wider U.S. system that operates chiefly with the English language as one of its primary tools in commerce, popular cultural activities, and so forth.

Historically, difficult economic times such as those that followed the Great Recession that began in 2007 are not typically kind ones for immigrants to the United States, especially those who have not mastered its dominant language. For better or worse, explicit and implicit language policy in public schools and elsewhere, such as in certain jobs, has traditionally been impacted by nationalism. Although not at all a good and decent human quality, in the actual world this makes sense because when resources become scarce, people who share commonalities, such as cultural background and its accompanying languages of difference, often band together and exclude those who are unlike them. By extension, schooling reflects a "language as a problem" mind-set, and English is now viewed as the dominant language of instruction in schooling. As a result of this dominant ideology, schools have predominantly moved toward instructional programs designed for English learners at various levels of language development in English-Only settings.

INSTRUCTIONAL PROGRAMS AND ENGLISH LANGUAGE LEARNERS

English language instructional programs used in schools include SEI, Sheltered English, or Specially Designed Academic Instruction in English (SDAIE), submersion, and pull-out/push-in. SEI is legally mandated in states that have passed English-Only laws such as California, Arizona, and Massachusetts. English language acquisition is where instruction is conducted in English and there is minimal native language support. Students are expected to learn their academic content in English within a year. Further, No Child Left Behind (NCLB) (2001) legislative mandates require English learners to acquire English rapidly. Classroom teachers have created and adapted various interpretations of SEI. Nonetheless, and according to Wayne E. Wright and Daniel Choi (2006), teachers need additional clarification and research regarding the distinct differences, if any, between SEI and mainstream classroom practices where students are expected to either sink or swim.

SEI or SDAIE is a program intended first and foremost to educate students exclusively in English while concurrently teaching subject area topics. There is some evidence that this approach has positive learning effects for secondary school students who possess intermediate English language proficiency. Sheltered instruction provides various structural supports based on the linguistic needs of the English language learner. For example, as its name implies, students are sheltered from the comparatively stark circumstances afforded by the mainstream English-Only classroom, and instruction is modified in terms of delivery, use of visuals, customized printed texts that match the level of the reader, and other media experiences. A submersion program, which is commonly referred to as a "sink or swim" curriculum approach, advances with the idea that English language learners will acquire English most rapidly when thrown into the mainstream waters of the regular classroom without any special support or modifications in the curriculum.

Pull-out programs are also as the name implies. Students are taken at designated and scheduled times away from their regular education classrooms to receive additional instructional assistance related to English language development from someone such as an English as a second language (ESL) teacher, language specialist, teaching assistant, or a qualified volunteer. Conversely, push-in is a program where the ESL teacher or teaching assistant works with students on English language development within their regular classroom. In these cases, ideally the specialist or assistant will typically collaborate with the classroom teacher on the design and implementation of developmentally appropriate instruction for the language learners.

Newcomer programs are created by some school districts and focus on the needs of newly arriving immigrant students. Like other programs mentioned previously in the present section, these programs consist of beginning English language development with an emphasis on content-specific instruction. Although not occurring as frequently as some of the other English-Only programs, at local levels there are schools that integrate English-Only learning with support for families as they adjust to living in the United States, a point picked up subsequently.

PEDAGOGY AND ENGLISH LANGUAGE LEARNERS

As shown previously in this counterpoint essay, there are a number of English-Only curriculum designs operating in U.S. schools. Yet with curriculum there is also instruction, and schools need to integrate research-based knowledge into classrooms and offer the best possible practices for English language learners. Two examples of how teachers can possibly bring this research into practice include the inquiry as curricular framework and family-led literature discussions, discussed in the following sections of this essay.

Inquiry as Curricular Framework and English-Only Learning

The challenge of effectively meeting the linguistic needs of English language learners in an English-Only environment requires curriculum and instruction that avoids rote and repetitive learning. Instruction needs to be planned methodically and crafted in challenging and critical ways. Inquiry needs to be an integral part of the curriculum and can be based on Paulo Freire's (1970) notion of problem-posing and problem solving. Inquiry requires learners to reflect and ask questions in systematic ways. Knowledge systems comprise strategic and domain-specific structures that people use to make sense of their world such as those of physics, botany, and accounting. Various sign systems offer students multiple ways of communicating and creating meaning not only through language but also through music, art, drama, gesture, and movement, which are as critical for English language learners as they are for all learners.

In English-Only classrooms mandated by law, instruction can include themes such as fairness, sense of place, milestones, and points of inspiration. Broad themes can be used as the frameworks for organizing the curriculum and are derived from questions based on experiences that children whose first language is not English will find meaningful and connected to their lives. Knowledge can drive the themes and comes from the children's rich communities and background, knowledge of their families, and knowledge of their languages and cultures.

State and local school district standards can be connected to these themes in English-Only classrooms. All children enter the classroom with funds of knowledge (Moll, Amanti, Neff, & Gonzalez, 1992) and with multiple ways of knowing that involve math, drama, music, art, and/or movement as ways of inquiring, reflecting, thinking, learning, and communicating (Van Sluys & Reinier, 2006).

In English-Only classrooms, drama can be used to take abstract concepts such as discrimination and make those concepts more tangible. It can enable children to experience firsthand some of the power struggles of historical figures from the past. These dramatic experiences can then be related to issues of discrimination that immigrant children have experienced. Children can discuss the challenges of standing up for the languages they speak and translating for their families in difficult situations. In these ways and in spite of English-Only school environments, students can inquire, learn, and possibly transform situations through which their cultural heritages are diminished or ignored.

Family-Led Literature Discussions

Immigrant families whose children attend English-Only schools can use dialogue as a way of knowing within their written and oral responses to the literature in their homes. Families can read and discuss books that are bilingual in their native language and English or in just their first language or in English. Home conversations can move children to draw on their linguistic and cultural resources. Families can use family-led literature discussions to encourage children's literacy in their first and second languages within the context of home and outside of the English-Only context of school. Indeed, in the case of English-Only schooling environments, primary languages can be strengthened and sustained with long-term planning to include the voices of families. Linguistic knowledge of families can be strengthened by using children's literature, oral stories, environmental print, and family response journals. Children's literature can be selected to represent the identities of the children who are represented within the classroom.

CONCLUSION

English-Only is a reality for English language learners in the United States as they move toward mastery of academic content. For better or worse, laws are passed regularly that legally bind educators in terms of their freedom to support English language learners in their primary language. As Mickey Imber and Tyl van Geel (2010) maintained, the Fifth Circuit Court of Appeals legally binds schools within its jurisdiction "to make a genuine and good faith effort consistent with local circumstances and resources, to remedy the language deficiencies of their students" (p. 171). The law does not specify the pedagogical approaches that are needed. In fact, English-Only is one of the so-called remedies to language deficiencies. This has led to increasing numbers of state governments taking control of this deficiency issue by crafting their own English-Only mandates, and with present economic issues, education budget cuts, and so forth, these mandates will likely translate to expansions of English-Only curriculum and instruction in U.S. public schools. As a result, and at least for the present time, educators are faced with the challenge of supporting multilingual learners without capitalizing on their primary languages. Sometimes, and in some localities, these challenges can be faced and teachers supported with multimodal resources. However, regardless of its merit, or lack of merit, English-Only is here to stay and will only expand as diverse language populations likewise will increase in schools. Nonetheless, inquiry approaches to learning in English-Only classrooms can provide the possibility of moving curriculum and instruction forward in critical ways that honor English language learners' funds of knowledge that include their primary languages.

FURTHER READINGS AND RESOURCES

Bernhardt, E. B. (2010). *Understanding advanced second-language reading*. New York: Routledge.

Bourdieu, P. (1986). The forms of capital. In J. G. Richardson (Ed.), *Handbook of theory and research for the sociology of education* (pp. 241–258). New York: Greenwood Press. Retrieved March 19, 2011, from http://econ.tau.ac.il/papers/publicf/Zeltzer1.pdf

Freire, P. (1970). *Pedagogy of the oppressed*. New York: Seabury Press.

Greene. J. (1998, March 2). *A meta-analysis of the effectiveness of bilingual education*. Retrieved June 7, 2010, from http://www.languagepolicy.net/archives/greene.htm

Imber, M., & van Geel, T. (2010). *A teacher's guide to education law* (4th ed.). New York: Routledge.

Labov, W. (2010). Unendangered dialect, enendangered people: The case of African American Vernacular English. *Transforming Anthropology, 18*(1), 15–28.

Moll, L., Amanti, C., Neff, D., & Gonzalez, N. (1992). Funds of knowledge for teaching: Using a qualitative approach to connect homes and classrooms. *Theory Into Practice, 31*(2), 132–141.

Nieto, S. (1999). *The light in their eyes: Creating multicultural learning communities*. New York: Teachers College Press.

ProEnglish. (2011a). *Mission*. Retrieved May 18, 2011, from http://www.proenglish.org/about-us/mission

ProEnglish. (2011b). *Official English map*. Retrieved May 18, 2011, from http://www.proenglish.org/official-english/state-profiles

Rossell, C. H., & Baker, K. (1996). The effectiveness of bilingual education. *Research in the Teaching of English, 30*, 7–74.

Slavin, R., Madden, N., Calderón, M., Chamerberlain, A., & Hennessy, M. (2010). *Reading and language outcomes of a five-year randomized evaluation of transitional bilingual education* (Technical report submitted to the Institute of Education Sciences). Washington, DC: U.S. Department of Education.

Van Sluys, K., & Reinier, R. (2006). "Seeing the possibilities": Learning from, with, and about multilingual classroom communities. *Language Arts, 83*(4), 321–331.

Wiley, T. G., & deKlerk, G. (2010). Common myths and stereotypes regarding literacy and language diversity in the multilingual United States. In M. Farr, L. Seloni, & J. Song (Eds.), *Ethnolinguistic diversity and education: Language, literacy, and culture* (pp. 23–42). New York: Routledge.

Wright, W. E., & Choi, D. (2006). The impact of language and high-stakes testing policies on elementary school English language learners in Arizona. *Education Policy Analysis Archives, 14*(13), 1–56.

COURT CASES AND STATUTES

No Child Left Behind Act of 2001, 20 U.S.C.A. §§ 6301 *et seq.*

8

Are the challenges and opportunities in contemporary diverse classrooms being met?

POINT: Loukia K. Sarroub, *University of Nebraska–Lincoln*
COUNTERPOINT: Lisa Patel Stevens, *Boston College*

OVERVIEW

Cultural diversity suggests the multiple and different ways groups of people share attitudes, perceptions, values, and practices. This overview examines a variety of the typically identified groups who share these four dimensions of culture. Although convenient for organizing this introduction, there are often significantly overlapping aspects between these major groupings, and indeed, there are infinite variations of cultures and many minority alliances whose listings are far outside the scope of a single chapter.

In many regions of the United States prior to and during the 20th century, a visible marker that signified cultural differences was racial categorization. Although there have been different racial categories used for various purposes, such as the identification of Asian Americans during World War II for internment by the U.S. government, the most salient racial division has been that between black and white, which was a catalyst for the civil rights movement. These lines of race were remnants of other cultural divides, such as those between the North and South or master and slave. Even now, what is often described as racial barriers marking these black and white historical divides remain apparent such as in how many of the urban centers on the Eastern Seaboard are organized and separated. These geographic zones have enormous effects on how public schools are constituted.

Other salient cultural divides in the United States are indicated through language, which is likely the most intimate aspect of cultures, as addressed in the point essay of the present chapter. Notwithstanding the numerous languages that became part of the United States during the great wave of immigration of the early 20th century, until recent years, a principal border between languages was found in areas occupied by people who had at one time or another been touched by various colonial land acquisition practices, such as those embedded in the histories of Texas and Arizona. In fact, in North America there are dozens of indigenous languages situated alongside colonial ones, such as Spanish, French, and English. In this vein, cultural diversity is often signified through infinite variations of languages, such as the southern drawl of English or among those whose native countries are Spain, Argentina, and Mexico who pronounce Spanish words differently. It is also this variation that marks the ongoing debate between what has been defined as Ebonics or African American Vernacular English (Delpit & Dowdy, 2002). While the cultural differences among people who share a language or its variation are immense, in the United States they are often lumped into umbrella categories, such as Hispanic.

Economics and class separate cultural groups in the United States as well. During the Great Depression of the 1930s, material resources were placed under greater oversight of and by the federal government to, in part, assure some degree of economic stability or social security, and gradually during modernity, schools became increasingly supported by governments. In the wake of the more recent Great Recession, economic divides have been a source of much discussion, especially as people have lost their homes while corporations have reaped what are for many people inconceivable profits. These factors not only affect personal lives but also public school cultures. For instance, when the so-called housing bubble burst and home prices declined, so too did the property tax income of states and counties. As a result, educational funding diminished in many regions of the country, which subsequently has led to lost human and material resources for public schools—many of which were already grossly different in what they were afforded due to regional class differences. The long-term effects of these economic issues on schools, teachers, and children are yet to be seen.

The cultures marked by different economic classes is indicative of cultures of politics, which are dividing lines that are visible in recent multimedia maps of voting trends that show red Republican zones alongside the blue ones of Democrats. Less dominant are the cultural values of other political groups, such as the Libertarian Socialists and Green Party, and the values of growing numbers of independent people who do not wish to be affiliated with a political party or the scores of citizens who seemingly do not value the U.S. electoral process and thus choose not to participate in it. Like economics, political capital and power exercised by various groups greatly influence education policy and the values, attitudes, and practices of school cultures.

Associated with debates of salient and different political values and perspectives, at least as early as Thomas Jefferson's famous letter to the Danbury, Connecticut, Baptist Convention in 1802, is separation between church and state in the United States. Yet, the cultures of religions have had enormous effects on U.S. schooling—a topic taken up in an entire volume of the present book series. Values and beliefs held by religious cultures, such as those found in the Ten Commandments and how the universe was purportedly created or evolved, are some of the most publicized and debated issues in schools and courtrooms of certain areas of the United States, especially the Bible Belt.

In addition, gender issues and cultural values commonly ascribed to gender subjects have influenced, and will continue to influence, education and other social and political practices in the United States. For example, it was only during recent decades that women gained access to education in certain professions and ranks, and they remain disproportionately underrepresented in major corporate positions, the natural sciences, and so forth. On the other hand, men are a minority in occupations such as those of nursing and public school classroom teaching. Nonetheless, even what had seemed to be a clear categorical division between male and female sexes has become increasingly blurred. In this vein, sexual preferences, transgender ways of being, transsexuality, and so forth have increasingly become topics of education conversations.

Education in itself results in the formations of various cultures, such as the culture of schools, higher education, the academy, and so forth. Further, age, desire, and preferences influence the formation of other cultural groups, such as youth culture and popular culture, topics taken up in another chapter of the present volume (Chapter 13). Indeed, culture is most of all a multiplicity.

The following two essays underscore novel and powerful dimensions of the multiplicity of cultures and education. Unlike many of the essays in the present volume, both authors chose to write in the first person. This is not coincidental because culture is based on identifications—what allows one to articulate the "I" of group alliances and identity. In contrast, scientific writing style, such as that of the American Psychological Association (APA)—which is the standard for much professional publication in education—typically pushes the author "I" to the side, which can give an inaccurate view of how subjectivity influences research and writing. Such narrative approaches, as shown in the subsequent essays, provide a space for subjects rather than simply objects and push against the academic canon. This also denotes the degree of reimagination that many people believe is needed for education research, policy, and practices—a theme that both authors share. Also a part of this reimagination is how language evolves, which is shown subsequently in how authors create neologisms to express ideas that are not part of the common lexicon. For example, "minoritized" is a word used in the counterpoint essay to show how minority subjects are formed (see also Deleuze & Guattari, 1975/1986).

In the point essay, Loukia K. Sarroub of the University of Nebraska–Lincoln uses vivid accounts of her research experiences with Yemeni Americans to show how the complexities of cultures and identities are too often misunderstood. Much of her focus is on how language works in different spaces and for various purposes. This is shown through her own imaginative writing and her call to find ways to reach beyond stereotypes and visualize different ways for us to transact in and with education communities and beyond. Sarroub concludes that the answer to the question of whether the challenges and opportunities in contemporary diverse classrooms being met is mixed. She feels that schools have good intentions and have adequately addressed the history and social constructions of minority groups but undermine the links between language and culture, how language constitutes those we talk and write about and those we represent in textual and visual ways.

Pushing against the grain in the counterpoint essay that follows, Lisa Patel Stevens from Boston College responds in the negative. Taking a critical pedagogy position, she points out how past education practices that seemingly celebrate diversity are often superficial ones, and she offers concepts and practices that can move education toward a valorization of diversity to extend present views of culture. She suggests that education needs to engage teachers and students in topics such as the struggle for legitimacy, xenophobia, protectionism, and global economic power. Valorization, Stevens contends, requires teachers and students to move beyond foods, fashions, and festivals to discuss how we should transact with and resist laws of exclusion, how such laws erode an inclusive social order, and what more equitable edicts and practices would promote.

A. Jonathan Eakle
The Johns Hopkins University

POINT: Loukia K. Sarroub
University of Nebraska–Lincoln

As I begin this essay, I am reminded of Edmond LaForest, a prominent Haitian poet who could not make sense of his colonized identity as either French or Haitian and who in 1915 stood on a bridge, "tied a French Larousse dictionary around his neck, and leaped to his death. This symbolic, if fatal, grand gesture dramatizes the relation of language and cultural identities" (Kramsch, 1998, p. 65), of the communities in which we live, and the communities in which we imagine we would like to live. LaForest's death acquired new meaning when recounted in 1985, at a time when linguistic and cultural rights were starting to be viewed as basic human rights. This has been especially true in light of the hegemonic spread of English around the world and its propagation of global consumerist ideologies.

By way of quick example, think of the following: American English is often characterized by metaphors linking time to money: We "spend" time—we don't pass the time as Spanish speakers and other indo European language speakers do; we say "time is money," "the buck stops here," "put your money where your mouth is." It's no wonder that our language and culture of time/money make us eat faster and everywhere (hence the now-worldwide phenomenon of fast food on the go and in the car) or that we argue about the comparative values we use to explain our choices—that it's not the length of time we spend with our children but the quality of time that counts. While I do not focus this essay on the linguistic imperialism of English or the French, for that matter, my point in sharing LaForest's sad fate is to show the significance of language and culture in connection with identity and education and in connection to the communities we construct, sustain, and imagine for ourselves.

STEREOTYPE AS COMMUNICATIVE PRACTICE?

As we individually and collectively imagine the communities within which we would like to live, considering the theme of the present essay is especially appropriate given the current global and political situation and the ways in which various discourse communities in the United States and abroad interact. The notion that the opening of minds might move us beyond stereotypes is an intriguing proposition. Immediate questions that spring to mind are as follows: How do we do this? How do we open minds? How do we become aware of the stereotypes we share? How do we move beyond them?

It seems to me that first there must be a critical awareness of how people, institutions, and governments interact with one another. How are thoughts, ideas, mandates, policies, laws, and traditions communicated? How are power and authority negotiated, and who benefits from these negotiations? By beginning with these questions, not only do we begin to open minds but we also begin to open hearts, for we do live in a world where there exists extreme miscommunication along with other extremes such as poverty, disease, and limited educational opportunities.

For example, some years ago I conducted fieldwork in a Yemeni American community in the Detroit, Michigan, area. As part of my fieldwork, I would often accompany the youth in the area on their various errands. On one occasion, I went with Asya and her father to buy new tires for their car. We left the relative safety of the neighborhood, in which everyone knew everyone else, and ventured out into the business area of Dearborn, Michigan. On our arrival at the tire shop, the receptionist took one look at Asya, who wore a head scarf and long dress, and at her father, who had a mustache. She proceeded to ignore them completely after she caught a glimpse of me in the background. She crooked her finger at me, and said, "Are you with them? What do they want?"

Sociolinguists might spend hours analyzing this contextual scene, its paralinguistic elements, and how this receptionist's questions embody the power dynamics at play. Basically, as anthropologist Michael Agar might say, the receptionist displayed a #1 mentality, wherein anyone who looks different from the expected norm cannot communicate and more importantly *cannot think* as well. Agar (1994) also argued that Americans are often guilty of the #1 mentality, in part because most do not speak a language other than American English and therefore their understanding of cultural and imagined realities are confined to the values expressed by their language. Now Asya and her father, who are Americans, understood the situation within seconds. They asked to see the supervisor, explained to him what had occurred, told him that the receptionist was disrespectful, and then said that they would go elsewhere to look for tires.

The tire shopping example illustrates how complicated and complex the building of community is. We might begin with becoming critically aware of how we use language to communicate with others, but the stereotypes linger and can suffocate any hope for understanding. Sociolinguists define stereotype as the "conventionalized ways of talking and thinking about other people and cultures" (Kramsch, 1998, p. 131). Scholars of language do not impose a negative or positive value on stereotypes because one universal that characterizes all languages is that speakers tend to find the most efficient ways to express themselves, and this means that all speakers categorize the world in various ways for the sake of efficiency. Outside of sociolinguistics, a stereotype connotes negativity and creates a distance between *us* and *them,* between *our* culture and *their* culture.

Among the Yemeni American youth I studied, I found plenty of stereotypes about what it meant to be American or Yemeni, or Arab, and at the core were questions of identity and what Benedict Anderson calls "long distance nationalism" among immigrants where the present-day homeland is more imagined than it is real. Stereotypes may index a truth at a given moment, but because "cultures are fundamentally heterogeneous and changing . . . and are a constant site of struggle for recognition and legitimation" (Kramsch, 1998, p. 10), stereotypes create a false reality that gives credence to the myth that a culture is static rather than dynamic, that people cannot think outside of the categories they've constructed to explain the world as in the case of the tire shop receptionist.

While stereotypes do exist, it is also clear that schools continuously evolve to address them, often struggling to define what legitimate practices might be when linguistic, ethnic, cultural, socioeconomic, and/or national diversity is represented in the student body. For example, in one high school in Dearborn, Michigan (Sarroub, 2005), administrators and teachers went to great lengths to address miscommunication between the school district and the Arab community in southeastern Michigan, differences in participation and interaction among their European American and Yemeni American students, demands for religious accommodations, and gendered and cultural accommodations for dress in various classes, etc. The majority of the staff were white middle-class teachers who for the first time in the inception of the high school were teaching a population of Yemeni American and Yemeni youth quite unlike themselves. The curriculum was revisited; lunch menus were debated; PE classes were assessed for appropriateness; and more importantly, teachers were positioned and positioned themselves in favor of accommodating diversity or not in favor of accommodating diversity. Teachers talked about treating everyone in the same way, thus buying into a classical liberalism that did not address individual and collective differences. The youth themselves lobbied for change and reform in the school to address religious practices. My point is that there is potential for change when communicative practices are put in place to foster such change, even when the challenges seem insurmountable.

PARTICIPATION IN COMMUNITIES OF PRACTICE

How do we move beyond stereotypes? In the past several years, many of us have paid close attention to the presidential campaigns of George W. Bush and John Kerry and then John McCain and Barack Obama. Their interactions and advertising campaigns have been as much about language use as they have been about the war and devastation in Iraq, the domestic economy, health care, and other issues. For example, Bush admitted that Austrian native Arnold Schwarzenegger is more articulate than he (Bush) is in English, and the media resoundingly endorsed Kerry as the more effective speaker and communicator. The candidates' individual messages about what they "plan" or imagine the United States and the world to be have also been cast differently, with one candidate using metaphors of fear, safety, and war and the other focusing on safety, communication, decreasing the deficit, and global community. The candidates argued until the elections, and their arguments gave evidence for another problematic metaphor in American English: Argument is war. For example, American English speakers say, "Your claims are *indefensible*," "He *attacked* what I said," "She was *right on target*," "OK, go ahead, *shoot*," "He'll *wipe you out*," "I *won* that point." The United States is a competitive nation, and its language illustrates this. One might say that there is little subtlety in our words or in the actions they express. The advent of Obama in national politics disturbed ideologies of competition because his discourse advanced notions of unity and togetherness.

In 1971, in the song "Imagine," John Lennon sang about imagining a world without countries, a place with no killing and dying or religion, a place where people live peacefully. His dream in the song of a people living as one is a powerful political precedent and educational one. In many places in the United States, schools have figured out or are figuring out how to engage students in learning regardless of the teachers' or students' backgrounds. This is an important aim of equitable and accessible education for all.

I've always liked Lennon's song even though I don't necessarily advocate for no countries. After all, if we were all the same we wouldn't have much to talk about today. "Imagine" provokes a set of images that allow us to speak of a world that is more open, where people share, where there is no war. As idealistic as Lennon's song sounds, it reminds me of Harvard educator Marcelo Suárez-Orozco's (2001) definition of globalization. He defined it as follows:

> . . . as a process of change, generating at once centrifugal (qua the borders of the nation state) and centripetal (qua the post-national) forces that result in the deterritorialization of important economic, social, and cultural practices from their traditional moorings in the nation state. (p. 347)

According to Suárez-Orozco, large scale immigration is a world issue and is transforming Africa, Asia, Europe, and the Americas: "Roughly 30% of Frankfurt's population is immigrant. Amsterdam by the year 2015 will be 50% immigrant" (p. 349). Leicester, England, is the first city in Europe where "whites" will no longer be the majority. Japan needs immigrant workers to maintain economic vitality. Africa has the largest numbers of refugees in the world. In the United States, the fastest growing sector of the child population is immigrant children (Suárez-Orozco, 2001). The world is changing, perhaps not becoming one as in Lennon's song, but significantly changing such that linguistic, social, and cultural practices have more immediate consequences and will be called into question.

My own research is concerned with what it means to be successful in public schools and how American-born and immigrant youth become literate in and out of school. I study why it is that youth in high school cannot read and how institutions such as schools, government, families, and community organizations accommodate one another. I've found that in general there is no question that families and schools have the best intentions with regard to their children and students, but they are not necessarily prepared or educated enough to understand one another and the systems they inhabit, especially in the Midwest, where non-Western immigration is a relatively new phenomenon. The reality of public education today is that it is fraught with social issues that influence the ways in which students learn and communicate. Further, as Davis Guggenheim pointed out in his 2010 documentary, *Waiting for "Superman,"* the social problems experienced by both schools and families exist within an organizational infrastructure meant to deal with an industrial rather than postindustrial economy. For example, the United States has a decentralized school system "financed mainly by local property taxes [that] ensures the perpetuation in schools of the local social class structure and local ethnic and racial distribution" (Kramsch, 1998, p. 83). Further, in 1998, alarming trends were reported by a national study among 20,000 randomly selected U.S. teenagers, and here I quote directly from the report:

> Foreign-born youth experience fewer physical health problems, have less experience with sex, are less likely to engage in delinquent and violent behavior and are less likely to use controlled substances than native-born youth.... Among foreign-born youth, statistical analysis showed the longer the time since arrival in the U.S., the poorer was the adolescents' physical health and the greater the likelihood of engaging in risky behaviors. (Migration Dialogue, 1998, p. 3)

The United States is certainly the land of economic opportunity and education, but the questions remain for whom and how? In the past several years, we've witnessed worldwide divisiveness, and neoconservative (in the United States and Europe) and fundamentalist movements (Mideast and Southeast Asia) that largely stem from cross-cultural miscommunication about cultural and religious norms, especially in immigrant communities; the failure of educated individuals to take humanitarian and proactive steps to build rapport rather than to destroy; and the further corruption by consumerist ideologies of socially minded welfare systems, such as the lack of universal health care for citizens or anti-immigration laws that favor some populations over others.

Going beyond the stereotypes to create our imagined communities requires critical awareness and a collective enactment of communicative practices within our communities. Communicative practices reflect "institutionalized networks of relationships, defined by nationality, family, school, workplace, professional organization, religious organization, and all their expected roles and statuses, values, beliefs, and ideologies" (Kramsch, 1998, p. 83). In the early 1990s, a new line of thinking emerged, redefining what community means. Going beyond the idea of community as a group with a common repertoire or shared codes, theorists Jean Lave, Etienne Wenger, Penelope Eckert, and Sally McConnell-Ginet suggested "communities of practice" defined as "an aggregate of people who come together around mutual engagement in an endeavor" (Eckert & McConnell-Ginet, 1992, p. 464). The idea is that people are engaged together in some project and that all of us in one way or another, as Lave and Wenger (1991) argued, are "legitimate peripheral participants" in these projects. In other words, we are all constantly learning new ways of speaking and interacting as we enter into collective endeavors, no matter how far we are from communities in which our participation is peripheral or minimal.

CONCLUSION

I began my essay with the sad account of the Haitian LaForest's real and symbolic death by French dictionary, a death reflecting the ambiguity of an occupied identity in flux, where a sense of community did not seem possible. Whatever layers of disillusionment pervade our lives, we can still productively imagine and enact communities that reflect a generosity of spirit both in action and talk. This edited volume, including the essays of Jonathan Eakle and Lisa Stevens, testifies that many, if not all of us, have cast aside and reinvented ourselves, the communities, and the nations to which we belong. Are the challenges and opportunities in contemporary diverse classrooms being met? Many educators have good intentions about thoughtfully representing *all* and *everyone*, but euphemistic expressions and the emergence of extreme politically correct talk have served to hide the tapestry of diversity. Schools seem to have adequately addressed the history and social constructions of legally recognized minority groups while simultaneously undermining the links between language and culture, how language constitutes those we talk and write about and those we represent in textual and visual ways. However, honoring the difference and diversity within and among human beings and the communities we imagine and eventually enact will be an ongoing project in the 21st century.

COUNTERPOINT: Lisa Patel Stevens
Boston College

I work with recently immigrated youth living in Boston. As I write this essay, these youth are in the midst of preparing for the rapidly approaching school year. They are perhaps purchasing school supplies; mapping the public transportation route to the high school that they will attend; savoring the last few days of their summer break from schooling; or if they have not yet attended school in the United States, wondering what it will be like here, what will be expected of them, and how they will manage to get by as newcomers. At the same time, their teachers, mostly white, female, and middle class, are working through existing curricular frames and pedagogical approaches designed to promote school-defined success. I mention these youth and their teachers because in answering a question such as the one of the present essay, being specific helps. It helps keep us centered on who education is for explicitly and implicitly, how it must have disserved and might serve diverse populations of youth, and where past efforts have faltered. From these critical points, we as educators might assess how well our education work is being done.

While these people are prepping for the start of a new academic year in 2010, there were a few political issues dominating U.S. media worth mentioning, particularly in relation to immigrant populations. First, there was the highly debated and hotly contested proposal to build an Islamic Cultural Center about four blocks from the former site of the World Trade Center towers in New York City. Some protested the location of this center as disrespectful to the memories of those who died during the terrorist attack of 9/11. Others bemoaned these protests for a lack of regard for religious freedom and free speech afforded through the U.S. Constitution. Alongside the Islamic Center debates, the state of Arizona was fighting federal government intervention to stop two proposed pieces of legislation that target immigrant populations: one that obligated police officers to question those who appear to be in the country without government sanction about their legal status (Support Our Law Enforcement and Safe Neighborhoods Act, 2010) and another proposal that prohibited ethnic studies courses in Arizona's schools (Prohibition of Seditious Ethnic Studies Act, 2010). In the point essay to this question, Loukia K. Sarroub drew in examples of communities, institutions, and people outside of schools, underscoring the symbiotic relationship between people, schools, and societies. These social contexts echo in the explicit curricula of the United States, including multiculturalism, and in the implicit absences and silences of white privilege and long histories of education as colonization. To put it mildly, diversity issues are anything but a comfort zone in the American landscape.

I must respond to the question in this chapter of meeting the challenges and opportunities of contemporary diversity in light of the surrounding and constitutive historical, social and political contexts of education. These issues and events, such as the ones I mentioned earlier, provide just some of the necessary foundation for the question of whether today's schools are meeting the challenges and opportunities. Because schools are situated in society and also reflect the society that surrounds them, they have the potential to engage with the ideas, values, and actions of that society. Also schools have the obligation to prepare students for these surrounding contexts. It is particularly in light of preparing racially minoritized and white students for social contexts that I answer an emphatic no to the question of whether schools are adequately meeting the challenges and opportunities of a diverse contemporary society.

HOW WILL OUR OUTCOMES BE MEASURED?

To meet the challenges and opportunities of diversity appropriately, it is usually taken to simply mean that schools should reflect, in their curricula, materials, and perhaps their pedagogy, a diverse student and societal population. Not only are U.S. schools not achieving this goal—given the present contextual backdrop and the history of our country's social reproduction of class, race, cultural, and gender inequities through schooling—this particular goal is an abysmally low one. It obligates schools, which are mostly staffed by white middle-class professionals, to represent diversity, which is often talked about in and of itself, but not necessarily the diversity found in schools and classrooms. There are three potential and co-influential locations where this representation can occur: pedagogy, assessment, and curriculum. Teaching and learning, or pedagogy, in the United States has remained a largely teacher-centered, banking-like approach (Freire, 1970), through which teachers seek to deposit traditional knowledge into the assumed empty or miseducated minds of students by use of their positions as authority figures. In turn, students are evaluated, with increasingly high-stakes ways for them and their teachers, via linear, standardized assessments that preserve knowledge as static and neutral.

In short, pedagogy and assessment remain largely reflections of white middle-class cultural practices.

The most frequent location of any kind of representation of diversity is in some curricula but not all curricula. The historical and social contexts of diversity in math and science education have been, and remain to be, all but absent from core standards movements (National Black Education Agenda, 2010). In an English class, though, you might find a section in the textbook entitled something like "Global Voices," and see entries taken from authors such as Martin Luther King, Jr.; Zora Neale Hurston; Sandra Cisneros; and Amy Tan. While these are outstanding authors who have much to lend to the social and literary education of today's youth, the sprinkling of their work in a largely Euro-centered textbook amounts to merely a symbolic representation of diversity. Furthermore, this diversity is not necessarily reflective of the constituents in the school or community. Add to that mix that much of this literature is mainly taught by teachers who come from different home cultures than these authors; who themselves are the products of a banking model of education steeped in Eurocentric curricula; and the inclusion of these authors' works usually does not include a deep understanding of the social contexts of their lives, the effect of their work on the past and present, and how their works might represent different worlds than those represented in canonical texts. Without this kind of engagement, a more typical cursory engagement with excerpts of great works, amounts to merely token symbolization, one that serves to center and legitimate the central white male European authors who make up the canon (Moreton-Robinson, 2008).

Such token symbolic representation, where only a few persons, at best, are taken to represent entire groups, is actually more corrosive than it is helpful to the edification of diverse student populations. Students learn, through the symbolic smattering of culturally diverse referents, that diversity is ancillary, an afterthought that ironically works to more firmly center European-delineated contributions to American thought, history, and events and easily subsumed under a few taken to represent a diverse many. In its worst moments, multiculturalism is manifested in a limited "foods, fashions, and festivals" approach where cultures are reduced to visible token symbols meant to stand for the collective, contested, and complicated histories that are endemic to all peoples. For students from nondominant class, ethnic, and gender backgrounds, they mistakenly learn that they, in turn, must also be ancillary—or at best complementary—but certainly not central members in American schools and society.

When the focus is on the canonical curriculum of the American ruling class, schools lose the opportunity to engage with the ways in which diversity issues are being met in the larger society. More simply put, how does a short and disintegrated textbook section such as "Global Voices" help immigrant and native-born youth interact, for example, with vehement, and at times, violent protests to Islamic culture in the United States? When there is such token engagement with diversity, although it is in some senses gesturing toward diversity, we are ill-equipping children and youth to understand the vicissitudes of identity, group membership, and civil rights that are at the core of polemic debates such as that concerning the Islamic Cultural Center in New York City mentioned previously in this essay. Rather, the goal remains more one of how to maintain the traditional curriculum and pepper it with representations of diverse peoples, or assimilation. To actually engage with diversity as opportunity would require a different set of goals.

MEETING DIVERSITY'S CHALLENGES AND OPPORTUNITIES

Although a very common question in schools and other education institutions, the question that guides the present essay is an ironically sad reflection of the state of multicultural education in the United States. It reflects a cosmetic approach to multiculturalism that has marked efforts to revise Eurocentric curricula and pedagogy in public schools. Asking the question is often the beginning and end of attention to diversity that paradoxically reflects an all too common invocation of diversity as a challenge.

Multicultural education, as a movement and field of study, is built on the premise that American society is pluralistic and that education should serve this pluralism. A major goal of multicultural education is "to reform the school and other educational institutions so that students from diverse racial, ethnic, and social class groups will experience educational equity" (Banks, 1993, p. 25). However, multicultural education has most often taken this concept of equity to simply mean a superficial representation of cultural diversity. This manifestation is directly connected to the vast majorities of teachers and teacher educators coming from dominant Eurocentric backgrounds. Put simply, this response reflects far more of the shortcomings and miseducation of teachers and teacher educators than it reflects of the students in today's classrooms.

The goal of meeting the challenges of diversity most often seeks to position white educators with opportunities to provide culturally minoritized students cultural referents in curricula. In the end, it does nothing to interrogate or change cultural structures of power, thereby reifying existing power structures. Without a doubt, inclusive education that draws from a variety of cultures (e.g., ethnic, class, gender, and sexual identity) is a must for all students, but I aver that this goal is in some ways even more important for students from dominant, or majoritized, backgrounds. While some students have been miseducated to believe that their cultures are ancillary, other students have been simultaneously miseducated to believe that their cultures are inherently the smarter and more valuable contributors to society (Nieto, 2008). Rather than seek to represent the cultures in front of a particular teacher or school registrar, true diversity in education should seek to engage all learners in the active learning of knowledge as a multifaceted, contested, alive, and pliable process that can only come from various perspectives. In this sense, diversity is itself an opportunity, one that is essential to avoid monocultures of thought and practices, which ultimately lead to their demise. Ecologically speaking, a monoculture is the agricultural practice of producing or growing one single crop over a wide area. From a capitalist point of view, this is great. You make all the cogs and widgets that the machine needs to grow, harvest, and sell the single crop—efficiency at its smoothest. However, from a more longitudinal and deeper view of biodiversity and sustainability, monocultures are not such great things. Overproducing a single crop undermines the ability for any ecosystem, necessarily made up of different parts, to survive. Create a monoculture, and you may as well start making collectors' editions of calendars, because for that ecosystem, time is limited. Jared Diamond named monocultures as one of the four fundamental threats to biodiversity. E. O. Wilson addressed overharvesting in his warnings against a system of five threats to biodiversity. And predating any European patterns of agriculture, indigenous communities in the Americas, the South Pacific, and Asia thrived on heterogeneous agricultural crops that fed back into the lands' abilities to produce foods appropriate to those climates.

For the immigrant youth I've been mentioning, of course, many educators would prefer that they be taught by teachers who understand and perhaps even reflect their backgrounds; learn about their own histories alongside the histories of other peoples; and who actively shape their curricula, pedagogy, and assessment practices to reflect themselves and their cultures. For immigrant youth and other youth from nondominant backgrounds, the inclusion of these cultural referents is but a partial start. This is the second aspect in which we are falling short of tapping the potential possibilities of diversity, but if we changed our manner of thinking we could change our manner of being.

In considering the opportunities that diversity presents, I urge us to consider if students' various cultural identities are valorized through education. Our focus on multicultural education must make a move from the too-benign goal of representation to a goal of valorization, one in which all stakeholders are educated to understand that increasing the value of diversity in the social order is a collective vested interest, particularly in societies that claim any kind of democratic value system. Particularly given the social contextual backdrop and infusion into schools, how are students engaged in learning about themselves and the world around them that valorizes them through these processes? How are we equipping them with the conceptual tools and strategic muscles they need to best understand and counter the social realities of xenophobia?

Valorizing students' cultural identities will necessitate a project of actively valuing and determining with intent the manifestation of multiple cultural identities in a collective, in a school, in a classroom, and beyond. It will mean that teachers and students from the dominant culture engage with the legacies of this culture. This must happen alongside students from ethnic, gender, and class minority backgrounds who must learn about their own legacies, each of these populations uncovering these legacies where they've been silenced. This will be painful, but in the face of multicultural education that has been far too nice while legacies of colonization, slavery, and subjugation continue to pulse through our lives, a little pain is called for.

WHAT VALORIZATIONS OF DIVERSITY IN EDUCATION MIGHT LOOK LIKE

It is, in fact, because of the glaring failure of American schools to represent diversity that I believe the ground is fertile to cast aside symbolic parity as our ultimate goal and retool for valorization in education. Valorization, though, will mean an entirely different educational process for teachers, students, administrators, and parents. And it will mean work, not necessarily more work, but very different and deeper work from what schools typically include in a "foods, fashions, and festivals" approach to multiculturalism.

For example, a valorizing education would engage teachers and students in topics such as the struggle for legitimacy, xenophobia, protectionism, and global economic power that are some of the themes of Arizona's proposed restrictive legislation, mentioned in the opening section of this counterpoint essay. It would require teachers and students to research the histories that have led to these legislative moves that equate ethnic solidarity with upheaval of social order and ethnicity with illegality, connecting the similar language and tone of the Arizona legislation with the black code laws of the antebellum South. It would require that teachers and students discuss how to transact with and resist laws of exclusion, how such laws erode an inclusive social order, and what more equitable edicts and practices would promote. At heart through all of these discussions would be a goal of valorization in and through education, with all people involved with exploring their social contexts with a regard for how to nurture and grow healthy diversity. In short, it would actively engage with the social contexts of diversity.

Valorizing diversity in education will mean that different questions must be posed, such as the following:

- Who are the students and teachers in a given classroom/school/district?
  - What are the ethnic, gender, and class demographics?
  - How are these demographics reflective of the region's and nation's histories?
  - What is the socioeconomic status of these populations in the local, national, and global landscape?
- What is the history of these cultures in this region, nation, and in other regions and nations in the world?
  - What has been the interaction of these populations with ways of knowing?
  - What contributions and social ills have been part of these intertwined histories?
- What are the most pressing challenges and opportunities for these cultural identities?
  - What are the most pressing threats to their projects of healthy self-determination in a pluralistic society?
  - Where are those threats coming from, and how might they be engaged?
  - What are the contributions—past, potential, and current—that this cultural identity has to offer to itself and to a collective pluralistic society?

I offer these questions not as a template, model, or blueprint but as a contributing, working example of the types of social scientific questions that might mark a process of cultural valorization rather than simply a product of symbolic representation. Diversity can be seen to be an essential cornerstone from which a multifaceted, vibrant, and rigorous education arises but only if education is seen to be an emancipatory process rather than a formula for assimilationist banking of knowledge shaped by dominant groups and individuals in power. These are questions that arise when I imagine an emancipatory education for students, engaging in questions of why contexts around them are the way they are, how they might be different, what they can add to these contexts, and steps they will have to take to do so. I see teachers and students actively researching the world around them, who and what has shaped it to be as it is, and how they are active in those legacies. I can easily picture arguments; discussions; collective reading; and collective, contested writing. When I envisage these processes of valorization, I am hopeful. When I consider if schools have represented diversity, I sigh.

FURTHER READINGS AND RESOURCES

Agar, M. (1994). *Language shock: Understanding the culture of conversation.* New York: William Morrow.

Banks, J. A. (1993). Multicultural education: Historical developments, dimensions, and practice. *Review of Research in Education, 19,* 3–49.

Deleuze, G., & Guattari, F. (1986). *Kafka: Towards a minor literature* (D. Polan, Trans.). Minneapolis: University of Minnesota Press. (Original work published 1975)

Delpit, L., & Dowdy, J. K. (2002). *The skin that we speak: Thoughts on language and culture in the classroom.* New York: New Press.

Eckert, P., & McConnell-Ginet, S. (1992). Think practically and look locally: Language and gender as community-based practice. *Annual Review of Anthropology, 21,* 461–490.

Freire, P. (1970). *Pedagogy of the oppressed.* New York: Continuum.

Hanks, W. F. (1996). *Language and communicative practices.* Boulder, CO: Westview Press.

Kramsch, C. (1998). *Language and culture.* Oxford, UK: Oxford University Press.

Lave, J., & Wenger, E. (1991). *Situated learning: Legitimate peripheral participation.* Cambridge, UK: Cambridge University Press.

Migration Dialogue. (1998, July).The health and well-being of children of immigrants. *Migration News* [Electronic newsletter]. Available from http://migration.ucdavis.edu

Moreton-Robinson, A. (2008). Writing off treaties: White possession in the United States critical whiteness studies literature. In A. Moreton-Robinson, M. Casey, & F. Nicoll (Eds.), *Transnational whiteness matters* (pp. 81–96). Lanham, MD: Lexington Books.

National Black Education Agenda. (2010). *For Black America, we are still a nation at risk.* Retrieved September 1, 2010, from http://blackeducationnow.org/id17.html

Nieto, S. (2008). *Affirming diversity: The sociopolitical context of multicultural education* (5th ed.). New York: Allyn & Bacon.

Sarroub, L. K. (2005). *All American Yemeni girls: Being Muslim in a public school.* Philadelphia: University of Pennsylvania Press.

Sleeter, C. E. (2001). Preparing teachers for cultural diverse schools: Research and the overwhelming presence of whiteness. *Journal of Teacher Education, 52*(2), 94–106.

Suárez-Orozco, M. M. (2001). Globalization, immigration, and education: The research agenda. *Harvard Educational Review, 71*(3), 345–365.

Wenger, E. (1999). *Communities of practice.* Cambridge, UK: Cambridge University Press.

COURT CASES AND STATUTES

Prohibition of Seditious Ethnic Studies Act, Arizona House Bill 2281 (2010).

Support Our Law Enforcement and Safe Neighborhoods Act, Arizona Senate Bill 1070 (2010).

Do the arts in education enhance or distract from core curriculum and instruction?

POINT: Ellen Winner, *Boston College*

COUNTERPOINT: A. Jonathan Eakle, *The Johns Hopkins University*

OVERVIEW

The role of the arts in education is a long-standing debate. One central question posed for the arts is this: How should they be included in curriculum and instruction? In other words, should the arts be taught as a separate set of subject areas in schools; should they be incorporated into what is often called the core curriculum subjects of English language arts, mathematics, science, and social studies; or should the arts simply not be part of the discussion about core curriculum?

On one side of the debate, advocates for the arts argue that students benefit from time and opportunity spent working through arts activities within the subject areas of dance, drama, instrumental and vocal music, and visual arts. Put simply, the arts are taught as separate subjects because educators value what students can learn in these areas that is different from what they may learn in other subjects. Elliot Eisner's work has a rich history and theoretical background to advocate for the arts in schools in valuing the thinking of students as they learn to use paintbrushes and paint, musical notes and their voices, rhythm, language, and their bodies to compose their ideas. The body of Eisner's work points to the importance of understanding that the arts provide students with opportunities to imagine open-ended solutions and to use play as a generative activity for thinking and working; moreover, and perhaps most important, it points out that learning in the arts involves complex thinking that is informed by careful perception of the world and paying attention to emotions while learning to create and perform through music, dance, acting, and visual arts.

A different viewpoint in the debate still values the arts, but rather than having independent classes for teaching the arts as subjects, they are simply incorporated into a core curriculum that focuses on teaching through language and mathematical symbols. In this case, the arts are viewed as supplemental tools for supporting students' competencies in reading, writing, mathematics, science, history, and geography. In this approach, the focus is on teaching students in an interdisciplinary fashion. For example, an interdisciplinary school focus might invite visual arts into the classroom as a way of understanding a cultural or historical time period while learning about literature, politics, and history. Students studying a time period like this may view or listen to historical art pieces, but they may not necessarily construct an arts-based project; rather, their learning is likely to still be assessed through such mechanisms as writing or tests.

The sharp focus on standardized testing and performance in the United States has helped to support a third position in the debate about the role of arts in schools: If student achievement is measured via high-stakes assessments that are more often standardized tests than not, then there is little room, if any, in the curriculum for the arts. The arts are not core subject areas because they are perceived as being more about feelings and self-expression than practices located around observable, measurable acts of producing sentences, algorithms, and formulas. When characterized this way, the arts seem to not have rigor or require substantive thinking—the kind of thinking promoted in the media and by state and federal government representatives as what is needed to propel the nation into the 21st-century global marketplace. From this perspective, the arts are shaped as pursuits of the body and hands, not of the mind as one might pursue literature and calculus. Further, the arts present a distraction from the real purposes of school: to teach students the basics, the 3 Rs—Reading, wRiting, and aRithmetic. The results of support for this perspective are ever-present funding cuts to eliminate the arts as subject areas and the relegation of the arts to after-school activities. Indeed, by placing the arts as supplemental to core curriculum, it is not difficult to remove them from daily activities because students will still receive the important curriculum of learning math, science, English, and social studies.

Ironically, subjects of reading literature; of writing prose, poetry, and persuasion; and of calculating formulas and proofs in mathematics all depend on sensory input, of paying close attention to the world and to symbols, of developing nuanced solutions for complex problems—all examples of what students achieve when they work in the arts. Unfortunately, despite long-standing arguments valuing the arts, arts programs are still among the first to be considered for removal and ultimately dropped from school budgets when the economy worsens. Budget cuts of this magnitude eliminate positions for arts thus creating a vacuum of expertise in schools.

In the following essays, Ellen Winner (Boston College) and A. Jonathan Eakle (The Johns Hopkins University) discuss the value of the arts in schools. In the point essay, Winner contends that the arts not only enhance the curriculum but should be as much a part of education as math and reading. Winner presents the argument that students do indeed learn broad skills in arts classes. However, she takes on claims that learning in arts classes can be transferred into learning in other subject areas. Winner's argument is based on meta-analyses and subsequently lays bare the reality about whether studies can prove that students do use what they learn in arts classes as means for learning elsewhere. Although waiting for further evidence to substantiate claims of transfer, Winner presents her argument with the assumption that the arts are essential to curriculum and that an education without the arts is incomplete.

Eakle, in the counterpoint essay, states that the arts are, and should be, a distraction from the core curriculum and instruction. He poses a different perspective for understanding the role of the arts in education. After reviewing how art and education are currently defined and practiced in the public schools, Eakle shapes his argument around the idea that education and instruction are two different aspects of schooling, with education being a form of art and instruction being a matter of craft. To frame education as art, Eakle argues, is to value creativity and to resist the present state of affairs in order to innovate solutions for already-present, complex problems. However, schooling in his argument is focused on craft, on honing best practices, and the arts in such a conservation-minded perspective serve as distractions from the core curriculum. Eakle embraces the value of distraction from the core curriculum as a means to reenvision American schools and contends that, at least for now, the arts should remain a distraction to curriculum and instruction now used in most public schools.

Michelle Zoss
Georgia State University

POINT: Ellen Winner
Boston College

Why do schools teach the arts? This is a question often asked as public schools find themselves with fewer financial resources. A distinction has typically been made between the core essential subjects that schools teach and the optional subjects that schools can teach if they have enough time and resources, as well as students who are not lagging behind in the essentials. Linguistic and numerical literacies and science are typically considered essential and the arts optional. But the arts were not always split off from the core of education, as was the case in the medieval western university.

Arts advocates in the United States have tried to give the arts a more prominent role in the classroom by arguing that the arts can be used as a tool to strengthen the core—to help children learn to read, write, calculate, and so forth. These are arguments for "far transfer"—when learning in one subject area leads to improvements in another. Far transfer can be contrasted to "near transfer," when learning in one area leads to improvements in a closely related area (e.g., beginning reading and spelling).

It is often heard from arts advocates that the arts make you smarter. Every year, the Music Educators National Conference publishes data showing that SAT scores of students are positively related to number of music courses taken. A recent Gallup poll surveyed people about their beliefs in the benefits of music education. Eighty-one percent of respondents reported that participating in school music is associated with better grades and test scores and helps students do better in math and science.

Those who offer such instrumental reasons for teaching music or any other art form in schools reveal that they value the arts only as a means to a more important end—the enhancement of core skills. In addition, instrumental reasons inadvertently create a contingency between teaching the arts and improving student performance in other "core" areas. Further, despite the widespread belief among the public that arts education boosts basic skills, the evidence for these beliefs is weak or nonexistent. Nonetheless, in what follows preliminary evidence is shown that the arts do teach important skills that can enhance performance in other areas of the curriculum—just not those measured by the kinds of standardized tests currently used to track student success. Then, an argument is presented that the question posed in the title of this chapter begs the question because it implies a distinction between core curriculum and arts education—a distinction I argue against. The arts should not only enhance core curriculum but also should be as much a part of it as are math and reading.

INSTRUMENTAL ARGUMENTS HAVE LITTLE LEG TO STAND ON

In the early part of this century, a comprehensive study of what existing research on academic outcomes of arts education shows was conducted (Winner & Hetland, 2000). The claim was tested that studying the arts leads to some form of academic improvement. These uncovered studies were subject to a series of meta-analyses—statistical summaries of findings across many similar studies. Several studies tested the claim that an arts-rich education does not result in higher verbal and mathematics scores or grades, and these yielded 66 effect sizes that could be entered into a meta-analysis (Winner & Cooper, 2000). Arts-rich education was defined as schools in which students take a variety of art courses, or schools in which the arts are integrated into the "academic" curriculum. While a clear correlation was found between studying the arts and academic achievement as measured primarily by test scores, no evidence was uncovered from experimental studies that showed that studying the arts *causes* academic indicators to improve. Correlation findings can always be explained by noncausal mechanisms, and in this case, there are several plausible noncausal explanations. For example, high-achieving students may come from families that value well roundedness enough to urge their children to achieve academically as well as in the arts.

These meta-analyses revealed that the claims that arts education boosts core academic achievement are overstated, except in the case of classroom drama. But in this case, the leap from enacting stories to verbal achievement is an example of near transfer, since stories are of course verbal entities. In short, from these analyses there simply was no evidence that the kind of far transfer that would be entailed by other art forms, which appear on the surface to be unrelated to verbal and math skills, would lead to improvements in verbal and mathematical areas of the core curriculum.

WHAT THE ARTS DO TEACH

What, then, do the arts teach? Ask a person on the street and you will be told that the arts teach art. A drawing class teaches you how to draw; a music class teaches you how to sing. But do the arts teach any broader skills that might spill over into other areas? Perhaps they do but only when well taught. To find out, a study was conducted in five visual arts classrooms in two local Boston-area schools, one public—the Boston Arts Academy—and one independent—the Walnut Hill School for the Arts. In a project called the Studio Thinking Project, classes were videotaped and photographed; teachers and their students were interviewed as well. The research goal was to find out what visual arts teachers were trying to teach (besides trying to teach the techniques of drawing, painting, working with ceramics, etc.). Eight skills labeled "studio habits of mind" were identified that art teachers were striving to instill (Hetland, Winner, Veenema, & Sheridan, 2007). None of these skills would be picked up on a standardized test of verbal or mathematical reasoning. Six of these skills are broad skills that may well enhance performance in other areas of the curriculum and are also skills likely to be important for life, as described subsequently.

Observational Acuity

Visual arts students are trained to look, a task far more complex than a layperson might think. Seeing is framed by expectation, and expectation often gets in the way of perceiving the world accurately. Let's take a simple example: When asked to draw a human face, most people will set the eyes near the top of the head. But this isn't how a face is really proportioned, as students learn: Our eyes divide the head nearly at the center line. If asked to draw a whole person, people tend to draw the hands much smaller than the face—again an inaccurate perception. The power of our expectations explains why beginners draw eyes too high and hands too small. Observational drawing requires breaking away from stereotypes and seeing accurately and directly.

Over and over teachers in the study told their students to look more closely at the model and see it in terms of its essential geometry. Seeing clearly by looking past one's preconceptions is central to a variety of professions, such as medicine and law. Naturalists must be able to tell one species from another; climatologists need to see atmospheric patterns in data as well as in clouds. Writers need keen observational skills too, as do doctors. Thus, observational acuity is one of the candidate skills that may, if learned, enhance performance in core areas of the curriculum—with the best bet being the sciences.

Envisioning

Another pattern of thought observed being cultivated in art classes was envisioning—forming mental images internally and using them to guide actions and solve problems. "How much white space will you be leaving in your self-portrait?" asked Kathleen Marsh at the Boston Arts Academy (Hetland et al., 2007, p. 103). "How many other kinds of orange can you get?" asked Beth

Balliro, also at the Boston Arts Academy, as she nudged her student to move beyond one shade (Hetland et al., 2007, p. 49). In fact, teachers gave students a great deal of practice in this area: What would that look like if you got rid of this form, changed that line, or altered the background? All were questions repeatedly voiced by the teachers, which prompted students to imagine what was not there.

Like observing, envisioning is a skill with payoffs far beyond the art world. Einstein said that he thought in images. A historian has to imagine events and motivations from the past, the novelist, an entire setting. Chemists need to envision molecular structures and rotate them. The inventor—an envisioner par excellence—must dream up ideas to be turned into real solutions. Envisioning is important in everyday life as well, whether for remembering faces as they change over time, or for finding our way around a new city, or for assembling children's toys. Visualization is recognized as important in other school subjects: the National Council of Teachers of Mathematics (NCTM) and the National Science Education Standards both see visualization as essential to problem solving, but art classes are where this skill is most directly and intensively taught.

Expression

In addition, students in the study were urged to move beyond technical skill to create works rich in emotion, atmosphere, and their own personal voice or vision. As one of the drawing teachers said, ". . . what hits you first when you look at a work of art is not its technique but its evocative properties" (Hetland et al., 2007, p. 56). This suggests another candidate that is rich for further investigation: Perhaps learning to express in art spills over into evocative writing.

Persistence

During the research study, students worked on projects over sustained periods of time and were expected to find meaningful problems and persevere through frustration. Clearly persistence is a skill important in all areas of school and life, but whether persistence learned in art classes generalizes outside of that particular art class is yet to be shown.

Stretching and Exploration

Not surprisingly, during the study it was found that innovation was a central skill taught in art classes. Art classes place a high value on breaking the mold. Teachers encourage students to innovate through exploration—to experiment, take risks, and just muck around and see what can be learned. In ceramics, for example, capitalizing on error is a major consideration, says Balliro at the Boston Arts Academy. To a student struggling to stick clay together, she says, "There are specific ways to do it, but I want you guys to play around in this first project. Just go with that and see what happens and maybe you'll learn a new technique" (Hetland et al., 2007, p. 25). The teachers that were studied told students not to worry about mistakes but instead to let mistakes lead to unexpected discoveries. Many scholars will tell you that a willingness to play and explore is important for discovery, but again, whether the habit of exploration learned in art classes generalizes outside of that specific art class has not yet been shown.

Reflection

Most people don't think of art class as a place where reflection is central but instead as a place where students take a break from thinking. But during the study, frequently the teachers pushed their students to engage in reflective self-evaluation. They were asked to step back, analyze, judge, and sometimes reconceive their projects entirely. The teachers regularly asked students to reflect on their art: Is that working? Is this what you intended to do? Can you make this part better? What's next? In group critiques, students also learned to evaluate the work of their peers. Making such judgments "in the absence of rule" (Eisner, 2004) is a highly sophisticated mental endeavor.

Many people might be surprised to find such systematic emphasis on thinking and perception in an art room. In contrast to the reputation of the arts as mainly about self-expression and technique, the teachers in the study talked far more often about decisions, choices, and understanding than about feelings. Developing a habit of reflection is important for all academic endeavors, but again whether such a metacognitive habit learned in art classes generalizes outside of that art class must still be tested.

While arts teachers rightly resist making their classes like "academic" ones where students memorize the names and dates of artists, teachers of academic subjects might well benefit from making their classes more like arts classes—especially when it comes to the emphasis on public reflection that is noted in the art classes of the study. Math students, for instance, could post their in-process solutions regularly and discuss them together in a class critique. The findings just reported pertain to what teachers believe that they are teaching. The next step is to document the extent to which these skills are actually learned by students and then to find out whether any of these skills turn out to enhance performance in other academic areas.

CONCLUSION

There should not be a distinction between so-called core subjects and arts education and hence any implication that the arts are less important than other subjects. The definition of *core* means essential. Thus, from a perspective of values and as suggested by the qualitative data presented earlier in this essay, the arts are indeed core subjects for schools to teach. The arts are as important as the humanities and the sciences, and an education without the arts is incomplete. The arts are a fundamental part of being human and have been around longer than the sciences (the earliest humans carved flutes out of bird bones and painted images).

A second answer to the question is empirical, and it awaits further evidence. The habits of mind found through the Studio Thinking Project suggest qualities that visual arts teachers strive to teach. Current and future research may well show that these habits of mind are indeed learned in arts classes and that one or more of these habits spill over into other areas of the curriculum. And in a recently completed dissertation of theater training conducted by Thalia Goldstein, it was found that experience impersonating characters on stage serves to strengthen empathy skills in adolescents as well as theory of mind skills—the ability to understand what someone else is thinking and feeling. These skills were not improved in the control group of students studying other forms of art. Certainly these two social-cognitive skills of empathy and understanding others are skills that many would agree are core to success in life.

The arts all involve making—an activity rarely expected in non-arts classes. What if students in all subject areas had to make a work of art to demonstrate their understanding? What if they had to make a drawing to demonstrate the mathematical principle of the golden section or if they had to compose a melody that mutated over time to demonstrate the principle of evolution? It is a good bet that infusing the arts into the curriculum in this way would not only demonstrate understanding but would also enhance it.

COUNTERPOINT: A. Jonathan Eakle
The Johns Hopkins University

Art is integral to education, but it distracts from core curriculum and instruction. To some readers, this statement may seem to be a contradiction. Yet its logic rests in what presently counts as education and how art is commonly perceived by many public school educators and policymakers in the

United States. The following lines of this essay define art, education, and instruction. The next explain how misuses of these concepts have led to misunderstandings in educational settings. The essay closes with how a reimagination of the relations of education and art is critical for schools in the United States and beyond.

ART, CRAFT, EDUCATION, AND INSTRUCTION

The words *art* and *craft* mean different things to different people. So, too, is the case with the varied meanings that are given to *education* and *instruction*. Complex concepts behind such words often slip by without careful consideration. However, there are centuries-old arguments attempting to distinguish these critical concepts. For instance, scholars such as Gordon Graham (2002) place education under the umbrella of philosophy—from the Greek *philosophia*—the love of wisdom. To those who subscribe to this definition, the goal of education is the cultivation of curiosity and the development of individual or group capacities. On the other hand, the concept of instruction assumes that there is a knowledgeable other such as instructor, trainer, and/or lecturer who is capable of successfully transferring ideas, information, and practices to pupils. This is not to say that education is superior to instruction or vice versa but rather that there is a marked difference between the two concepts and their application.

The concepts and practices of art are burdened by a similar problem. Art is often confused with craft. Nonetheless, art, as with education, is about curiosity, and more often than not, art involves individuality and subjectivity. To be sure, artists can sometimes weave narratives, make social commentaries, entertain, and so forth. Yet more to the heart of the matter, artists search for juxtapositions of forms, lines, sounds, space, and so forth, which capture sensations (Eakle, 2007). Conversely, craft involves relatively discrete material processes and procedures, such as mixing colors from a standard color wheel to arrive at a desired hue, reflectance, and intensity, or using particular musical notes to replicate chords of a favorite song or applying glazes to add degrees of luminosity to a piece of pottery. Further, the concept of craft has been used to describe objects that are produced through a range of processes from the reproduction of a pattern arranged from a prescribed template or a priori style, as is the case with commercial needlepoint and skilled furniture production such as the crafts of the Shaker tradition.

Adding to the misunderstanding between art and craft is that sometimes craft objects are elevated to the status of art in museums that display the mundane. For example, the crafting of toaster appliances has been the focus of several museum displays in the United States and is the object of an online museum. This is an idea somewhat related with the Dada "anti-art" movement of the past century. Akin to school instruction, the discrete processes of craft can be methodically transferred from teacher to pupil and in its best sense from master to apprentice—as is the case with the silversmith's craft. Aligned with the differences introduced earlier in the present essay between education and instruction, some people, such as the Dadaists and Pop Art practitioners, attest that art is not superior to craft or vice versa. However, more often, art is reserved to creative products that are those most valued by cultures.

THE ARTS ARE—AND SHOULD BE—A DISTRACTION FROM CORE CURRICULUM AND INSTRUCTION

Keeping the distinctions of art and craft—as well as those between education and instruction—in mind, the purpose of this section of the essay is to situate the arts in current public school practice. In doing so, this section advances general scholarly arguments about the arts and contemporary schooling and policy in the United States.

Especially during the past century in the United States there has been a recurring divide between so-called traditional and progressive schooling. The former is generally associated with teacher-centered, direct instruction and the latter with student-centered curricula. Carrying the banner of traditional, direct instruction during recent decades, Jeanne Chall (2000) reflected on an urban school curriculum that exposed children to art, such as cultural events at museums, theater performances, and so forth. In the end, she concluded that such progressive practices as this urban school's art initiative had not contributed to what she described as meeting the nation's "academic achievement challenge."

Chall's (2000) line of thinking was, and continues to be, fueled by reports of risks for academic failure faced by the United States, which are supported by scientific data compiled to demonstrate the achievement gaps in reading, math, science, and so on. In short, ongoing underperformance of certain groups of students such as African Americans has been attributed by some policymakers and scholars, at least in part, to progressive trends in schooling that were earmarked by practices such as arts-based curriculum and the whole language movement (see Shapiro & Purpel, 1998; Chapter 5, this volume). In this vein, what counts as education research and effective school and classroom practice has recently been the sole purview of a particular, and arguably narrow, application of medical science concepts and the methods and procedures related with such concepts. For instance, from this view it is believed that by use of proper formulae of instruction, the student (patient) is treated and cured of ignorance in a targeted subject area, such as mathematics. On the label of prescriptive instructional measures are brand names that are difficult to dismiss, such as No Child Left Behind (NCLB) (2001) and What Works Clearinghouse, and the brands come with advice that reads like a prescription label: If taken as directed, the treatment will produce desired effects.

From this narrowly defined medical model of treatment/instruction, it stands to reason that there follow standards (see the Assessment chapter of the present volume, Chapter 4)—points of reference that compare a unit to what is deemed normal, such as body temperature; the elemental weight of hydrogen in relation to that of oxygen; or the ability of a pupil to correctly solve a quadratic equation at a given point in time and in a particular controlled space, such as a quiet classroom container or testing center. Standards, another tool of science, are based on the assumption that eventually schooling can be flattened out to a level surface of best practice—an equal plane where all children can achieve a normal educated state of being. This crafting of *best instructional practice* by definition assumes that all other practices are inferior to it.

Further, the medical model of treatment/instruction in U.S. public schooling calls for preventive measures and regular examination to determine the health of the patient (student). To meet these instructional objectives, there are experts—including statisticians, policymakers, and other government operatives—who carefully craft and dispense curriculum and instruction for public consumption. The agents of these experts are instructors and trainers whose goals are to relay the curriculum and instruction and also, as Foucault (1977) suggested, to produce disciplined and compliant citizens. Not only does the content and manner of instruction lead to disciplinary learning but it is combined with carefully honed and implemented behavior management techniques, frequent examinations, surveillance ranging from human hall monitors to miniature video recording devices, and so forth. To be sure, designing, producing, and distributing instruction in U.S. public schools has become an increasingly complex craft. Nevertheless, it is just that: craft.

On the other hand, art involves individuality, subjectivity, and creative production, and it does not fit in the narrowly defined medical-like model of present-day schooling in the United States. In fact, by its very definition, art threatens the status quo and by extension the standardization concepts and procedures of the present public school curriculum and instruction. Unlike craft, art never condones complacency, normality, or the status quo. Thus, art and its agents at best distract from the disciplined order of crafting and delivering instruction, and for better or worse, art can be a source that resists the public education agenda. Art is about freedom and expression rather than conformity and repetition, which are hallmarks of craft.

CAPITALISM, ART, AND THE CRAFTING OF CURRICULUM AND INSTRUCTION

Leveling out the plane of public school curriculum and instruction to a homogeneous one could, on the surface, be considered a democratic project. However, in the United States, the careful crafting of curriculum and instruction also involves hierarchical economic dimensions. For instance, some scholars argue that public school resources are allocated in ways that maintain differences between economic communities, which has only been amplified during the recent recession. In this vein, differences in schooling are sometimes maintained by property values, taxes, and local borders. At other times, the wealthy seek out costly private rather than public education for their children—as in the cases of the current and past U.S. presidential families. To be sure, there are enormous differences in the economic resources available to and across various U.S. school districts that affect the possibility of meaningful instances of both instruction and education.

In lean economic times, such as during the recent U.S. recession, art is often the first casualty of budget cuts. At the time of the present writing, the art capital of New York City is faced with nearly a one-third reduction of municipal funding of the arts. Further, in 2007, required federal funding for the arts in public education was repealed. For FY2011, the Obama administration proposed consolidating the arts in schools with other topics, such as civics, economics, American history, and foreign language assistance. Although the arts are not excluded in the forthcoming federal budget, the administration's so-called well-rounded education proposal is arguably a way to further position the arts in the margins of what really counts the most in U.S. public schooling—on the surface, as a means to become more competitive in a global economy through enhanced curriculum and instruction in science, mathematics, and new technologies. In short, and following Chall's (2000) general argument about curriculum and instruction, the arts are considered as a distraction from these types of competitive goals or, in the least, a drain on increasingly scarce financial resources. Scarcity leads to conserving actions and not simply economic ones, as taken up subsequently.

CONSERVATION OF VALUES

To conserve is to resist change and maintain a steady state of affairs. Because art does not condone the status quo, it stands against conservative agendas in schooling, government, and beyond. In the 1980s, the confrontation between the arts and progressive notions versus conservative instructional perspectives came to light through what is commonly known as the "culture wars" (Williams, 1999). During that time, U.S. Senator Jesse Helms; conservative National Endowment for the Arts (NEA) chairperson Lynne Cheney, the wife of former vice president Dick Cheney; the Christian Coalition; and others attempted to curb funding to the NEA (Koch, 1998). The salient arguments against the NEA hinged on economics and financially supporting values inconsistent with conservative religious ones, such as those standing overtly outside mainstream heterosexual or religious beliefs and practices. Arguments evolved that pitted what the religious right perceived as the founding fathers' purported conservative values against the First Amendment of the U.S. Constitution and the freedom of expression. The latter is the hallmark of art, and the former is what has become an increasingly powerful force in public school curriculum and instruction, among other things.

In short, the cutting edge of art pushes boundaries and stands in stark contrast to efforts to conserve the past. In fact, given the histories of modern and contemporary art movements, such as those of the Cubists, Expressionists, and Surrealists, art is closer to anarchy than the preservation and conservation of traditional values. Without doubt, art distracts from conserving institutional values, such as those that drive much of current U.S. public schooling.

THE REIMAGINATION OF ART AND EDUCATION

If public schooling in the United States could be conceived as education rather than as instruction, as defined and outlined in the opening section of the present essay, then art would have a critically central place in the curriculum. In fact, by its definition, art not only enhances education but it is also intimately connected to it. And, with political and social calls for creativity and innovation—hallmarks of art—it seems tantamount to reimagine what art is and what it can do. On the leading edge of calls for this reimagination is the European Union, who designated 2009 as the Year of Creativity and Innovation. This is not surprising because Europe is the home to two of the most established arts-influenced education methods: the Montessori and Waldorf approaches. Of the latter, Rudolf Steiner (1996) spoke of the "incomplete and imperfect" person as the actual medium of the arts and that the goal of education is transforming students into accomplished and ethical human beings (p. 16). In this regard, teachers are artists and education is an art. By extension, teaching is about the individual, and it is not a craft.

The reimagination of art and education would require capacities that may well be outside of the possible under current government mandates and directives, but as taken up in other essays of the present volume, they are certainly part of a collective desire of many educators. Perhaps the art movements of the past, which occurred through small groups of individuals in grass roots, can be models for disrupting and resisting conservative trends that hold the nation and its schools apart from creativity and innovation. Such a movement could also create what has been uttered through time yet seemingly forgotten by many people: that there is indeed an art of education. Until then, the arts should remain a distraction to the current and prevailing tide of conservative curriculum and instruction found in U.S. education policy and many school practices.

Further Readings and Resources

Chall, J. S. (2000). *The academic achievement challenge: What really works in the classroom?* New York: Guilford Press.

Eakle, A. J. (2007). Museum literacy, art, and space study. In D. Lapp, J. Flood, & S. B. Heath (Eds.), *Handbook of research on teaching literacy through the communicative and visual arts* (2nd ed., pp. 177–186). Mahwah, NJ: Lawrence Erlbaum.

Eisner, E. W. (2004). *The arts and the creation of mind.* New Haven, CT: Yale University Press.

Foucault, M. (1977). *Discipline and punish: The birth of the prison* (A. Sheridan, Trans.). New York: Pantheon Books.

Graham, G. (2002). *Universities: The recovery of an idea.* Charlottesville, VA: Imprint Academic.

Hetland, L., Winner, E., Veenema, S., & Sheridan, K. (2007). *Studio thinking: The real benefits of visual arts education.* New York: Teachers College Press.

Keinanen, M., Hetland, L., & Winner, E. (2000). Teaching cognitive skill through dance: Evidence for near but not far transfer. In E. Winner & L. Hetland (Eds.), The arts and academic achievement: What the evidence shows. Double Issue of *Journal of Aesthetic Education, 34*(3–4), 295–306.

Koch, C. (1998). The contest for American culture: A leadership case study on the NEA and NEH funding crisis. *Public Talk: Online Journal of Discourse Leadership.* Retrieved January 17, 2012, from http://www.upenn.edu/pnc/ptkoch.html

Shapiro, H. S., & Purpel, D. E. (1998). *Critical social issues in American education: Transformation in a postmodern world.* Mahwah, NJ: Lawrence Erlbaum.

Steiner, R. (1996). *Rudolf Steiner in the Waldorf School: Lectures and addresses to children, parents, and teachers.* Hudson, NY: Anthroposophic Press.

Williams, M. E. (Ed.). (1999). *Culture wars: Opposing viewpoints.* San Diego, CA: Greenhaven Press.

Winner, E., & Cooper, M. (2000). Mute those claims: No evidence (yet) for a causal link between arts study and academic achievement. *Journal of Aesthetic Education, 34*(3–4), 11–75.

Winner, E., & Hetland, L. (2000). The arts and academic achievement: What the evidence shows. Double Issue of *Journal of Aesthetic Education, 34*(3–4).

COURT CASES AND STATUTES

No Child Left Behind Act of 2001, 20 U.S.C.A. §§ 6301 *et seq.*

10

Should the primary focus of gifted education be on teaching advanced and accelerated curricular content?

POINT: Carol J. Mills and Linda E. Brody, *Center for Talented Youth, The Johns Hopkins University*
COUNTERPOINT: Rosa Aurora Chávez-Eakle, *Washington International Center for Creativity, Washington Center for Psychoanalysis*

OVERVIEW

It seems reasonable for schools to provide opportunities for capable students to pursue advanced and accelerated curricular content and at the same time assist students who are highly sensitive and capable of creative thought to understand and develop their abilities. To be sure, there is a limited amount of time in a day and a limited number of things one can teach. Yet advanced content and thinking skills, such as creative thinking, are certainly not mutually exclusive. In fact, it could be argued that one cannot effectively teach either one without the other.

Benjamin Bloom (1985), in the seminal *Developing Talent in Young People,* described the development of talent in various fields as going through three stages: (1) falling in love with the area of talent, (2) learning the principles of the discipline, and (3) going beyond mastery to original contributions. He went on to argue that developing talent needs different types of teaching at the different levels. First, students need teachers who are encouraging and motivating, then, those who are exacting, and finally, those who are able to push students beyond their own levels of excellence to contribute something new. Even very talented students will not develop to the third stage without appropriate teaching or coaching. Thus, it is clear that students do need opportunities to work with teachers or mentors at an appropriate level for their developing talents. It is also clear that those teachers or mentors need to be able to take them beyond mastering even the most advanced content.

Terry Tao (2010), an eminent graduate of the Johns Hopkins program for radical *acceleration* of mathematically gifted youth, has argued on his blog about gifted education that there is no silver bullet that is the best educational accommodation for all gifted students. He argued that acceleration, along with other options, has both advantages and disadvantages that must be examined in light of the particular child's needs and interests, "both academic and nonacademic."

For example, there are many very intelligent students who do not show early and exclusive interests in one content area. They may have interdisciplinary interests, extreme sensitivity, and/or interests in areas that are not as conducive to acceleration such as art, global justice, or spirituality. Such students may respond better to in-depth and broadened explorations of their interests rather than linear acceleration.

Young students who have not yet shown clear talents and sustained interests in particular areas need opportunities to explore educational options and topics with breadth as well as depth. They are still developing physically, cognitively, and affectively, so their particular talents and interests may not be developed to the point where a need for acceleration is clear.

Even for students whose talents and interests are clear at an early age, education need not prematurely narrow their scope of investigation. One highly gifted individual who grew up in the Cold War days of the 1950s to 1960s was targeted in middle school and early high school because of his high intelligence and aptitude for science. He was accelerated in grade and guided into science for weapons development. It was only years later that he realized he had never been given a choice about his career trajectory; he had been fast-tracked into an area in which he did not really have an interest. After quitting his government job and living as a farmer for several years, he eventually found his way back into science in a physics program, but his interests and experiments have nothing to do with weapons technology.

Another young man won a national science competition as an adolescent. The recognition of his talent earned him opportunities for scientific research at a university. He was excited by the possibilities and advantages that he was given, but he was not ready to commit to a life of scientific research. That was just one of his many interests. An equally compelling interest—one that he does not see as mutually exclusive—is filmmaking. He hopes to create programming to excite young people about science. Although his parents and science mentors actively guided him toward pursuing a science major and career, he resisted the pressure and is enrolled in what he describes as a transdisciplinary degree program that combines his science and arts interests. It has not been and is not easy for him to forge this unconventional path. However, he resists the pressure to push him forward in one area of interest and talent at the expense of his other interests and talents.

These experiences may not be as uncommon as they may seem. Robert and Michele Root-Bernstein (2001), authors of *Sparks of Genius: The Thirteen Thinking Tools of the World's Most Creative People,* interviewed top scientists and artists about their creative processes. From the interviews, the Root-Bernsteins concluded that individuals at the top of what seem like such disparate fields really see their processes of creation as very similar. Moreover, many top scientists have artistic avocations and vice versa. These individuals do not see their interests as competing; rather, they see them as complementary. For such individuals, academic acceleration, without the opportunities to investigate their other passions, would be a reductionist rather than a facilitative education.

However, this is a false dichotomy. Acceleration and enrichment are not mutually exclusive, just as they are not necessarily companions. Some students' needs clearly dictate radical acceleration in the area or areas of advanced ability, and others need more moderate acceleration along with enrichment. One cannot have meaningful process without content and vice versa. So, as Tevye, from *Fiddler on the Roof,* would say to both sides of an argument, "You're right, and you're right." Acceleration and enrichment, advanced content and thinking skills, critical and creative thinking, mentors and metacognitive awareness, as well as play are all important components of good programs for gifted students. How much of each and to what degree is an ongoing issue in education.

The debate in this chapter is concerned with whether the primary focus of gifted education programs should be on teaching advanced and accelerated curricular content. In the point essay, Carol J. Mills and Linda E. Brody of the Center for Talented Youth at The Johns Hopkins University contend that the needs of gifted students cannot be met in regular education; thus, it is necessary to present such students with advanced curricular content. Further, they state that the degree of curricular adjustment and modification must be matched to each child's academic ability and development. Rosa Aurora Chávez-Eakle of the Washington International Center for Creativity and the

Washington Center for Psychoanalysis concludes that teaching advanced curricular content is part of the process but should not be the focus of gifted education. Chávez-Eakle argues that gifted education should focus on helping students understand and realize their creative potential and talent. This, Chávez-Eakle contends, will lead to mastery of curricular content, provide students with the skills they need for self-fulfilling and productive lives, and enhance their motivation for continued learning.

Bonnie Cramond
University of Georgia

POINT: Carol J. Mills and Linda E. Brody
Center for Talented Youth, The Johns Hopkins University

While the field of gifted education has generated numerous theories of intelligence and often lacks consensus about how to identify and serve highly able children, there is considerable agreement that the goal should be to produce students and, ultimately, adults who will make innovative and creative contributions to society. How this goal is reached has fueled considerable debate about which educational programs and practices will be most effective in developing students' talents and stimulating creative output. For example, the question of whether enrichment or acceleration should be advocated remains unresolved by many, though most educators have embraced both practices as useful for talent development.

A related question has to do with whether gifted students benefit from direct instruction in the creative process or whether it is more important to provide access to advanced curricular content in order to achieve the stated goal. Schools that offer special enrichment programs for gifted students often teach brainstorming, creative problem solving (CPS), and other related skills in the hope and expectation that the skills mastered will transfer to academic content areas and lead to creative solutions. However, there is little evidence that this transfer occurs, and when the enrichment program becomes the only accommodation offered to students with advanced academic abilities, this is particularly problematic. This essay presents the position that, based on both research and programmatic evidence, gifted education should focus *primarily* on providing advanced and accelerated curricular content to students who are academically gifted. Without this accommodation, students are unlikely to be motivated or sufficiently prepared to excel on a high enough level to be creative.

GIFTED EDUCATION: DEFINITION AND INTENT

The federal definition of gifted students was originally developed in the 1972 Marland *Report to the Congress*. Since then, the definition has been modified several times, so that the current definition in the No Child Left Behind (NCLB) Act (2001) includes students capable of high achievement in intellectual, specific academic, creative, artistic, or leadership domains. The definition states that these students need services not ordinarily provided by the school. Although this federal definition, as well as definitions embraced by most states, recognizes these various types of giftedness, in reality the world of gifted education primarily deals with students who are intellectually or academically talented. Aside from special schools for the arts, rarely are school-based gifted programs identifying and serving students who are solely gifted in the areas of creativity, leadership, or the arts. Even schools that offer instruction in the creative process through enrichment programs are typically providing it to students who have been identified on their intellectual or academic strengths.

The present essay addresses gifted education as it applies to students who are primarily identified as intellectually or academically gifted. These students may also be creatively gifted. These are not mutually exclusive domains; in fact, they are often closely linked. However, the discussion here is not directed at students who might excel on a test of *divergent thinking* but do not also have high intellectual and/or academic abilities. As a way of providing clarity about the nature and scope of their services to their constituencies, many school systems are beginning to use the term "Advanced Academic Program" instead of "Gifted and Talented Program," which suggests a renewed emphasis on academic instruction.

In the case of general intellectual ability or specific academic ability, depending on how this ability is manifested in any given child and the level and nature of regular instruction in the child's school, there may or may not be a need for special services, instructional modifications, and/or curricular adjustments. In most schools, the general education program should be broad enough and deep enough to meet the academic needs of the largest number of students—with perhaps some minor adjustments and differentiation. Gifted education, on the other hand, is usually based on the premise that this is not the case for some number of students (which has variously been defined as the top 2% to 3%, top 5%, or even the top 20%, depending on the school and the definition of gifted being used). Regardless of where the line is drawn, it is important to remember that as a child's ability falls further along the continuum of the upper end, even within the group of students designated as gifted, the greater the need for differentiation and intensity of services as related to academic content and instruction.

Recently, the gifted education community has begun to discuss how the Response to Intervention (RTI) model, which is usually applied to students with learning disabilities, might be applicable to identifying and serving gifted students with differentiated needs. This may be a promising approach if implemented so that strengths, not just weaknesses, are recognized and addressed. The RTI emphasis on universal screening to target students in need of specific instructional support, differentiation of instruction including fluid, flexible grouping; multiple means of learning; demonstration of learning; and progress monitoring of learning through multiple formative assessments across the entire school and education program for all children is a good basis for beginning to serve the needs of gifted students. The model's use of needs-based interventions is highly defensible and shows a recognition that there is a continuum of specific abilities/disabilities present in any group of students and that increasingly more intensive and specific interventions are necessary to respond to this continuum.

The RTI model and the individualization of instruction it stands for represent good educational practice that acknowledges individual differences in instructional needs. It is reminiscent of Johns Hopkins Professor Julian Stanley's advocacy for using what he referred to as Diagnostic Testing followed by Prescriptive Instruction (DT–PI) with students who already know considerable content and for "helping students learn only what they don't already know." This approach provides students with an appropriate level of challenge, avoids the boredom involved in having to repeat work they have already mastered, and encourages motivation to excel at a high level. It is hard to imagine creativity resulting when students are bored with the core content.

THE JOHNS HOPKINS TALENT SEARCH MODEL

Julian Stanley's unique contribution to gifted education was to introduce the necessity for above-level assessment to determine the full extent of a child's ability along a continuum and to demonstrate that students who exhibit advanced reasoning abilities can master, and should be provided with, advanced academic content in order to achieve their potential. The Center for Talented Youth (CTY) at The Johns Hopkins University is based on the model of talent identification and development that evolved from Stanley's pioneering work with the Study of Mathematically Precocious Youth (SMPY), which he founded in 1971.

SMPY arose out of Stanley's experience with a middle school student who was astounding his teachers in a university-based summer computer science course. When the eighth grader scored at the level of students entering Johns Hopkins on university admissions tests and his school refused to acknowledge and accommodate his academic needs, Stanley facilitated, having him enroll full-time at Johns Hopkins, where he was highly successful in spite of entering at such a young age. A similar experience with several other students led Stanley to believe that there must be other students languishing in their schools with unmet academic needs, and he subsequently launched talent searches where students with above-level reasoning abilities could be identified on the basis of above-level specific aptitude tests. The range of performance results that were found showed that it is no longer possible to consider all the children in the top percentile ranks on any particular ability as homogeneous. When above-level testing is used to assess the full extent of a child's academic ability, researchers find that large within-group differences in cognitive reasoning emerge among students who "hit the ceiling" on in-grade level tests. With this information, as educators, we are faced with the incontrovertible reality of how different from each other these children can be.

With the knowledge of these large within-group differences at the top end of the distribution of cognitive ability, it is impossible to ignore the fact that some children need more than what is provided in the regular instructional program. Indeed, it is obvious that some children need *vastly* more than what is provided in the regular instructional program. Since SMPY was first established, numerous strategies have been identified and programs developed to meet the needs of students who exhibit above-grade-level academic abilities, and early entrance to college is no longer the only way to accommodate them. CTY was established in 1979 to aid in identifying and serving these students; programs at Northwestern University, Duke University, and elsewhere utilizing the talent search model have followed. The hallmark of all these programs, however, is the opportunity for high-ability (i.e., gifted) students to study advanced and accelerated content in their area(s) of strength.

Research supports the principles and practices incorporated in this approach to talent development. In particular, the short- and long-term validity and predictability of using an above-level specific aptitude test to identify students ready to master content at a higher level and faster pace than their same-age peers has been well established. In addition, the efficacy of providing academically advanced students with accelerated and advanced content is well supported by numerous research studies. But does it foster creativity?

Now that early talent search participants are adults, it is possible to evaluate their level of creative production in their chosen career fields, and studies suggest that these individuals have done more—much more—than learn content. For example, research on SMPY participants by David Lubinski and Camilla Benbow (2006) and their colleagues at Vanderbilt University has shown that, as a group, the creative productivity of high-scoring students years later is exceptional, with an unusually high proportion developing patents or earning the ranks of tenured faculty, positions that require creative contributions in their respective fields.

One eminent product of this approach to talent identification and development is mathematician Terence (Terry) Tao, who has won both the Fields Medal (often called the Nobel Prize of mathematics) and a MacArthur "Genius" Award for his creativity in mathematics. Terry's exceptional mathematical abilities were identified at a young age through above-level testing, and he was provided with a very individualized educational program (IEP) to meet his needs, including consistent access to advanced content in mathematics throughout his childhood. Could Terry have reached this level of achievement in his field without being given access to advanced mathematical concepts when he was ready and eager to learn them? It is highly unlikely. In fact, numerous studies of eminent mathematicians point to the importance of having had access to advanced content at young ages, to being exposed to mentors and role models, and to having been able to reach the peak of their profession at relatively young ages, as critical to their creative output as mathematicians.

AN EDUCATIONALLY SOUND APPROACH TO GIFTED EDUCATION

There is much support, therefore, that the most educationally sound and reasonable approach for students who exhibit above-grade-level abilities and/or content knowledge is to provide them with access to advanced content that is an appropriate match for their ability and achievement levels. Although this is usually referred to as acceleration, it simply means placing students at the level and pace that is developmentally appropriate for their educational needs, not racing toward any specific goal. Most importantly, it can refer to acceleration in a single subject area, if that is appropriate, not necessarily in grade placement.

Students who are presented with material they already know learn mainly that school is unresponsive and that effort is not valued. On the other hand, those who are presented with material that they cannot grasp become disabled by their discouragement. Between these two extremes lies a zone of appropriate challenge that spurs both new learning and a zest to master the difficult. The need for providing advanced students with appropriately advanced curricular content seems clear.

Of course, there is more to learning than the accumulation and regurgitation of information, so once again we must emphasize that this is not a race to finish the curriculum in a hurry, and CPS within content areas should clearly be encouraged. Though essential, acceleration is just the beginning—the launchpad for meaningful learning to take place. In a recent article by Ronald A. Beghetto and James C. Kaufman (2009) titled "Intellectual Estuaries" the authors recommended that academic learning and creativity become overlapping goals that are simultaneously pursued. Clearly, a good education program should encourage (indeed, expect) students to explore, interpret, and make personal meaning out of the academic content offered. But when the content is so elementary and is not matched to the students' current level of knowledge and understanding, there is no motivation to use information in a creative way or an opportunity to find new understanding. The extension of knowledge that leads to increased breadth and depth of content acquisition and understanding is at the heart of the rationale for providing advanced learners with appropriately matched advanced academic content.

Within the content area, the emphasis should be on active learning and putting knowledge to use in independent and creative ways. But the creative process is only meaningful when it unfolds within an academic discipline and with a sufficient knowledge base from which one can make meaning. For example, students with exceptional ability and interest in the sciences must first gain the necessary content background to comprehend the relevant scientific principles at a sufficiently high level before they can use this knowledge in creative and innovative ways. The many CTY students who are award winners at the International Science and Engineering Fair (ISEF) or the Intel Science Talent Search over the years provide clear evidence that when high-ability students are exposed to advanced curriculum content, they can and will apply their knowledge creatively. But we can presume that their achievements could not have been as exceptional without a solid foundation of advanced content knowledge and the passion for the subject that can only come with a deep understanding of it.

CONCLUSION

In the end, the question comes down to what is the most defensible and educationally sound approach to meeting the needs for exceptionally able learners. Based on years of research evidence and programmatic experience, the answer to this question seems clear. Gifted education must of necessity be about teaching advanced curricular content to academically gifted students whose academic needs cannot be satisfied by the regular education program. The degree of curricular adjustment and instructional modification should be matched to the individual child's level of academic ability and development. This approach is most defensible when it is linked to specific ability such as mathematics or verbal skills rather than general intellectual ability even though this should not be ignored. While engaging students in creative tasks early in their development may feed their inclinations for spontaneity and associative and fluent thinking, it potentially limits their ability to engage in deeper thinking and reasoning in a chosen area if it becomes the ongoing focus of instruction in lieu of advancing in the content.

Although providing academically gifted students with advanced curricular content is necessary, it is not sufficient if done in a vacuum with the only goal being to complete as much material as possible within the least amount of time. Advanced level content must be embedded in a well-designed and broad-based curriculum, delivered by a teacher who has a deep understanding of the content area and who provides an open and flexible environment where students are guided, encouraged, and provided with the opportunity to explore, extend, and apply the knowledge they have gained. We believe this curriculum is the most defensible way to meet the educational and intellectual needs of academically gifted students, which should be our primary motivation for adopting it. In addition, this approach has the highest probability for achieving the goal of producing students and, ultimately, adults who will make innovative and creative contributions to society.

COUNTERPOINT: Rosa Aurora Chávez-Eakle
Washington International Center for Creativity,
Washington Center for Psychoanalysis

The aim of this essay is to show why gifted education should not be focused only on teaching advanced and accelerated curricular content. Instead, the focus of gifted education should involve helping students to better understand and realize their potential and talents, particularly their different ways of thinking and experiencing diverse stimuli by teaching them to use creative methods and processes. In using such a process approach in gifted education, students learn to understand and realize their creative potential and learning advanced information follows. As a result, and as argued subsequently, gifted students can develop skills that are useful for productive and self-fulfilling lives.

UNDERSTANDING GIFTEDNESS

Early approaches to giftedness considered high IQ as the parameter for identification. However, recent research has shown that gifted students also perform highly on creativity assessments and that creative thinking and creative skills were predictors of gifted achievement in adulthood. One of the leading creativity researchers in this area, E. Paul Torrance, conducted longitudinal studies in which he followed his gifted and talented participants for over 50 years, demonstrating the relation between creativity and giftedness (see Torrance & Sisk, 1999).

One of Torrance's greatest achievements was the development of several valid and reliable psychometric instruments for creativity assessment that remain a standard for the identification of gifted and talented children. For Torrance, the goal of gifted education is to provide students better chances to achieve their potentialities, and being creative is a key component of this potential. Creative individuals are able to see gaps in information, find new and innovative solutions where there seems to be no solution; they are able to tolerate ambiguity and uncertainty, they are open and tolerant, and they display original thinking. Further, Torrance discovered that during crises or challenging circumstances creativity was critical for survival. In this vein, the World Health Organization has noted that creativity is an important requirement for resilience.

In spite of Torrance's compelling research findings, children who are gifted are often misunderstood and ridiculed; these students understand and feel that they are different but are uncomfortable with these differences, which sometimes translates into isolation from others and low sense of self-esteem (in spite of having exceptional abilities). If such children are not afforded opportunities to realize their creative potential through understanding and capitalizing on their creative processes, they are at risk of turning away from their talents and conforming to lives of mediocrity. Or worse, they might use their talents for destructive goals such as malevolent creativity (the use of creativity to destroy or harm other humans, animals or the environment such as the production or weapons and torture instruments) or even crime.

Therefore, a key focus of gifted and talented education should be to help gifted children understand the ways that they are different, learn to feel comfortable with it, and realize and understand the processes involved in their creative thinking to use and share their creativity for the benefit of others and themselves.

THE RELEVANCE OF CREATIVE THINKING

Thinking creatively involves particular cognitive processes. The style of thinking involved in most academic and intelligence assessments leads to a single "correct" solution, which was labeled by creativity research pioneer J. P. Guilford as *convergent thinking*. In contrast, Guilford's research showed that creativity involves a different style of thinking—one that produces a number of different possible solutions. He described this different cognitive style as divergent thinking. In this vein, Arthur Koestler discovered that creative thinking involves connecting unrelated elements or ideas in a novel way, which he called *bisociation*.

Along this line of research, Albert Rothenberg investigated the cognitive processes used by Nobel Prize awardees during their creative processes. Rothenberg found that they superimpose discrete entities, such as visual or other kinds of mental representations, which he denoted as the *homospatial process*. Highly creative individuals also actively conceive multiple opposites or antitheses simultaneously, which he called the *Janusian process*, named after the Roman god Janus, who had two faces looking in opposite directions. In fact, Rothenberg observed that most major scientific breakthroughs and artistic masterpieces involve Janusian thinking. Individuals who actively formulate antithetical ideas at the same time and are able to see all the opposite faces of an idea become able to achieve outstanding results. A good example of this kind of thinking are the theories related to the nature of light. For years, scientists debated between two contradictory positions: light as waves as opposed to light as particles. There was no point of conciliation between these two groups. Instead, Louis de Broglie was later able to conceive both positions simultaneously while explaining the duality of light both as a particle and as a wave, and his insights about the nature of electrons became one of the bases of quantum physics.

Similarly Silvano Arieti showed that creativity involves the integration of *primary process* (the kind of thinking present in dreams) and *secondary process* (logical thinking) at the same time, which he called the *tertiary process*, the "magic synthesis," as he described it, where dream cognition and logical thinking produce creative outcomes. Poetry is a great example of this process, and there are many examples in science as well. For instance, August Kekulé was able to integrate a dream of whirling snakes with his thoughts and inquiries about the structure of benzene and thus elucidated the model of the benzene ring, which was a pivotal breakthrough for the field of organic chemistry. In the same respect, Albert Einstein's daydreaming about riding a comet led to the further development of his theory of relativity.

Colin Martindale later showed that primary process cognition is related to right cerebral hemisphere activation while secondary process is related to left hemisphere activation. Rosa Aurora Chávez-Eakle and collaborators have recently provided evidence that creative thinking involves simultaneous activation of both sides of the brain at the same time, particularly in brain areas that participate in cognition, emotion, working memory, novelty response, imagery, multimodal processing, and pleasure. These findings could be useful for educators designing educational tools, strategies, and lessons seeking to develop their students' potential.

UNDERSTANDING DIFFERENCES IN GIFTED AND TALENTED STUDENTS

Martindale, Kazimierz Dabrowski, and other creativity researchers have shown that gifted individuals tend to react more intensively to stimulation. Dabrowski identified these patterns of intense responses as overexcitabilities, which he argued are critical components of one's potential for development and allow individuals to become authentic and autonomous. There are five types of overexcitabilities: (1) emotional, (2) sensual, (3) intellectual, (4) imaginational, and (5) psychomotor.

Overexcitabilities have been found to be indicators of creative potential and giftedness in several parts of the world. A child with high emotional overexcitability displays intense emotional sensitivity and high empathy; is able to feel others' emotional states with intensity; and will be moved to tears by music, art, or nature. Emotional overexcitability involves joyful appreciation, but it also involves the ability of experiencing emotional pain in a more intense way. The educator can help children who have this quality to transform their intense emotions into symbolic representations.

Children with high sensual overexcitability are able to have an enhanced experience of the senses of sight, smell, taste, touch, and hearing. And they are intensively moved or repulsed by these experiences. These children benefit from multimodal learning experiences. Intellectual overexcitability is easily recognized in the classroom because it involves constant thinking and reflection. Students with high intellectual overexcitability love knowing and learning, are curious, are constantly searching for answers, are always formulating theories, and are independent thinkers.

Children with high imaginational overexcitability are fantastic players of vivid imaginative games that often include vivid stories and atmospheres. They frequently have imaginary friends and are able to vividly visualize the best and the worst of any situation. These children are terrific learners when the educator is able to involve their imagination in their activities. Finally, psychomotor overexcitability is higher in gifted children when compared with gifted adults. These children cannot stay still, and they always want to do physical things. Important for teachers to know is that in some cases students with this quality might be misdiagnosed as having attention deficit/hyperactivity disorder (ADHD).

Differences in temperament and character also have been documented among gifted individuals when compared to general samples. According to Rosa Aurora Chávez-Eakle, M. del Carmen Lara, and Carlos Cruz, highly creative individuals display exploratory behavior when encountering novelty; are optimistic and tolerant of uncertainty; pursue their goals with intensity; display responsibility; are directed to their goals; are able to use resources; are self-accepting and congruent; and they display empathy, tolerance, and integrated consciousness. One of the goals of gifted education should be to help children and teachers understand these traits and behaviors so they can use them to facilitate learning processes. For instance, exploratory behavior often facilitates going deeper in the search of knowledge, which can lead to exploring advanced curricular content.

Further, the self-directedness and persistence of gifted students could be useful to accomplish complex projects, and their cooperativeness could be helpful to engage them in collaborative learning and activities with other students and also with professionals from a given field. Moreover, their persistence enables them to pursue their interests in spite of challenges or even rejection.

TEACHING AND FACILITATING THE CREATIVE PROCESS

A variety of methods, techniques, and strategies are useful to facilitate creative thinking to be used in classrooms. Creative problem solving (CPS) and the Incubation Model of Teaching are two exemplars. CPS is a method to make creative processes more visible, explicit, and deliberate by organizing the creative approaches to problem solving, therefore enhancing effectiveness. CPS uses research-based techniques, such as brainstorming, future problem solving, and creative role playing.

CPS contains components and stages that correspond with the stages of the creative process, using divergent thinking and convergent thinking tools. The CPS stages involve clarifying a challenge, usually one of personal interest to the participants. For this purpose, relevant information is gathered. The students generate, propose, and select ideas that allow them to understand, visualize, and overcome the targeted challenge, and subsequently they develop solutions and plans. During all of the stages of CPS, students process advanced content as required.

CPS components and stages offer endless possibilities to enhance learning. For example, during a science lesson about sea mammals, Maria, a sensitive and usually shy student, timidly expressed her concern about whales being killed and asked if that could be stopped. Her question captured the attention of other students. The discussion was encouraged by the teacher, and soon the question became a class concern. The first stage of CPS involves precise clarification of a problem or challenge. Soon thereafter, the students were invited to brainstorm using specific divergent thinking rules such as deferring judgment, striving for quantity, welcoming unusual or even wild ideas, and building on others' ideas. In 3 minutes, the 12 students of the classroom generated over 150 ideas. At that point, the teacher introduced convergent strategies and the students selected the most viable and interesting ideas to them—improving and combining the ideas when possible. During this process, the students realized that they needed to learn more information about the whales; search advanced content sources regarding whale biology, behavior, evolution, and neuroscience; and also regarding the history of whale fishing and killing, socioeconomic and cultural aspects, and environmental repercussions. The students dived into deep content but not as a requirement; it was *their* search. In addition, some expressed their desire to contact experts in these various fields. Finally, the students created a plan for action that involved group work inside and beyond the classroom.

A second way to teach and facilitate the creative process is the Incubation Model of Teaching developed by E. Paul Torrance. This model involves three stages:

1. *Before the lesson*—the goal is to heighten anticipation to create the desire for learning, engaging students' attention, stimulating curiosity and imagination, and enhancing intrinsic motivation.

2. *During the lesson*—the purpose is to deepen expectations. What was anticipated in the first stage must be fulfilled, and new expectations are created so students will want to go deeper into what is being taught.

3. *After the lesson*—this stage involves strategies to keep the creative and the learning processes going even after the lessons or the courses are over, and sometimes during a lifetime.

The three stages of the Incubation Model of Teaching have as a consequence learning advanced curricular content, but this model involves much more than that. Some could say that this model describes what happens in other good models of teaching. The Incubation Model of Teaching, as envisioned by Torrance, provides teachers with the tools necessary to leap from the good to the great; in other words, it enables them to become great teachers who are capable to inspire and motivate students and to keep them thinking even years after the lesson is over. The key of this model is that it precisely enhances and facilitates a particular stage of the creative process known as incubation, which is when things become suddenly connected (even if we are doing or thinking about apparently unrelated matters) and the "aha moment occurs," the insight when creative breakthroughs happen.

THE IMPORTANCE OF MENTORS

Having the opportunity to learn directly from a mentor who is an expert in a field of interest is often a more determinant learning experience than simply introducing and reviewing advanced subject area content. With a mentor, children are able to express and develop their own ideas, questions, proposals, and interests at a more advanced level than what schools can typically offer. In short, through mentorship learning can become personal and meaningful. Additionally, mentors can help children to become better able to see, understand, value, and enjoy their potential while providing the opportunity of being immersed in a field of interest collaborating with real life professionals. The examples are countless. Take, for instance, the case of Thomas Hart Benton and Jackson Pollock; the latter took the former's lessons and made the next "creative leap beyond" into abstract expressionism and drip painting. Beethoven learned from Joseph Haydn. Socrates mentored Plato who mentored Aristotle who mentored Alexander the Great. Stephen Hawking acknowledged that it was because of his mathematics teacher and mentor Dikran Tahta that he became interested in the fields of physics and mathematics.

Teachers can also function as mentors when personally focusing on the particular needs and interests of children. If adults are attuned, children become aware of their own capacities to create. As a result, children become able to build and use internal resources and to develop their intuition and self-confidence. However, if their experiences with adults are negative, all of the frustrations that the children cannot handle become impingements, and individuality and creativity can be deeply affected. If during a learning experience children are devalued and experience shame, this experience of shame not only harms their developing personalities but also can result in blockages in the creative process that often continue throughout adult life. What Peter Fonagy described in caregivers can be applied to mentors and teachers as well: Adults serve as mirrors wherein children can find coherent, creative sense of the self; what is seen by children in this mirror is what they become able to see in themselves. Being teachers and mentors involves great responsibility.

SERIOUSLY, PLAY!

If we take education seriously, it is imperative to consider the critical effects of play on cognitive, affective, and creative development. Play involves the basic components of the creative process such as combining and generating new possibilities, experimentation, and exploring the limits of reality and fantasy. Moreover, play is crucial for the development of healthy personalities. In support of this notion, highly successful artists, scientists, and other domain-specific experts often describe that playlike activities and processes related to their work are critical for being able to accomplish their goals in novel and original ways.

On the other hand, if play is ignored or disrupted children often experience deep distress. If the school environment is too strict or if playing is devalued, children become frustrated and distressed. Consequently, as Eric Rayner (1978) has shown through his research, such children may begin to torture others, developing ruthless actions that involve sadistic, unempathic, cold, and cruel behaviors. Unfortunately, these attitudes and behaviors could continue through adult life. Thus, if play is prevented in order to gain additional time for covering curriculum content or for any other reason such as testing students' skills or to avoid interactions among students, this could have a harmful and negative impact on children's personality and creativity development and on their mental health. In contrast, good sessions of play leave children calm and satisfied and lead to creative rather than destructive behaviors in the short and long term.

CONCLUSION

Implicit in this essay is that close collaborations between experts in creativity and experts in advanced curricular content could be extremely synergic and fruitful in not only developing children's potential but also in creatively solving problems that exist in today's world and that will undoubtedly emerge in the future. Along this line, teaching advanced curricular content is part of the education process (and also a consequence), but it should not be the focus of gifted education. Rather, the goals and focuses of gifted education should be to help students understand and realize their creative potential and talents; to assist students and teachers to understand that giftedness often involves different ways of thinking and experiencing diverse stimuli that offer unique opportunities for in-depth learning experiences; to teach and learn a variety of thinking methods and processes, particularly those related to creative thinking, such as those found in the CPS approaches to learning and the Incubation Model of Teaching. These methods lead to learning advanced curricular content; provide students with the skills that will be useful for a productive and self-fulfilling life; and enhance students' motivation to continue learning after the lesson or their formal schooling is over, to involve other key strategies, in particular, mentoring opportunities with experts in a field of interest to the student, and to foster play and playful attitudes.

Further Readings and Resources

Beghetto, R. A., & Kaufman, J. C. (2009). Intellectual estuaries: Connecting learning and creativity in programs of advanced academics. *Journal of Advanced Academics, 20*(2), 296–324.

Bloom, B. (1985). *Developing talent in young people.* New York: Ballantine Books.

Kulik, J. A., & Kulik, C.-L. C. (1984). Effects of accelerated instruction on students. *Review of Educational Research, 54,* 409–426.

Lubinski, D., & Benbow, C. P. (2006). Study of mathematically precocious youth after 35 years: Uncovering antecedents for the development of math-science expertise. *Perspectives on Psychological Science, 1,* 316–345.

Marland, S. P. (1972). *Education of the gifted and talented: Report to the Congress of the United States by the U.S. Commissioner of Education and background papers submitted to the U.S. Office of Education* (2 vols.). Washington, DC: U.S. Government Printing Office.

Rayner, E. (1978). *Human development: An introduction to the psychodynamics of growth, maturity, and ageing.* Boston: Allen & Unwin.

Root-Bernstein, R. S., & Root-Bernstein, M. M. (2001). *Sparks of genius: The thirteen thinking tools of the world's most creative people.* New York: Mariner Books.

Stanley, J. C. (1980). On educating the gifted. *Educational Researcher, 9,* 8–12.

Tao, T. (2010). *Advice on gifted education.* Retrieved September 26, 2010, from http://terrytao.wordpress.com/career-advice/advice-on-gifted-education

Torrance, E. P., & Safter, H. T. (1990). *The incubation model of teaching. Getting beyond the aha!* Buffalo, NY: Bearly.

Torrance, E. P., & Safter, H. T. (1999). *Making the creative leap beyond.* Buffalo, NY: Creative Education Foundation Press.

Torrance, E. P., & Sisk, D. (1999). *Gifted and talented children in the regular classroom.* Buffalo, NY: Creative Education Foundation Press.

Vehar, J., Firestein, R., & Miller, B. (1996). *Creativity unbound.* Williamsville, NY: Innovation Systems Group.

Wai, J., Lubinski, D., & Benbow, C. P. (2005). Creativity and occupational accomplishments among intellectually precocious youths: An age 13 to age 33 longitudinal study. *Journal of Educational Psychology, 97*(3), 484–492.

Court Cases and Statutes

No Child Left Behind Act of 2001, 20 U.S.C.A. §§ 6301 *et seq.*

11

Should there be alternative special education curricula, or should students with special needs be part of mainstream classroom instruction?

POINT: Timothy E. Morse, *The University of Southern Mississippi*

COUNTERPOINT: Margie W. Crowe, *The University of Southern Mississippi*

OVERVIEW

The question of where students with special needs should receive instruction or what type of instruction students with disabilities should receive is not new. In 1975, Public Law 94–142, the Education for All Handicapped Children's Act, later reauthorized as the Individuals with Disabilities Education Act (IDEA), outlined service delivery in terms of the least restrictive environment (LRE) and the continuum of placements. The mandate for the LRE requires "to the maximum extent appropriate" students with disabilities be educated alongside their peers. If students with disabilities are removed from the general education classroom setting because of the severity of their disabilities, school officials must document that all supplementary services, accommodations, and modifications have been seriously considered in an attempt to include the students.

Recently, a national panel of experts was tasked with determining ways to offer multidisciplinary teams a range of options when determining the most appropriate LRE for each student in planning his or her individualized educational program (IEP). The IEP defines the specially designed instruction and the supplementary and related services needed by the student to benefit from instruction. Legally, school boards are required to maintain a range of placements along a continuum of most to least restrictive ranging from special schools to general education classrooms. The procedures set in place in 1975 attempt to ensure that students identified in need of special education services receive proper instruction, to the maximum extent appropriate, with students who are identified as not being in the range of children who achieve normally. These mandates provide students with special needs access to the general education curriculum.

The No Child Left Behind (NCLB) Act (2001) emphasizes not only access to the general education curriculum but also that students with disabilities should make adequate yearly progress (AYP). With the inclusion of students with disabilities in statewide and districtwide assessment programs, it became clear that students with disabilities would be held responsible for the same coverage of the general education curriculum and be expected to master the same academic standards as general education students. The NCLB mandate also requires that all students should have teachers who are highly qualified in the content area they teach. However, few secondary-level special education teachers are highly qualified in the content areas they teach; this lack of "highly qualified" qualifications in content areas by special educators is believed to have influenced the increased placements of students with disabilities in general education classrooms with special educators serving as coteachers. Some special education scholars suggest that federal policies related to accountability and highly qualified educators serve as a catalyst for the movement toward less restrictive placement to continue. The question becomes whether this movement toward full inclusion is beneficial for students with disabilities.

Other scholars suggest that the place where instruction happens is not what makes education effective or beneficial. Effective teaching strategies and an individualized approach are the more critical ingredients in "special" education. Neither of these approaches is necessarily associated solely with one particular classroom setting. The most effective instructional approach for a student identified as one with special needs recognizes that schools must provide the most appropriate education regardless of type or degree of disability. The type of instruction and where it is offered is determined by reviewing the learning needs of the student. Failure to recognize the special needs of the student diminishes the opportunities of that student with disabilities to have an appropriate education. "Special education is intensive, urgent and goal-directed and it is delivered by a uniquely trained teacher. . . . The role of the special education teacher is to teach what could not be learned elsewhere" (Zigmond, 1997, pp. 379, 384–385).

There have been developing views of special education. Some experts identify special education as "specially designed instruction" that meets the needs of exceptional children. Others advocate instruction that is direct and intense and with accommodations provided in regular classroom settings. Recently, Margo Mastropieri and Thomas Scruggs (2007) referred to providing accommodations and modifications as providing differentiated instruction. Differentiated instruction is based on the notion that "all learners do not necessarily learn in the same way and it refers to the practice of ensuring that each learner receives the methods and materials most suitable for that particular learner at that particular place in the curriculum" (p. 126).

As suggested in the following essays, numerous strategies for differentiated instruction are available to help general educators meet the needs of their students. However, Elizabeth A. Swanson (2008) suggested that although differentiated instruction is viewed as a path to provide access to general education curriculum and appropriate instruction for students with disabilities in fully inclusive classrooms, there is a gap between research and practice. Naomi Zigmond, Amanda Kloo, and Victoria Volonino (2009) also hinted at the need for more "special instruction" provided within the general education classroom. Many in the field of special education cannot support the elimination of a continuum of services for students with disabilities and the special education instructional practices offered by special educators.

The issues surrounding special education are as complex as the alphabet soup of acronyms that pervade the field, such as IEP, LRE, and NCLB. And, to be sure, the law requires that no child is left behind nor is excluded, which on its face is not debatable in an ethical society. Yet, in an essay that follows, Timothy E. Morse (The University of Southern Mississippi) argues that current legislation and policy may run the risk of creating a one-size-fits-all approach to education that in actuality holds back the success of students with special needs. In fact, he maintains that IEPs and so forth are evidence that alternative curricula in some cases best serve student needs. While standard curricular frameworks might provide a goal for all students, Morse insists that such curricula cannot adequately address the diversity that exists in American schools. Conversely and using the same concept of "fit," in the opposing essay, Margie W. Crowe (The University of Southern Mississippi) advances the idea that the vast majority of students with disabilities can be best educated in the mainstream. Crowe states that educators should apply means and methods to differentiate among students no matter how extreme, within certain bounds, their abilities may seem. She responds that such inclusive practices might be difficult in some cases for teachers to address the same level of content and processes with all students; however, other benefits, such as social and cultural ones, she argues, outweigh the possible challenges.

Laurie U. deBettencourt
The Johns Hopkins University

POINT: Timothy E. Morse
The University of Southern Mississippi

The importance of curricular decisions that are made on behalf of children with disabilities cannot be overstated. For some of these children, namely those with the most significant disabilities, educators always will be able to identify more skills that they need to master than educators will have the time to teach them. Hence, determining what skills to teach these students is of utmost importance. Further, educators know that students will learn what they are taught in school as is reflected in their curricula and will be less likely to master skills they are not taught.

Insofar as the purpose, or mission statement, of the IDEA, the federal legislation directing the provision of special education services to children with disabilities who are determined to be eligible to receive these services, is to prepare the incredibly diverse population of eligible students for postschool employment, further educational opportunities, and independent living, there are numerous reasons for arguing in favor of teaching individualized, alternative curricula to these students rather than standardized, one-size-fits-all curricula. These reasons include the nature of certain disabling conditions, stipulations in the IDEA, provisions in the NCLB Act (2001), historical unemployment rates for individuals with disabilities, limitations on the amount of diversity that can be addressed in a classroom, and the historical lessons that should have been learned from the need to pass the IDEA. Accordingly, these reasons are elaborated in the remainder of this essay.

Before expounding on the various reasons in favor of teaching alternative curricula to special education students, it is necessary to define the term *curriculum* since numerous definitions for this term have been offered in the literature. For the purposes of this discussion, the term *curriculum* refers to the skills or behaviors educators target for students to acquire. This term does not refer to the instructional strategies and materials instructional personnel will use, nor the scope and sequence of instruction.

NATURE OF A DISABILITY

Regarding arguments in favor of teaching alternative curricula to special education students, the primary argument in favor of doing so is because the inherent nature of a disability clearly calls for this approach. For instance, mental retardation, by definition, is a disability that results in significantly subaverage general intellectual functioning that exists concurrently with deficits in displays of adaptive behavior, which is also referred to as the performance of activities of daily living. Hence, the performance of adaptive behaviors refers to being able to independently complete essential life-sustaining tasks such as shopping for groceries, preparing meals, eating, and maintaining personal hygiene skills, such as brushing one's teeth, bathing, and administering medication.

A curriculum, such as one that focuses almost exclusively on teaching academic skills from the traditional content areas of reading/language arts, mathematics, and science, will, to some extent, address the academic needs of students with mental retardation but will not adequately address the adaptive behavior deficits they experience. These deficits can only be addressed through the provision of direct instruction that targets a student's acquisition of these skills.

Likewise, the core characteristics of a number of other disabling conditions necessitate the teaching of a curriculum to these students that is specific to their needs but is not addressed by a mainstream academic curriculum that focuses on the teaching of traditional academic content. Examples of these conditions, and the resulting curricula needs, are as follows:

1. Students who are visually impaired, particularly those who are blind, must be taught orientation and mobility skills in order to be able to travel independently.

2. Students who are deaf and unable to profit from oral language must be taught another mode of communication, such as sign language.

3. Students with a speech impairment that results in an articulation disorder must be taught skills that will enable them to pronounce words clearly.

4. Students identified as having an emotional disturbance may need to be taught how to overcome irrational fears or phobias.

5. Students with autism, a disability that is defined by the display of core social interaction and communication skill deficits, need to be taught skills that will enable them to interact with their nondisabled peers.

Insofar as public schools are the institutions in American society that are configured, within a universally accessible educational system, to provide necessary instruction to all of our nation's children, schools must provide the means necessary to teach the aforementioned students the core skills they lack as a result of their particular disability. The offering of appropriate curricula serves as the foundation for meeting these students' needs. Conversely, only offering/teaching a standardized curriculum that has a traditional academic focus, such as the curricula that have been developed by states for the purpose of addressing the provisions of the NCLB Act (2001), will not address the presenting needs of many special education students, nor the purpose of the IDEA that was described previously.

STIPULATIONS IN THE IDEA

Beyond the stated purpose of the IDEA, several stipulations in it combine to provide a second argument in support of teaching individualized, alternative curricula to special education students. The IDEA requires school personnel to address both the academic and nonacademic needs of each child with a disability. To this end, the IDEA calls for comprehensive evaluations that address all areas of need that result from a student's suspected disability and that the resulting evaluation data be used to write students' IEPs and serve as a baseline measure against which future progress can be measured. Further, within the IDEA the term *special education* is defined, in part, as specially designed instruction that addresses the content, or curriculum, that is taught to a child with a disability.

The IDEA and its accompanying regulations are devised via a legislative process in which all affected constituencies, including educators, parents of children with disabilities, and advocacy groups for the disabled are involved. The resulting product, then, can be viewed as a form of expert validity. Consequently, the IDEA's requirements for an IEP to be written on behalf of each special education student that addresses, as necessary, the child's specific needs (that may include functional performance skills that are not included in the general education curriculum) serve as proof that individualized, alternative curricula for some special education students are warranted.

In fact, the enactment of the IDEA (which was originally titled the Education for All Handicapped Children Act when it was first passed in 1975) resulted from an acknowledgment that the traditional curricula taught in schools were not appropriate for some students with disabilities. One segment of this population was students with relatively significant disabilities for whom schools claimed they were not equipped to address their functional performance needs and displays of maladaptive behaviors. The second segment of this population was students with relatively mild disabilities who were permitted to attend school but whose needs were not truly being met in the mainstream curricula.

NO CHILD LEFT BEHIND'S ALTERNATE CONTENT STANDARDS

Earlier in the present essay, the influence of the NCLB Act on curriculum development was mentioned. Key provisions in this law call for states to set challenging content standards in core curricula areas, including reading/language arts, mathematics, and science; administer rigorous tests of students' achievement of these standards; and enforce near universal participation of all students in grade-level assessments. Together, these provisions can be interpreted as an attempt to create a standard, mainstream general education curriculum. Yet, along with this attempt, there is an acknowledgment in the NCLB Act that such a curriculum—whether it is ultimately established at a national level or set separately by states—will not be appropriate for all students. Rather, the NCLB Act allows for an extremely small percentage of students who are classified as significantly cognitively disabled for assessment purposes to work to master alternate achievement standards in the content areas.

This aspect of the law argues in favor of individualized, alternative curricula for special education students even within traditional core academic content areas. This is to say, some students with disabilities can work to achieve skills that comprise the various core academic content areas, but these skills will be considered to be less rigorous and foundational than the skills their nondisabled, same-age peers will work to attain. Students with relatively mild disabilities will work from content area curricula that may be 2 to several years behind their same-age, nondisabled peers while, on the other hand, students with more significant disabilities will work from content area curricula that consist of basic, foundational skills, such as those taught in preschool through second grade.

Moreover, additional examination of the NCLB Act reveals further support for arguments on behalf of individualized, alternative curricula for special education students. Even as the law has been aligned with the IDEA, the elements of the IDEA that call for addressing the functional performance needs of students with disabilities have remained intact. Thus, even though the statewide assessment systems that have been established under the NCLB Act (2001) do not address the functional content that may comprise part of a student's curriculum, the fact that this content is to be addressed, as warranted, in a student's IEP in accordance with both the IDEA and the NCLB Act is evidence that such an alternative, individualized curriculum is necessary in some instances.

HISTORICAL UNEMPLOYMENT RATES

The historical employment data, as it pertains to individuals with disabilities, can serve as the basis for another argument in favor of the teaching of individualized, alternative curricula to special education students. As noted previously, one of the purposes of the IDEA is to prepare students with disabilities for future employment. One reason for this provision has been reported unemployment rates as high as 75% among this population. These circumstances lead to the inclusion of provisions in the IDEA calling for transition planning for secondary students with disabilities that requires not only the identification of future employment/vocational goals by a student but also the planning of an individualized course of study to enable the student to achieve these goals. Additionally, some advocates for these students have called for the use of local ecological inventories whereby potential jobs could be task analyzed for the purpose of determining the skills a special education student would need to master to be able to perform the job. Given the economic diversity that exists within and between states (e.g., in the state of Texas alone, ecological inventories in separate communities could result in task analyses for industries such as cattle ranching, seafood, and financial services), the creation of individualized, alternative curricula for special education students and the subsequent teaching of these curricula to enable them to obtain one of the stated purposes of the IDEA are necessary.

DIVERSITY LIMITATIONS IN CLASSROOMS

Recently many states have sought to reduce class size in an attempt to enhance the effectiveness of their teachers' instruction. Likewise, emerging research seems to indicate a correlation between the number of students who attend a high school and critical outcome measures, including graduation and dropout rates. A closely related issue to relatively small class and school sizes is the student diversity that can be addressed by a single teacher in a classroom. Simply stated, the more diverse the students, the more difficult it becomes for teachers to differentiate instruction within core curricula, let alone to also teach other curricula that have been designed to address the unique needs of some special education students who have been placed in the classroom.

HISTORY LESSONS AND THE IDEA

Many readers are aware of this statement: "Those who are unaware of and/or do not learn the lessons from history are doomed to repeat them." This statement is particularly germane to this discussion of appropriate curricula for special education students. The IDEA was created because a one-size-fits-all approach to providing a public school education did not allow for some students with disabilities to be permitted to attend public schools because their needs, such as toileting, could not be met, while other students with disabilities were permitted to attend but were not provided an education that met their needs. Fast forward to the NCLB Act and its call for mastery by all of nearly universal academic content standards and we run the risk of recreating an environment that does not allow for the inclusion of all of our nation's students.

CONCLUSION

The establishment and teaching of a standardized curriculum to students with disabilities is a concept that literally has no basis in fact. Simply stated, this concept is predicated on an unfounded desire to teach a student population some people apparently wish we had rather than the student population we actually teach. In other words, a standardized curricula would be appropriate for students who begin their schooling experience having already acquired a similar foundational skill set, possess similar capabilities for learning such as for total content and rate of learning, advance through developmental stages at the same rate, demonstrate nearly identical work ethics, maintain and generalize skill performance identically, and have in place support systems within the home that are almost identical in terms of their value for an education and efforts to support a child's acquisition of it. Clearly, this reality does not exist. In fact, educators in the United States are faced with quite the opposite. The movement within preservice teacher education programs to develop teachers' skills to present differentiated instruction is evidence of this fact.

The multiethnic society that is the United States presents its public school system, which allows for universal access by its students, with an incredibly diverse population to educate. This diversity is furthered by federal legislation that mandates every child with a disability, irrespective of its severity, be permitted to attend school and be provided with an individualized, free, appropriate public education. In this context, the term *individualized* refers to an instructional program that has been designed to meet the unique needs of a particular child. Hence, federally mandated special education services actually create an educational system—within a school system—that must craft individualized, alternative curricula for students. Thus, while standardized curricula can be established and designated as a marker toward which educators want students to work, these curricula never have, and arguably never will, be able to adequately address the incredible diversity that characterizes the student population in America's public schools.

At the end of the day, we all must recognize that disability is a part of the human condition. As such, its unique manifestations should be celebrated, recognized, and supported as necessary. To pressure teachers to do otherwise creates a cognitive dissonance that is unsettling to them and results in inappropriate instruction to their students.

COUNTERPOINT: Margie W. Crowe
The University of Southern Mississippi

There are few absolutes in education. However, one absolute is that all decisions concerning students with disabilities served under the IDEA are predicated on plans that are individually designed, executed, and assessed specifically for those children. In order to remain in compliance with IDEA, there can never be one universally applicable plan for *all* students with disabilities. It is important to remember that IEPs for students with disabilities must be just that—individualized. The educational program must be designed to fit the child, not the other way around. Even so, that does not mean that students with disabilities cannot be educated in the mainstream. Rather, the vast majority of students with disabilities can, and should, be educated alongside their peers who do not have disabilities.

Should there be alternative curricula for students receiving special education? Yes . . . but maybe not. The traditional approach to developing curricula for students with disabilities has been greatly dependent on the disability itself. Very often assumptions are made concerning the learning capabilities of students based on the specific qualifying IDEA disability categories. For example, students who have been diagnosed as having autism are placed in autism classes. The setting and, in some cases, the curricula in these classes are determined by the label used to qualify the students who are in need of services. There is great value in considering what research reveals about learning modalities, teaching strategies, and curricula characteristics of a specific disability. Such research is not stand alone. Rather, this research should be a part of the total context from which students with or without disabilities are educated. It is equally important to consider: the intent and content of IEPs for students receiving special education services, other elements of the IDEA such as "supplemental aids and services," the continuum of placement options, and the atmosphere of general education and special education in the context of the NCLB Act.

The real challenge of special education is determining how to equip students with disabilities with the required academic abilities while meeting their real-world, functional, and unique needs. At the same time, this is also the challenge of general education. The goals of both programs are the same but it is rather the "how" that is often required to be different. This "how" is, in a large part, the curriculum itself. Curriculum is generally considered to be the organization of ideas and concepts that are planned and presented with the intent of educational outcomes. A plan or framework of learning is necessary for all students. Those receiving special education are served through the complex crafting of IEPs.

INDIVIDUALIZED EDUCATION PROGRAMS

IEPs are the overall game plans or strategies to provide appropriate services to students with disabilities. By law, IEPs are written by multidisciplinary teams based on multiple assessments. These IEPs must express how disabilities affect students' abilities to participate and progress in the general education curricula. The assumption is that the general education curriculum is the core in which all students are to be engaged. Based on this assumption, as well as data derived from multiple sources on the manner in which the disability is manifested in the individual student, written documents—known as IEPs—are devised stipulating what services are to be provided, who will provide the services, where the services will be offered, how long the services will be offered, and what will constitute success. IEPs are the projection of what students should be able to accomplish during the described time. Federal law clearly mandates that students receiving special education services under IDEA are to be exposed to typically developing peers and general education curricula to the maximum extent possible.

IEPs must include statements of program modifications, accommodations, related services, and supplementary aids and services intended to provide access to the general education setting and curricula to the maximum extent possible. The intent of the IDEA is a concert of educational implementation requiring that the assessment data gleaned in the process of determining eligibility be correctly used, by a problem solving, proactive, and collaborative team of experts (including parents) to create appropriate goals based on the functional needs of students as well as the core general education expectations, including behavior and social skills. This is a complex task. These skills will be acquired, under the best of circumstances, in general education classrooms using general education curricula to the maximum extent possible. This expectation must be supported by the provision of manpower and other resources to support the students and provide the supplemental aids and services as required by the IDEA.

Clearly, this approach requires an ongoing, collaborative undertaking on behalf of the student. For many reasons, one of which is resources, this has been reduced to a more restrictive setting with alternative curricula because it is a ready answer to a complicated and resource-consuming issue. It is apparent and important to note that the intent to provide these services to the maximum extent possible would require that few students with complex medical needs and/or very severe disabilities receive specialized services. Yet this area of the continuum of LRE is actually very small and cannot account for the current number of students who are often quickly served in these settings with alternative curricula. The practice of systematically using alternative curricula creates students without many of the basic skills. In short, it would be a mistake to discard *all* alternative settings and curricula in an attempt to involve *all* students *all* of the time in the general education setting. Further, it is also a mistake to act quickly and without very careful regard in making decisions reducing the exposure of students to the social, peer-rich, age-appropriate learning with supplementary aids and services.

SUPPLEMENTAL AIDS AND SERVICES

The importance of supplementary aids and services has been underscored by law. First mentioned in concert with Section 504 of the Rehabilitation Act of 1973, supplementary aids and services were most importantly defined in the IDEA (amended in 1997) as those services and materials provided in a regular education setting that enable students with disabilities to be educated to the maximum extent possible with their nondisabled peers. In the 2004 revision of IDEA, the scope of intent was widened to include improving access to the educational spectrum including academic, nonacademic, and extracurricular activities. This provision includes all services in terms of training for general education teachers, use of specialized technology or materials, and the services of related service personnel such as speech and language services, occupational therapy, and others. This can include direct and indirect services. Specific applications of supplementary aids and services may include environmental adjustments such as preferential seating, planned seating, modified room arrangement to accommodate specific necessary equipment; specific levels of support exemplified by related service personnel, paraprofessional instructional support; instructional pacing, specific materials needed in the forms, for example, of large print, braille, assistive technology; assignment modification, testing accommodations, modifications in presentation of subject matter as illustrated by taped lectures, primary language instruction; social interaction support such as social skills curricula; self-management techniques including calendars and assignment books; and specific or specialized training needed for staff.

The IDEA mandates supplementary aids and services in a good faith effort to make the general education curricula and settings available to students with disabilities. Supplementary aids and services may include modification of local school policy such as attendance, discipline, and transportation policies as it affects the individual student. At the very heart of supplemental aids and services is the intent to provide those services to prevent a student with a disability from being removed from age-appropriate class settings solely because of a needed modification in general curriculum. The U.S. Department of Education (ED) states in the *26th Report to Congress* on the implementation of IDEA that approximately 85% of students with disabilities in elementary and middle school are receiving some sort of supplementary aids and services, modifications, and/or adaptation as indicated in their IEPs. This is a tremendous outlay of resources with the single intent to successfully access general education settings and curricula.

CONTINUUM OF PLACEMENT OPTIONS

Also central to the IDEA are the concepts of providing services in the LRE and the availability of a continuum of placement options. In other words, settings must be provided in which students with disabilities can be successful with the most access to general education curricula and age-appropriate peers. This continuum of placement options for students must include the range of choices from inclusion in general education classrooms with consulting services to the most restrictive of residential or hospital-based services. Where the instruction takes place is of less importance than how and what takes place. The seduction of inclusion is hard to ignore in a NCLB atmosphere, however, modified, supported curricula delivered in an appropriate setting is bedrock to the intention of the IDEA.

GENERAL AND SPECIAL EDUCATION IN A NO CHILD LEFT BEHIND ATMOSPHERE

The NCLB Act (2001) is a major piece of federal legislation that has dramatically changed the landscape of general and special education services. The NCLB Act requires the closing of academic gaps between various subgroups. This seems to be impossible for students with some disabilities, but it is nonetheless an assumption of the NCLB Act and the IDEA. Having established that comprehensive and dynamic individualized educational planning facilitated with appropriate supplementary aids and services as well as modifications is foundational to serving students with disabilities, as well as options available for placement, it is important to consider the elements of planning the curricula specifically. Planning is not a standardized process but is dependent on a number of related issues. Planning requires using data to determine what needs to be done to maximize student learning within the context of the unique constraints of the student's disability. This maximization requires an adaptive fit or individualizing the approach for students with disability and can be determined only by analyzing specific learning needs. While major revisions in curricula based on individual needs may be required, the limits often imposed by quickly designed or improperly monitored curricula may serve to underestimate the learning potential of a student.

The goals of special education are to produce individuals who can be as independent as their disabilities allow and to facilitate quality in that independence. Academic learning in traditional settings may have a low possibility of success, but supporting this learning with modifications and supplemental services increases the possibility of success. Due to the fact that the requirements of the NCLB Act are of paramount importance it may be, for example, that students with severe disabilities may well not be successful at literacy but enjoy the experience in different formats. Any change in behavior should be the work of learners. Learning constitutes changes in behavior so educators should under any circumstance consider carefully which skills are most required and important to teach. Carefully sequencing and refining objectives based on task analysis and determining ways to authentically assess learning is best practice under any circumstance. Modified general education curricula emphasizing specific selected elements may be the answer while maintaining high expectations and avoiding arbitrary ceilings for expectations. Learning becomes valuable when it can be transferred between settings or generalized. The task of learning is not complete until students can generalize their learning across settings. Learning as a behavior is not part of the usable repertoire for any student unless it is generalized. The supported core learning in general education with modifications and adaptations is best learned within the context of the give-and-take of general education.

Differentiation has been popularized in the general education community with the onset of the NCLB era. Rarely does the special education teacher have a situation that allows for teaching multiple students in the caseload the same way or with the same materials. The NCLB requirement of diminishing the gaps between subgroups in general education is expressly supportive of the needs of students with disabilities. In effect, this is the fit also necessary for the construction of effective individual education plans. One major element of differentiating instruction also ensuring fit is asking a student to do only what they are ready to do. This concept of fit also requires that students connect learning to what they need from the real world and what they care about.

Teachers ensure fit by using small-group instruction, reading partners, text at varied reading levels, rubrics individualized for the student, instruction in small increments or mini-workshops, learning contracts, product and task options, and varied homework assignments to make learning an individualized experience. This requires flexibility with time, seating arrangements, groupings, and other classroom elements. Solid differentiation requires consistent and careful assessment to assess student abilities but also student need from which teachers adjust their teaching. Differentiation is nothing new to the mind-set of special educators, and now it is a common concept in general education settings.

CONCLUSION

The vast majority of students with special needs should be part of mainstream classroom instruction. A key element of the IDEA is its mandate that every student with a disability is to be educated in the LRE for that student and that removal from the mainstream can occur only when necessary for the student to receive special education services. While some students have disabilities that may require highly specialized services that are best provided out of the mainstream, most special education students will benefit from inclusion in regular education classrooms with exposure to the regular education curriculum.

If the elements of the IDEA are used as they are intended with the IEP process carefully considered, monitored, and executed while supported by supplemental aids and services and related services, the vast majority of students can successfully receive all or the majority of their educational experience in settings with typically developing peers. As general education acclimates to the NCLB mandates, the atmosphere for students with disabilities gets more complicated in regard to testing. However, the focus of closing the gap by differentiating instruction in the general education setting to engender successful learning on an individual basis creates a ripe climate for students with disabilities. Alternative curricula for students with disabilities is philosophically a different curriculum specifically designed to meet specific needs. Differentiated, a general education strategy is designed to specifically meet the learning needs of students. Never before has there been a time and mind-set that is more collaborative in nature. This same collaboration is the essence of effective educational planning.

As surely as buying a diet cookbook and placing it on the shelf does not guarantee weight loss, having an IEP does not guarantee appropriate educational planning or curricular access. The framework for using the core curricula is legally there. The execution is often encumbered with many "in the trenches" realities. Many times due to a lack of training or knowledge and expediency, the shortcuts of adopting alternative curricula become the answer. Solid collaborative planning and execution of differentiated instruction with supportive supplementary aids and services including modifications and related service support can and should meet the needs of many of the students who are currently using alternative curricula. The framework of the IDEA requires a continuum of options for the LRE for all students with disabilities. This neither changes nor does it establish the requirement for alternative curricula for some specific students. At the same time, this does mandate judiciously limited use of the alternative curricula. With all the opportunities and possible combinations available within individualized planning, such as modifications, supplementary aids and services, and continuum of placement options, providing alternative curricula for any students not requiring the most specialized of care seems nothing less than a shortcut or compromise.

FURTHER READINGS AND RESOURCES

Browder, D. M. (2001). *Curriculum and assessment for students with moderate and severe disabilities.* New York: Guilford Press.

Brown, L., Nietupski, J., & Hamre-Nietupski, S. (1976). Criterion of ultimate functioning and public school services for severely handicapped students. In M. S. Thomas (Ed.), *Hey, don't forget about me! New directions for serving the severely handicapped* (pp. 2–15). Reston, VA: Council for Exceptional Children.

Donnellan, A. M. (1984). The criterion of the least dangerous assumption. *Behavioral Disorders, 9*(2), 141–150.

Ford, A., Black, J., Schnorr, R., Meyer, L. H., Davern, L., Black, J., et al. (1989). *Syracuse community-referenced curriculum guide for students with moderate and severe disabilities.* Baltimore: Paul H. Brookes.

Kauchak, D., & Eggen, P. (2003). *Learning and teaching: Research-based methods* (4th ed.). Upper Saddle River, NJ: Pearson.

Mastropieri, M., & Scruggs, T. (2007). *The inclusive classroom: Strategies for effective instruction* (3rd ed.). Upper Saddle River, NJ: Pearson.

Swanson, E. A. (2008). Observing reading instruction for students with learning disabilities: A synthesis. *Learning Disability Quarterly, 31,* 115–133.

Tomlinson, C. (2008). The goals of differentiation. *Educational Leadership, 61*(2), 6–11.

Webber, J., & Scheuermann, B. (2008). *Educating students with autism: A quick start manual.* Austin, TX: Pro-Ed.

Westling, D. L., & Fox, L. (2008). *Teaching students with severe disabilities* (4th ed.). Columbus, OH: Merrill/Prentice Hall.

Wolery, M., Ault, M. J., & Doyle, P. M. (1992). *Teaching students with moderate to severe disabilities: Use of response prompting strategies.* White Plains, NY: Longman.

Zigmond, N. (1997). Educating students with disabilities: The future of special education. In J. Lloyd, E. Kameenui, & D. Chard (Eds.), *Issues in educating students with disabilities* (pp. 377–390). Hillsdale, NJ: Lawrence Erlbaum.

Zigmond, N., Kloo, A., & Volonino, V. (2009). What, where, and how? Special education in the climate of full inclusion. *Exceptionality, 17,* 189–204.

Court Cases and Statutes

Individuals with Disabilities Education Act, 20 U.S.C. §§ 1400–1482 (2006).

No Child Left Behind Act of 2001, 20 U.S.C.A. §§ 6301 *et seq.*

12

Should moral values be a topic in public education?

POINT: Ralph D. Mawdsley, *Cleveland State University*

COUNTERPOINT: A. Jonathan Eakle, *The Johns Hopkins University*

OVERVIEW

Should moral values be a topic in public education? According to Ralph D. Mawdsley (Cleveland State University) in the point essay, moral values are a set of traits and viewpoints embedded in religion, particularly Christianity, that used to be reinforced and enforced at schools until public education became prevalent with Progressive, democratic, and multicultural viewpoints; therefore, according to Mawdsley, the only way to return to these previous values is to "use the legal system aggressively," as he describes it, so the teachers can be the ones who "make rules, give commands, and punish disobedience." On the other hand, A. Jonathan Eakle (The Johns Hopkins University) in the counter-point essay questions whose moral values we are talking about when we talk about morality; and shows—through historical analysis—how "moral values" have been appropriated by conservative right-wing groups imposing their viewpoints by use of legal, economic, and political means. This counterpoint essay suggests that to reach beyond an antiquated progressivism, public education needs to construct a new ethics.

The question "should moral values be a topic in public education?" unleashes a passionate debate because it is based on a definition of morality as a set of principles or values. Such a definition can become ambiguous, biased, not clearly evidenced, and not equally acceptable to different members of a society because moral codes are developed in the context of our relationships to others and in the context of our cultural surroundings (Javier & Yussef, 1995). Moreover, as pointed out in the counterpoint essay, this could involve imposing a set of values that not do necessarily result in ethical behavior.

Many feel that moral development is a process that begins early in life in the context of the interactions with our caregivers, and its purpose is the modulation of our interactions toward oneself and others in order to ensure the survival of all the members of the society. In that context, moral development can be viewed as a relevant task in education. Furthermore, since there are various levels of moral development some might argue that a goal for education should be to ensure that all students reach a high level of moral development, and this cannot be achieved by imposing a single set of values.

Lawrence Kohlberg (1981) concluded that there are six stages of moral development, three levels with two stages each:

1. *Preconventional level:* In its first stage individuals obey to avoid punishment and because authority is assumed to be right, rules are interpreted literally without involving any judgment. In a second stage of this preconventional level, individuals follow rules but do so to serve their own interests (you do this for me and then I will do that for you).

2. *Conventional level:* In this third stage, individuals' sense of what is right depends on others' approval, but shared feelings and needs are more important than self-interest, idealizing generosity, helpfulness, and forgiveness. Later in Stage 4, behaviors that contribute to social functioning and order (e.g., work hard, following rules) are the ones most valued. Here is where critical thinking is not at odds with morality; on the contrary, it allows people to move towards an autonomous morality (Piaget, 1932/1965) where rules are understood, questioned, and improved for a joint social purpose.

3. *Postconventional level:* This is the highest level of moral development. In this fifth stage, individuals place value not in specific laws but in the process that they serve, such as individual rights or democratic principles. In Stage 6, the highest of the postconventional level, what is right is defined by ethical principles that are above specific laws, and social order is valued unless it violates ethical principles. Jesus; Gandhi; Martin Luther King, Jr.; Mother Teresa, but also many other exemplary individuals from diverse cultures and diverse religious backgrounds have reached this level of moral development. Carol Gilligan (1982) suggested that this level is reached when affective components are also taken into account. This is a relevant remark because the first attempts to consider moral development as an educational goal included only cognitive methods (Broderick & Blewitt, 2006).

Contemporary developmental psychoanalytic theories and observations, which integrate emotion, cognition, and behavior, provide valuable information about how and when meaningful, attuned interactions stimulate optimal moral development (Rayner, Joyce, Rose, Twyman, & Clulow, 2005). Children need boundaries and rules while they move from a premoral stage to a heteronomous morality, but the developmental pathway should not end there. Moreover, it is important to point out that moral education is not synonymous to religious education. In fact, it has been found that tolerant environments, where diverse family cultures are respected, promote moral development; in contrast, environments that enforce rules through guilt and humiliation form individuals that conform to authority but at the same time are capable of sadistic acts (e.g., school bullying and other violent acts). Sadism can even become institutionalized when teachers themselves enforce control by frightening their class (Rayner et al., 2005).

In this chapter, scholars debate the issue of whether moral values should be taught in the public schools. Ralph D. Mawdsley, a professor of education law at Cleveland State University, argues in the point essay that the teaching of moral values should be returned to the public schools but acknowledges that such an approach faces an uphill battle. After reviewing much of the litigation on issues involving religion and public schools, Mawdsley concludes that the only way to do this may be to use the legal system aggressively. A. Jonathan Eakle (The Johns Hopkins University) takes the opposing position in the counterpoint essay. Eakle raises the question of whose moral values are to be taught if moral education is part of the instruction in public schools. Eakle concludes that instead of returning to past values and their contradictory double standards that the public schools should construct new ethics.

Rosa Aurora Chávez-Eakle
Washington International Center for Creativity,
Washington Center for Psychoanalysis

POINT: Ralph D. Mawdsley
Cleveland State University

"The centrality of moral education remained an article of faith from the creation of the public school system in the 1830s until the last decade of the century" (McClellan, 1999, p. 23). Particularly at that time, educators in public schools were expected to reinforce the moral education of the homes with the added effect of creating a common culture and preserving harmony and order for the greater society. The values projected in American public schools eventually became a combination of traditional Protestant morality with a 19th century concept of good citizenship that emphasized attributes such as self-restraint, industry, honesty, kindness, punctuality, and orderliness. At the same time, contrary to other Western countries that provided state support for religious education, American public schools responded to the diversity in society by replacing sectarian doctrine in public schools with a muted nonsectarianism that emphasized commonly accepted factors on which all could agree—"the ten commandments, the golden rule, and the redemptive power of Jesus Christ" (McClellan, 1999, p. 33). Broadly speaking, educators in public schools went on to teach topics consistent with the Protestant religion while reserving to the home and the churches the task of indoctrinating students with special doctrines identified with particular religions (McClellan, 1999). Against this historical backdrop, then, the main premise of this point essay is that moral values should be returned as a topic of instruction in American public schools, although such an approach faces an uphill battle.

HISTORICAL BACKGROUND

The generalized change in the religious emphasis in American public schools coincided with a significant increase in the number of children in public schools, especially in secondary schools, where the emphasis on instructing students in social, academic, and vocational skills in preparation for college or careers crowded out religious instruction. An increasing number of immigrants in the 19th century who adhered to the Roman Catholic faith found themselves at cross-purposes with the Protestant-influenced public schools. While some public school systems attempted accommodations, such as reading from the Roman Catholic Douay version of the Bible and removing any anti-Catholic commentary that could offend students of that faith, educators in most public schools continued to read only from the (Protestant) King

James Version of the Bible, to use prayers that had a distinctly Protestant quality, and did not recognize holidays of solely Catholic significance.

Largely, in response to anti-Catholic sentiment, Catholics, beginning in the latter half of the 19th century, pursuant to the dictates of the Third Baltimore Council in 1884, created their own schools and expanded them well into the 20th century into what is still the largest system of private education in the United States. However, these private schools furthering Catholic doctrine created a new set of problems regarding values and education—to what extent should public tax dollars be expended to support Catholic schools?

In 1875, Congressman, then senator, and Republican nominee for president James G. Blaine of Maine proposed, but a year later U.S. Congress very narrowly failed to pass, the anti-Catholic Blaine Amendment to the Constitution that would have banned all financial support for what it described as "sectarian schools." Even so, from both before and after the attempt to pass the Blaine Amendment, individual states took the initiative such that more than 30 states amended their state constitutions to ban aid to sectarian schools more restrictively than that permitted by the Establishment Clause of the U.S. Constitution.

PROGRESSIVE APPROACH

Against this backdrop, during the 20th century, moral education in public schools became a contest between the use of codes of conduct emphasizing individual character traits versus a more flexible and critical approach to moral education. The former approach, rather than turning back the clock to the strong religious influence in public school instruction, used community organizations such as the Scouts, 4-H clubs, and Campfire Girls to develop codes of conduct that emphasized individual good behavior and moral growth. The latter approach, referred to as the Progressive view, and perhaps most typically exemplified by John Dewey and his followers, attacked the character traits approach as having produced poor results. Declaring that students needed an approach to moral education that was fluid and situational, the Progressives asserted that what was needed was "ethical flexibility and a pure sense of the relativity of values" (McClellan, 1999, p. 56).

Rejecting the notion that educators in public schools could teach specific moral precepts or encourage the development of specified character traits, the approach of the Progressives "hoped to cultivate in students both a quality of open-mindedness and a general ability to make moral judgments" (McClellan, 1999, p. 57). In effect, the shift in moral education went from individual character development to the ability of students to contribute to a humane and democratic society. Under the Progressive mantra, matters of private conduct were less important than students' contribution to social and political issues. "The good citizen, in [the Progressives'] scheme was not simply the person with the right intentions and a strong will but someone who could understand the social world and carefully calculate the social consequences of actions" (McClellan, 1999, p. 58).

Utilizing a pedagogy that emphasized problem solving and social learning, Progressives capitalized on a group pedagogy that used groups not to reinforce moral codes and individual character development, as in the past, but "to teach democratic decision-making and to help children break from tradition and create novel solutions of their own" (McClellan, 1999, p. 58). The consequential and drastic shift in thinking under the aegis of the Progressive approach to moral development was that all subjects in the curriculum, especially social studies, "had a wide range of opportunities to shape character" (McClellan, 1999, p. 59). The pedagogical mantra became "critical thinking" that would lead to exploring community, state, national, and international affairs. The emphasis on critical thinking gave students the opportunity to abandon what they considered to be arbitrary and outmoded thinking to be replaced with an *ethical flexibility and sensitivity to situation* that allowed for *different moral responses* depending on the arena in which a problem arose.

The irony of the Progressive approach is that, while it avoided what were considered to be the pitfalls of individual character development, it created its own problems. "By denigrating tradition, weakening the authority of adults, and giving new legitimacy to peer influence, progressivism left students vulnerable to the tyranny of both the immediate group and the present moment" (McClellan, 1999, p. 60). More frightening though for the individual student is as follows:

> his chances to rebel or to do anything on his own hook are practically nil; ... rather he is in the position, hopeless by definition, of a minority of one confronted by the absolute majority of all the others. (Arendt, 1961, p. 181)

To assert that public schools should engage in moral education requires that one inquire as to the nature of that moral education. The moral education that was taught during the 19th and early part of the 20th centuries focused on the character development of individual students and involved considerable input from parents. Character development relied on the moral pressure of the group to assure that the conduct of individual students accorded with desirable character traits. Progressive moral education also saw moral education in relationship to other students but solely for the purpose of assuring that student responses changed depending on the ethical issues at hand. The role of parents was supplanted by public schoolteachers who, as paid employees, could be directed to present moral relativism. Thus, while character development viewed student decision making in terms of personal traits such as honesty or reliability, Progressive moral development viewed student decision making in a social and political context with terms such as *social justice* or *multiculturalism.* In effect, the moral development approach of the Progressives, one can argue, came to be identified with the mantra "it all depends."

RETURNING MORAL VALUES TO EDUCATION

One does not need to argue for a return to Progressive moral development in public schools since it is already firmly entrenched. However, to return to individual character development would be a daunting task. Since the U.S. Supreme Court conferred constitutional rights on students and teachers in *Tinker v. Des Moines Independent School District* (1969), the main method for effecting change in public schools has become litigation. Moral values have since become attached to constitutional rights. Legal issues related to moral development have become diffused with a multitude of legal concepts—government speech, private speech, viewpoint discrimination, forum analysis, and hostility toward religion. The control of school boards over student expression has been framed by such concepts as disruption under *Tinker,* pedagogical content under *Hazelwood School District v. Kuhlmeier* (1988), lewd and vulgar content under *Bethel School District No. 403 v. Fraser* (1986), and antidrug rules under *Morse v. Frederick* (2007). With this kind of legal analysis, the relationship between school board control over schools and moral education has become purely ad hoc. Court decisions permitting student expression on moral issues, such as war, homosexuality, and/or religious messages are effective only until the next suit (Mawdsley, 2007). In effect, moral development has become like the thirsty person waiting for a few drops of liquid encouragement from the judicial faucet. Occasionally, the U.S. Congress intrudes as well and allows students to form clubs that have a common moral theme, such as Bible or gay rights clubs, to meet on school premises during noninstructional time pursuant to the federal Equal Access Act, which allows religious clubs to meet in public secondary schools during noninstruction time as long as other groups are permitted to gather. However, even this congressional effort at accommodating student moral compatibility can be undercut by the Supreme Court's upholding the nondiscrimination moral value of the educational institution (*Christian Legal Society, Hastings College of the Law v. Martinez,* 2010).

Missing from this moral development equation is the role of parents. Despite the Supreme Court's long-recognized constitutional right of parents to direct the education of their children in *Pierce v. Society of Sisters* (1925), that right does not intrude into the schools themselves (Mawdsley, 2010). Thus, while parents can make choices for their children to attend religious schools that are compatible with their own moral views, the right of parents to direct the education of their children does not confer a right to effect changes in public school curriculum or programs. As reflected by some high-profile litigation involving sexuality education in schools (*Parker v. Hurley*, 2008), even if school curricula introduces children to content that is contrary to the parents' moral views and, contrary to school board policy, no effort is made to secure parent permission, the parent has no constitutional claim (Russo, 2008). Such conduct serves to reinforce the notion that as much as one may want to have moral education in public schools, leaving such education to public schools is a hit-and-miss proposition.

However, to reinforce the ad hoc nature of the Supreme Court's viewpoint of moral development in public schools, the Court, effective with its decisions in *Lamb's Chapel v. Center Moriches Union Free School District* (1993) and *Good News v. Milford Central School District* (2001), permitted community religious organizations to have access to public school facilities during noninstructional time, as long as other nonreligious organizations are permitted. Thus, elementary school students are able to wait around after school to attend Good News Clubs that introduce children to moral values through Bible memory. Of course, school officials have the option, however draconian it may be, of stopping this moral incursion by simply banning all after-school use of its facilities by community groups.

CONCLUSION

The connection between religion and moral values that, over a century ago, undergirded character development now exists only in terms of students' constitutional rights. The moral viewpoints of parents are, at best, optional. Student efforts to express their religious views have encountered hostility toward religion by school teachers and administrators. The insistence by public schools on banning student religious expression for fear of offending the sensitivities of others ignores the impact of such denial on the sensitivities on the students desirous of expressing their views. Thus, to forbid or severely circumscribe student moral expression that recognizes the religious significance of religious holidays such as Christmas or that opposes conduct at odds with their religious views in opposition to abortion, for example, sends a clear message that the Progressive approach to moral education, unfortunately, is alive and well.

If moral education relying on character traits is to be returned to schools, the only recourse is to use the legal system aggressively to limit the undesirable effect of the Progressive approach. Despite generations of students who have imbibed the intoxicating liquor of Progressive moral education, we have produced neither a better society nor better citizens. We are probably too far along the constitutional right highway to follow the simple advice of Justice Clarence Thomas in his advocacy for the reversal of *Tinker* and the return of in loco parentis, a topic addressed elsewhere in this series as it relates to discipline, as the governing concept for the moral direction of students. Such a return, he is of the opinion, would effect a system whereby the teacher, in cooperation with the parent, "govern[s] [the] pupils, quicken[s] the slothful, spur[s] the indolent, restrain[s] the impetuous, and control[s] the stubborn. [The teacher is the person who] must make rules, give commands, and punish disobedience" (*Morse v. Frederick*, 2007, p. 414).

COUNTERPOINT: A. Jonathan Eakle
The Johns Hopkins University

The purpose of the counterpoint essay is not to take a devil's advocate perspective or to promote immorality. Rather, it is to deconstruct morality— an issue that cuts deeply into the national fabric. The reason that this moral slash is so deep is because behind the question of whether moral values should be a topic in public education is a much more important one: whose moral values?

WHOSE MORAL VALUES, NEW TIMES, NEW ETHICS

In the United States, "moral values" have been appropriated by conservative right-wing groups of people who divide morality into black and white, good and evil. They hold fast to their particular view of culture and the conservation of it even in the face of sweeping changes, such as the mass immigration of peoples who are rapidly appearing in our communities and schools. These conservative groups at times operate by legal and political means, such as through the statements or silences of Supreme Court Justice Clarence Thomas or the confessions and misstatements of former Alaska Governor Sarah Palin. More often than not in the United States, moral values are worn on the sleeves of religious groups as highlighted by the point essay of the present chapter, a point returned to subsequently.

On the other side of the aisle is the Left, who are typically defined as liberal. The roots of the split between conservatism and liberalism are immense, and as John F. Kennedy suggested, just as the conservative looks to the past, the liberal is about change and the future. The changes associated with liberalism include the redistribution of wealth from the few (e.g., a royal family) to the many—a motive of the liberal French Revolution—and the freedom of and from religious dogma and moral authority (e.g., of gods, kings, dictators).

In Kennedy's terms, those who hold to and wish to conserve the past and "moral values" are against the future and freedom. The hazards wrought by morality and how it has been twisted to promote conservative agendas in national debates over the past century are a threat to the opportunity for freedom and education—and to the Republic. Thus, at all costs moral values should not be a part of public schooling. Rather, the topic of education should be a *new ethics*—as argued in the closing of the present essay.

A BRIEF HISTORY OF THE MORAL "RIGHT" IN THE UNITED STATES

As every schoolchild learns, notions of religious freedom laid the foundation for the British colonization of North America. Nonetheless, religion is about opinion, and Thomas Jefferson warned of the disasters of a government ruled by opinion. Through his pivotal letter to the Danbury Baptists, he helped to establish a rational wall that separates church and state and, by extension, public education. However, that wall is an increasingly perforated one—so much so that an entire volume of the present series on education is devoted to various aspects of the religious tears to Jefferson's wall (e.g., should the Bible be taught in public school?). These penetrations are not new. For example, following the Progressive Era of the 1890s to 1920s, pious groups managed to usher in the Eighteenth Amendment, which prohibited the manufacture and transportation of alcoholic beverage and in effect curtailed its consumption. In short, to many members of those conservative groups, alcohol and establishments that served it, such as saloons, were connected to hedonism and sin.

This brand of moral values did not disappear with the repeal of Prohibition. In fact, during the late 20th century, pious forces gained in intensity resulting in what has come to be known as the "culture wars" (Donnelly, 2007). On the "right" side of this war, in the late 1970s, Jerry Falwell, a fundamentalist Christian pastor, established the Moral Majority, which set out a political agenda that among other things was based on the censorship of media materials, anti-homosexuality, banning abortion (even in cases of saving the life of the mother, rape, or incest), and an opposition to the Equal Rights Amendment, which proposed an equality of rights, such as equal pay for equal work, regardless of gender. As with Prohibition, morality was again used as a conservative hedge against cultural change. And at the center of the Moral Majority's goal was the reform of public education to align with Christian moral standards, which at the time were sometimes more generally referred to by the Right as "family values."

Falwell's Moral Majority gained momentum in the 1980s. Not surprisingly, the group became associated with other conservative causes; it supported Senator Jesse Helms's legislative call for school prayer and for curtailing funding to the National Endowment for the Arts (NEA) because of its support of projects not aligned with their moral agenda. In addition, Falwell claimed that the morality movement assured Ronald Reagan's election to the presidency and the wave of conservatism that followed. Because of the Moral Majority's interest in public education, Reagan appointed one of its founders, Robert Billings, to an administrative post in the U.S. Department of Education (ED), where he purportedly stated that no public school should be staffed by those who have not accepted Jesus as the savior of their soul (Pearce & Littlejohn, 1997).

The end of the Reagan era also marked the temporary decline of the influence of the Moral Majority and other Christian Right organizations on politics and by extension public education. However, in the early 21st century and with the support of conservative groups, George W. Bush was elected president. In some ways, his presidency mirrored the one of Reagan. Bush's second major governing initiative, after the No Child Left Behind (NCLB) (2001) education legislation, was to empower faith-based organizations to receive federal funding through the Compassion Capital Fund. Soon thereafter and following the 9/11 attacks, he used biblical phrases that divided good and evil, as had Reagan with his comments that cast the USSR as an "evil empire." Further, Bush has been criticized by scores of scholars and journalists for launching a contemporary crusade—a word Bush used—against Islam (Maddox, 2003). In similar regard, other conservatives have demonized the splits of good and evil. The rhetoric has become so much a part of the national discourse that even as Obama attempted to "change the script" from polarizing rhetoric during his campaign, he too used good/evil binaries to support U.S. military missions (Ivie & Giner, 2009).

THE FOG OF MORAL VALUES

Some people could argue that because of the double standard of the transcendent high moral claims made by U.S. leaders, including some educators, and the reality of decadent inclinations and practices that are immanent in U.S. society, it is an even more paramount reason to teach moral values in public schools. However, it is clear through its actions that any moral claim that the United States—and a main delivery system of its concepts and culture: the public schools—might have is dubious, at best. Nonetheless, this does not mean that educators should promote hedonism. On the contrary, they should dispense with the worn, tarnished, and value-laden notions of what has become known as "moral." Although perhaps useful during a far past time, there are simply too many contradictions between what has been deemed moral through U.S. dogma and what has actually unfolded in its practices, which include mass killing; rampant desiring; and malicious—and sometimes legalized—stealing, among other things. As Nietzsche concluded, we are "human, all too human" and remain trapped in a fog of feeble moral values.

Do Not Kill

To those who do not strictly adhere to the ideology of the conservative Right, defining moral values can be like nailing JELL-O to a wall. Thus, as with the conservative impulse, a return to the past for definition and a few basics could be useful, and the often-voiced divide of good and evil is a ripe target. In these terms, evil, after all, is usually defined as destructive. And above all other actions, the murder of a human being is a destructive deed that has been denounced across cultures and time. Yet, the United States, while promoting moral values, may likely be the most destructive of all nations in history in terms of destroying human life.

Reports of civilian causalities during U.S. wars as a result of violent deaths vary greatly; however, it has been estimated that over 100,000 civilians have died because of recent wars in Iraq and Afghanistan, and at the time of this writing, conflicts have begun in Libya. Moreover, during the World Wars, estimated causalities are beyond belief. This is graphically shown in the documentary *The Fog of War* (Morris, 2003). The film is centered on interviews with Robert McNamara, who served as a key analyst of U.S. Air Force bomber efficiency and effectiveness during World War II and later as U.S. Secretary of Defense during the Vietnam War. McNamara laid out statistics comparing the incineration of Japan's cities to U.S. equivalents (e.g., 51% of New York destroyed), and he proposed the following:

> Proportionality should be a guideline in war. Killing 50% to 90% of the people of 67 Japanese cities and then bombing them with two nuclear bombs is not proportional. . . . If we'd lost the war, we'd all have been prosecuted as war criminals. LeMay [commander of the U.S Air Force] recognized that what he was doing would be thought immoral if his [sic] side had lost. But what makes it immoral if you lose and not immoral if you win?

As McNamara suggested, relying on moral edicts such as not killing is not easily reconciled with U.S. practices. Of course, shortcomings like these are simply fodder for the most radical of moralists to point out the decadent decline of the United States during recent decades and to call for moral reform. Nonetheless, tracing U.S. history from its inception and the treatment of Native Americans through the slavery of Africans to global militarism and so on highlights that occupying a moral high ground is not consistent with the centuries-old rhetoric of morality professed in many U.S. homes, churches, businesses, and schools of past and present.

Bodies, Temples, and Desires

Despite the freedom professed by U.S. institutions, such as schools, the individual body has been the target of not only bombs but also ongoing moral agendas and debates. Schools, governments, and public media censor nudity and sexual acts while violence is accepted more leniently. In this vein, utterances suggestive of body parts, body fluids, and the copulation of bodies are strictly regulated in the public media and classrooms. Nonetheless, during the 1970s a challenge to so-called immoral or obscene language censorship was mounted by comedian George Carlin. In a stand-up routine, he suggested there were "seven words that can never be said on television"—all of which involved the body. Even though these words have since made it into public broadcast media, in part because of free speech court challenges, uttering these seven words in today's U.S. public school settings still spells trouble.

Similarly, books have been, and continue to be, censored in U.S. communities and schools because of language denoting sexual activities and other issues of the body. Familiar titles of banned books include Henry Miller's *Tropic of Cancer,* D. H. Lawrence's *Lady Chatterley's Lover,* and J. D. Salinger's *Catcher in the Rye.* As a counterpoint to such actions, the American Library Association advocates the freedom to read what one wishes as a right guaranteed by the Constitution and promotes Banned Books Week each fall.

Digital media from the Internet is censored by schools, as well. One principal reason for this regulation is the astonishing proliferation of global Internet pornography, its multibillion dollar U.S. industry, and its enormous consumption by hundreds of millions of users. San Fernando Valley, California, is one of the major porn capitals of the world, which distributes its products not only digitally but through major U.S. television cable companies, parcel post, and so forth. While schools and governments attempt to control youth's viewing of bodies engaged in sexual activities in the wider community, there is what Chloe Woida (2009) described as a seemingly infinite crossing of digital borders and the widespread practice of the "undisciplined gaze." Conversely, and as detailed in the *Religion in Schools* volume of the present series, how the body is covered by clothing has also been deemed a moral issue in and out of schools. In their halls, schools seek to regulate sexual desire, such as the recent youth practices of "sexting" (sharing sexually explicit material, often self-produced and usually sent via cell phone), but functioning increasingly in the light of day is the massive production and consumption of multiple media that include various genres and modes of sexual practices in and for the U.S. public.

Do Not Steal

Echoing modern proclamations that ushered in the foundations of U.S. education and its accompanying preparation of workers for the factory and the mill, it is often professed that public schools should provide students with the means to be successful in the workplace. Because this mission falls short in certain corners of U.S. communities—especially urban areas with high percentages of economically distressed households—students frequently become disengaged with school, unmotivated to learn academic material, and their self-efficacy is tarnished. Not surprisingly, dropout and truancy rates of students in these localities are alarming. An explanation for these statistics is that children conclude that schools and their current academic curriculum and instruction do not deliver on their promises for a better life.

On the heels of this promise, however, are immanent and contradictory examples to what children are taught in school. At every turn, they learn that there are alternative ways to prosper in the capitalist arena. First, they see it firsthand on neighborhood streets, where, for instance, peers earn good money selling illegal commodities, such as cocaine. In spaces removed from their communities, news and entertainment media distribute and profit from sensational reports of Ponzi schemes, marginally legal applications of Wall Street financial instruments that few people can understand, and charges of nepotism and other fraud committed by U.S. Congress and others, including school officials, at the expense of the U.S. taxpayer. To be sure, all that was once deemed moral by commandment or other rules has been turned on its head in contemporary U.S. culture.

A NEW ETHICS

Instead of a return to past values and their contradictory double standards, cultures at large, and U.S. public schools in particular, need to construct a new ethics. First, this means reaching beyond progressivism, in part because its once powerful rhetoric has long been appropriated and deformed by those who wear labels such as democracy and morality on their sleeves. It also means accelerating past concepts such as the "minority of one," which, according to the author of the point essay of the present chapter is steeped in individualism and relativism and toward the minorities of the many (Deleuze & Guattari, 1986)—a movement of everyday people against fascism. These minorities can go about a collective dismantling of institutions and practices that are based in destructive modes of production and consumption. Although at first blush this could seem Pollyanna, the beginnings of this deconstruction have commenced through grassroots movements such as *Democracy Now!*, Greenpeace, and Occupy Wall Street (see also Whalen-Levitt, Chapter 14 of this volume). And although controlled in schools, the Internet and new technologies offer some of the means necessary to propagate this new ethics. In the end, local social networks can meld with broader ones, and communities can thus be formed whereby ethical, constructive—rather than destructive—human efforts might flourish.

FURTHER READINGS AND RESOURCES

Arendt, H. (1961). *"The crisis in education" in between past and future: Six exercises in political thought.* New York: Viking Press.

Broderick, P. C., & Blewitt, P. (2006). *The life span: Human development for helping professionals* (2nd ed.). Columbus, OH: Pearson.

Deleuze, G., & Guattari, F. (1986). *Kafka: Towards a minor literature* (D. Polan, Trans.). Minneapolis: University of Minnesota Press.

Democracy Now!: The war and peace report. http://www.democracynow.org

Donnelly, K. (2007). *Dumbing down: Outcomes-based and politically correct: The impact of the culture wars on our schools.* Melbourne, Australia: Hardie Grant Books.

Gilligan, C. (1982). *In a different voice: Psychological theory and women's development.* Cambridge, MA: Harvard University Press.

Ivie, R. I., & Giner, O. (2009). More good, less evil: Contesting the mythos of national insecurity in the 2008 presidential primaries. *Rhetoric & Public Affairs, 12,* 279–301.

Javier, R. A., & Yussef, M. B. (1995). A Latino perspective on the role of ethnicity in the development of moral values. *Journal of the American Academy of Psychoanalysis, 23,* 79–97.

Kohlberg, L. (1981). *The philosophy and moral development: Moral stages and the idea of justice.* San Francisco: Harper & Row.

Maddox, G. (2003). The "crusade" against evil: Bush's fundamentalism. *Australian Journal of Politics & History, 49,* 398–411.

Mawdsley, R. D. (2007). Sailing the uncharted waters of free speech rights in public schools: The rocky shoals and uncertain currents of student T-shirt expression. *Education Law Reporter, 219,* 1–23.

Mawdsley, R. D. (2010). Parents' right to direct their children's education: Examining the interests of the parents, the schools, and the students. *Education Law Reporter, 258*, 461–480.

McClellan, B. E. (1999). *Moral education in America.* New York: Teachers College Press.

Morris, E. (2003). *The fog of war* [motion picture]. Sony Pictures Classics. Flash index retrieved February 27, 2011, from http://www.sonyclassics.com/fogofwar/index-Flash.html

Pearce, W. B., & Littlejohn, S. (1997). *Moral conflict: When social worlds collide.* Thousand Oaks, CA: Sage.

Piaget, J. (1965). *The moral judgment of the child* (M. Gabain, Trans.). New York: Free Press. (Original work published 1932)

Rayner, E., Joyce, A., Rose, J., Twyman, M., & Clulow, C. (2005). *Human development. An introduction to the psychodynamics of growth, maturity and ageing.* London: Routledge.

Russo, C. J. (2008). "The child is not the mere creature of the state": Controversy over teaching about same-sex marriage in public schools. *Education Law Reporter, 232,* 1–17.

Woida, C. (2009). *International video pornography on the Internet: Crossing digital borders and the un/disciplined gaze.* UC Irvine: Digital Arts and Culture 2009. Retrieved February 27, 2011, from http://escholarship.org/uc/item/64x2343p

Court Cases and Statutes

Bethel School District No. 403 v. Fraser, 478 U.S. 675 (1986).

Christian Legal Society, Hastings College of the Law v. Martinez, 130 S. Ct. 2971 (2010).

Equal Access Act, 20 U.S.C.A. §§ 4071 *et seq.*

Good News v. Milford Central School District, 508 U.S. 384 (2001).

Hazelwood School District v. Kuhlmeier, 484 U.S. 260 (1988).

Lamb's Chapel v. Center Moriches Union Free School District, 508 U.S. 384 (1993).

Mitchell v. Helms, 530 U.S. 793 (2000).

Morse v. Frederick, 551 U.S. 393 (2007).

No Child Left Behind Act of 2001, 20 U.S.C.A. §§ 6301 *et seq.*

Parker v. Hurley, 514 F.3d 87 (1st Cir. 2008).

Pierce v. Society of Sisters, 268 U.S. 510 (1925).

Tinker v. Des Moines Independent School District, 393 U.S. 503 (1969).

13

Is there a place for popular culture in curriculum and classroom instruction?

POINT: Donna E. Alvermann, *University of Georgia*

COUNTERPOINT: Margaret J. Finders, *University of Wisconsin–La Crosse*

OVERVIEW

José is a gifted high school student who smiles as he watches his teacher Ms. Parrott standing on a chair while reciting a famous scene of Shakespeare's *Hamlet*. As she concludes the soliloquy, the teacher is pleased by the student's apparent enthusiasm for her performance and asks him what the opening lines about being and not being might mean. José responds, "Excuse me?" Little had Ms. Parrott realized that José's smile was derived from the electronic pulsing of his favorite band—Gogol Bordello—traveling up a thin white line from his nanotech device into his ear, which was strategically turned from the teacher's gaze to avoid detection.

This all too common exchange between student and teacher is used to introduce the present chapter because José's use of Gogol Bordello gypsy punk music shows that whether popular culture should be in the classroom is a moot point. It is—if not undercover such as in miniature music devices, comics wedged between textbook pages, or literally worn on sleeves of branded clothing, and so forth, then at least in the hearts and minds of most students. Whether popular culture should be a part of curriculum and instruction in schools is another matter and one of perspective and values, which are themes taken up in the two essays that follow.

However, as every student should discover, perspectives are multiple and plastic. Examining a snippet from the lyrics of "Immigraniada (We're Coming

Rougher)" that José was giving his attention to during his class can give a sense of this multiplicity and ever-shifting tide of perspectives and cultures. Its opening lyrics directly reference the great writer Franz Kafka in terms of fragmentation, social exclusion, and cultural disposal—deleted dimensions of migrant culture that are erased by fascist bureaucrats as they described it. The song goes on to imply invitational words to those seeking freedom that are carved into the Statue of Liberty in New York Harbor—a space where thousands of immigrants have passed. Lastly, the lyrics confront the myth of a univocal U.S. culture by resisting the double standards of a false plural ideology and the actuality of a heterogeneous U.S. culture, implicitly warning that because of these inconsistencies, migrants are arriving to America rougher and more cynical every time as the gypsy rockers suggest.

In Gogol Bordello's lyrics are themes and issues that are not only internationally popular among, and critically important to, many young people but also ones that cut into the fabric of the actual worlds that people of all ages today occupy. Immigrants to the United States, for instance, are lured to its borders by promises of freedom and work, but are sometimes stopped short of acquiring meaningful jobs through which they are able to freely live healthy and purposeful lives. In this vein, opening Gogol Bordello's (2010) online music video of this song is a quote by President Franklin Roosevelt that reminds those of majority positions in the United States—"You and I especially, are descended from immigrants"—which is followed by moving black-and-white images of people arriving during the early part of last century to Ellis Island. The online video concludes with another printed text theme of the American Civil Liberties Union: "No human being is illegal." Further, the reference in "Immigraniada" to the literary giant Kafka is by no means simply an ornamental one. In some respects, Kafka—like Gogol Bordello band members who come from several different countries and backgrounds, represent different age groups, genders, and so on—could be considered a gypsy punk. And, like the band members and their music, during his life, Kafka crossed multiple borders, including those of language, nation, and radical ideologies.

Sliced from its context whether in-school or out-of-school places, there simply might not be much difference in the reading of Shakespeare and Kafka or in perusing the same historical Ellis Island immigration pictures and presidential quotes in a school textbook versus a YouTube video. But in a wider context, what is shown marks an important border between modernity and what follows it. Kafka and gypsy punk are not about capturing exchanges between archetypes such as a father–king, mother–queen, prince–son. Instead, they are about creating a "sequence of intensive states, a ladder or a circuit for intensities that one can make race around in one sense or another, from high to low, or from low to high. The image is the very race itself" (Deleuze & Guattari, 1975/1986, pp. 21–22). This image-race is reminiscent of Lewis Carroll's *Wonderland,* which over time has crossed, "head over heels," from classic book formats to Disney cartoon, to a recent virtual world cinema production and beyond.

This intensive race of the gypsy punk band, Kafka, and Carroll is a real and local one. In the point essay, Donna E. Alvermann (University of Georgia) draws on these actual and local notions. There is no high culture in relief to low culture; there are only cultures. And as might be expected when describing a race of intensities, she highlights the resulting "blur" that happens when trying to stake out what popular culture is or is not. Taking that into account, Alvermann provides evidence and resources for how carefully designed professional development (PD) programs can assist teachers in integrating popular culture texts into their curricula, even in a standards-based school environment. Further, she addresses the critical issue of how capturing students' attention is perhaps one of the greatest challenges in education today as popular culture often holds much more meaning for youth than does what they perceive as antiquated school ideas delivered to them in equally outdated ways as if a teacher were delivering a script to pupils.

Taking another side of the issue, in her counterpoint essay Margaret J. Finders (University of Wisconsin–La Crosse) describes how importing popular culture into classrooms can be counterproductive. However, her point is not one of setting academic content above popular culture content or vice versa. She argues that at least in part the crux of popular youth culture is about resisting dominant institutional structures—and the messages, methods, and results of that dominance, such as those sometimes associated with typical public schools. By attempting to bridge what is important to young people in their out-of-school lives to what is deemed important by traditional academic standards, Finders points out that there is the risk of moving students even further away from important matters that could be taught and learned in classrooms and moreover, from those ideas and practices that could be the most useful and relevant ones in their futures beyond the school years.

A. Jonathan Eakle
The Johns Hopkins University

POINT: Donna E. Alvermann
University of Georgia

Popular culture, as defined in this essay, is not distinguished from high culture. This postmodern view of popular culture celebrates an end to elitism built on subjective notions of taste. From this perspective, popular culture consists of everyday practices that connect a group of people to each other in particular times and places. Examples of such everyday practices point to group and individual preferences in music; literature; art forms; movies; foods; news sources; games; TV shows; clothing; communication tools including texting, social networking, instant messaging, blogging, tweeting, and e-mailing; and lifestyles in general.

For many years, the idea of high culture as exemplified in reading Dante and Shakespeare, attending operas, or marveling at Michelangelo's ceiling in the Sistine Chapel was contrasted to low culture such as reading magazines, reading dime novels, listening to popular music on the radio, or watching cartoon flicks at the local movie theater. In some circles of society, low culture became a synonym for popular culture. By 1940, however, the line between high culture and pop culture in America had begun to blur. Perhaps nowhere is this more apparent than in the memorable image that film critic Neal Gabler (2011) captured in his contemporary tracing of cultural authority in America. According to Gabler, a telling moment in the easing of rigid distinctions between high culture and popular culture occurred when the classical conductor Leopold Stokowski shook hands with Mickey Mouse in the Walt Disney production of *Fantasia*. This symbolic gesture, Gabler claimed, showed how far popular culture had come in establishing its own niche in the American psyche. As Gabler illustrated, not even an icon of high culture was interested in maintaining the cultural divide of earlier times.

Somewhat parallel to questioning the arbitrary divide between high culture and popular culture is the current move to deconstruct concepts such as *informal* and *formal* learning. A common assumption, though sometimes left unstated in the research literature on integrating popular culture with formal classroom instruction, is that the divide between informal and formal learning environments is "real" and as such, needs to be bridged. Another assumption is that the type of learning thought to take place in each setting is qualitatively different. Yet in a yearlong study of informal learning during computer gaming and chatting online that involved a group of boys and girls, ages 9 through 13, in the Shared Spaces Project, Julian Sefton-Green (2003) concluded that informal learning, while vague in terms of its pedagogic structure, is coexistent with formal learning rather than being distinct from it. This finding, along with similar conclusions drawn by other contemporary scholars such as Kevin Leander and Jason Lovvorn (2006) in their research on schooling and online gaming, suggested that the time has come to move beyond a debate that would separate informal learning (context-as-sieve) from formal learning (context-as-container).

COEXISTENCE OF INFORMAL AND FORMAL LEARNING IN CURRICULUM AND INSTRUCTION

The coexistence of informal and formal learning is evident in studies of curriculum and classroom instruction where overlapping practices involving popular culture texts and literacy are taken for granted and even celebrated. Not surprisingly, popular culture texts, whether print-based, digitized, or hypermediated that are easily integrated into a school's existing curricula have a better chance of being considered educationally worthy than texts that lack this potential. Evidence in support of this claim comes from the following studies that were summarized in the most current volume of the *Handbook of Reading Research* (Kamil, Pearson, Moje, & Afflerbach, 2010): Eve Bearne and Helen Wolstencroft's (2005) research of a class of 8- and 9-year-olds who compared Red Riding Hood to Lara Croft, a character in a popular video game; Linda Labbo's (1996) study of a kindergarten class in which children used their knowledge of superheroes to compose their own computer-generated stories; Ernest Morrell's (2004) exploration of a high school English class that incorporated hip-hop in a poetry unit; and Jason Ranker's (2006) study of an 8-year-old boy's use of video games as a source of subject matter and form in his own writing and drawing.

Teachers in each of the foregoing studies were supportive of students' uses of popular culture texts in their classrooms. However, this was not the case in Kevin Leander's (2007) study of a high school in which wired classrooms provided students with laptop access to an unprecedented world of texts. Findings from Leander's study showed that teachers were uncomfortable with students' multitasking online literacies such as blogging, web browsing, and remixing texts, especially when such activity led to the production of popular culture texts that threatened school-sanctioned curricula and the teachers' authority.

More recent work, though, suggests that teachers who participate in carefully designed, long-term PD programs are comfortable in integrating popular culture texts into their curricula. One such example involved PD activities that advocate for a pedagogical awareness that takes into account the competencies and comfort zones of both students and teachers within a standards-based environment. *Bring It to Class: Unpacking Pop Culture in Literacy Learning* (Hagood, Alvermann, & Heron-Hruby, 2010) offers teachers and school library media specialists practical ideas and activities for introducing popular culture texts into traditional standards-based curricula. In that book, suggestions are offered for creating curriculum and classroom learning conditions that push against outdated perceptions some people have of teachers and school library media specialists. Rather than distancing themselves from graphic novels, anime, hip-hop lyrics, fan fiction, blogs, and the like, as if the plague had just announced itself, the teachers and media specialists in *Bring It to Class* balance their enthusiasm for using popular culture texts with a healthy dose of skepticism. They realize that these texts often fall outside the definition of what counts as literacy learning on high-stakes tests or in tradition-bound curricula that privilege print over other modes of communication.

Teaching in a multimodal, media-rich era where attention, not information, is often in short supply can make even enthusiastic and qualified teachers feel uneasy at times. Although they may sense the need to compete with 21st-century information communication technologies for their students' attention, they also recognize that in doing so they invite all manner of speculation, including whether or not mass media messages embedded in popular culture texts are negatively affecting young people's agency to think for themselves. Teachers, of course, can take some comfort in the counterargument that such embedded messages are grist for instruction in critical topics. Thus, there is value in providing opportunities for students to transact with popular culture texts in ways that show how *both* mass media producers and audience consumers maintain varying degrees of control over a particular text's meaning and its positioning of a particular reader, viewer, or listener.

INCREASED AWARENESS OF TEXTUAL POSITIONING

The perception that introducing popular culture texts into school curricula will undermine young people's ability to think for themselves is based on the supposition that audiences lack agency in interpreting messages embedded in media, such as rap lyrics, TV advertisements, graphic novels, and the like. Although this general distrust of audiences to think for themselves was largely discredited more than three decades ago by Stuart Hall (1981) and several of his colleagues at the Birmingham (UK) Centre for Contemporary Cultural Studies, the fear that popular culture texts will somehow make dupes of young children and adolescents lives on. Hall proposed that popular culture texts are neither inscribed with meaning guaranteed once and for all to reflect a producer's or author's, film director's, music arranger's intentions, nor are they owned solely by creative and subversive audiences. Instead, Hall's theory of *production-in-use* suggests that producers and consumers of popular culture texts are in constant tension with each other. It is this tension between forces of containment and resistance against such containment, Hall argued, that theoretically enables audiences to express meaning differently within different contexts at different points in time.

This belief in an audience's ability to express meaning differently, plus the definitional broadening of *text* to include moving and still images, sounds, and gestures in addition to a text's usual linguistic features are but two factors that account for increased interest in finding a place for popular culture in curriculum and class instruction. Other factors include the new information communication technologies, such as Web 2.0, that are interactive and capable of transporting both students and teachers into virtual worlds such as Second Life, Webkinz, and Meez where the distinction between online and offline spaces is sometimes blurred to the point that popular culture texts produced and consumed in one space for fun and relaxation often become objects of intense study and work in another.

Photo sharing and video sharing websites, such as Flickr and YouTube, respectively, make popular culture texts readily available for viewing and remixing. In fact, the ease with which multimodal content from these websites can be edited and remixed to create new texts contributes in no small way to young people's fascination with popular culture texts and the new literacies that they entail. In fact, it is this fascination with creating remixed online content that suggests the feasibility of making time and space for such activity as part of the regular curriculum. Doing so could conceivably increase students' awareness of how texts of all kinds (remixed as well as their required textbooks) attempt to position them to believe and act in certain ways and, just as importantly, how they have agency to push back against such attempts. Content area teachers who are open to considering the curricular implications of this pushback might consider incorporating into their instructional repertoire opportunities for students to integrate what they have learned from creating remixed texts during after-school hours with what they are required to learn from their subject matter texts. In this way, teachers are likely to find that adolescents who create derivative texts are neither mindless fans nor thoughtless remixers of existing media. An argument could be made, in fact, that engaging with all kinds of ideological messages (found in both popular culture and assigned classroom texts) is central to students learning to think for themselves. Likewise, maintaining a sense of agency in the "push–pull" tensions that can occur during textual positioning may be key to students developing skills and identities as critical readers of popular culture texts and their assigned content area textbooks.

IDENTITY CONSTRUCTION THROUGH USING POPULAR CULTURE TEXTS

One of the six strategies for teaching with popular culture texts that Richard Beach and David O'Brien (2008) encouraged involves students in the exploration of how race, class, gender, and other identity markers mediate mass-produced popular culture texts. For example, Beach and O'Brien pointed out that the discourse of whiteness prevalent in so many Hollywood films and television programs often becomes the invisible norm, which if taken up can foster negative or racist attitudes toward people of color. The politics of identity construction are alive and well. That such constructions frequently become visible through films, music, rap lyrics, and so on is yet another reason why popular culture texts have a place in a school's curriculum and its classrooms. Both are potential sites of engagement for moving toward a more just and equitable world.

Similarly, with popular culture texts, young people experience how authority and expertise are distributed across age, class, and gender lines to name but a few of the "old school" identity markers that continue to serve some youth well, and others not so well. The new ethos of 21st-century texts does not ration literacy "success" to scoring high on standardized tests that are typically renormed once the pass rate rises to an unacceptable level. Nor does it sanction the dominance of the book over other forms of text, such as fan fiction, manga, 'zines, anime, and online gaming in which multiple players perform certain roles in keeping with a particular game's storyline. Instead, as noted previously, identity construction through the use of popular culture texts is a process that encourages youth to explore how texts that position them in negative ways can be resisted or restructured in a more positive light.

Of course, as the principal investigators of a 3-year study aimed at verifying the degree to which media and popular culture texts find their way into classroom instruction, Andrew Burn, David Buckingham, Becky Parry, and Mandy Powell (2010) learned that there are valid reasons for why some students may not wish to explore their identities through popular culture texts introduced in the school curriculum. For sure, moves by educators (however well intended) that colonize young people's interests in popular culture texts are to be avoided.

Oftentimes students' online literate identities that incorporate popular culture texts, broadly defined, remain invisible to their teachers. This is disquieting, especially given the fact that a growing body of research suggests that teachers who make links to students' out-of-school experiences increase motivation and success in school learning. But this research aside, it makes little or no sense to ignore the considerable time young people spend each day on entertainment media. Some surveys, such as the Kaiser Family Foundation (2010) report, point to the fact that youths between 8 and 18 spend an average of 7 hours and 38 minutes daily on entertainment media. Moreover, the hours they engage in such media on a daily basis rise to over 10 when multitasking is taken into consideration.

What these numbers fail to show, however, is that adolescents are producers as well as consumers of popular culture texts. For example, a frequently cited report issued by the Pew Research Center's Internet & American Life Project (Lenhart, Madden, Smith, & Macgill, 2007) shows that 64% of young people between the ages of 12 and 17 who have Internet access in the United States spend a significant amount of their after-school hours creating web content, such as blogs and personal webpages. They also engage in social networking and playing video games, both of which require them to decode and encode a complex mix of images, words, sounds, symbols, and genre-specific syntax— skills that typically are not taught in traditional subject-matter classrooms.

Identity construction through the use of popular culture texts remains largely invisible to teachers because of potential and/or actual barriers associated with the authoritative role of institutional contexts. For instance, one such barrier is the prevailing sentiment that multimodal digital texts distract. This is unfortunate given the various affordances these kinds of texts provide during student-text transactions in content area classrooms. Pressures within schools to maintain standards; increase accountability; and deal with constraints related to time, resources, and testing also contribute to the notion that distractions of any kind are counterproductive. A second barrier is the tendency to employ needless and artificial dichotomies when thinking about youth, popular culture, and identity construction. For instance, school learning must be standardized whereas online learning can be customized. This artificial divide between in-school and out-of-school learning sends the message that teachers need not concern themselves with students' after-school interests and identity construction. Keeping students' online identity work with popular culture texts at bay simply reifies the notion that formal and informal learning are hardened categories.

PARTING OBSERVATIONS

Young people growing up today are experiencing a world that is increasingly less dominated by print-centric texts than the world that their teachers experienced a mere decade ago. In the current era of rapid page-to-screen shifts and easily accessible multimodal digital texts, the place of popular culture in curriculum and classroom instruction seems ever more assured. Yet some researchers, such as Adam Lefstein and Julia Snell (2011), have pointed to various trade-offs that can occur when teachers attempt to integrate popular culture texts with traditional schooling. Even so, these researchers are careful to note that genre mixing is not necessarily bad; it's simply more complicated than teachers may have been led to believe.

When perceptions of a school's institutional authority clash with young people's perceptions of their right to a certain degree of autonomy from adults' surveillance of their use of popular culture, tensions can erupt. For instance, through a school's positioning of teachers as experts on all topics and students (novices) on none, distrust can ensue. If these perceptions are acted on (e.g., new school policies heighten adult supervision over all matters dealing with the use of popular culture in the classroom), then the likelihood of teachers having opportunities to learn about their students' online literacy practices and identity construction is lessened.

In sum, it is this essay's contention that continuing to reify distinctions between which texts are suitable or unsuitable for formal and informal learning contexts—a binary that contemporary researchers are showing to be arbitrary at best—makes little sense. Given the rapidly changing times in which we live, drawing such distinctions also tends to limit what can be learned from treating contexts not as structured containers but rather as sieves through which social, cultural, institutional, economic, and political discourses animate one another and provide a sense of agency for both learners and teachers.

COUNTERPOINT: Margaret J. Finders
University of Wisconsin–La Crosse

There is an enormous chasm that separates the culture and experiences of teachers from many of their students. Often popular culture is called upon to bridge that gap. The purpose of this counterpoint essay is to raise some concerns that popular culture may not have the capabilities to do all that has been promised in much of current scholarship and pedagogical practices. When it comes to discussions on popular culture, it seems that teachers and youth alike may have been conned with simplistic notions of bringing popular culture into the classroom. There seem to be two extremes when it comes to discussions of popular culture in the classroom.

On the one hand, popular culture has no place in the curriculum because it glamorizes violence, portrays women as sex objects, and devalues education. It overemphasizes the importance of material consumption and denies the importance of hard work and sustaining relationships with family and friends. On the other hand, importing popular culture into the classroom has the potential that can somehow miraculously change power dynamics, liberate students from oppressive institutional practices, and enhance students' content knowledge and academic literacies. Both of these seemingly opposite discussions minimize the complexities of popular culture.

While the works of widely respected researchers such as Jabari Mahiri, Glenda Hull, and Anne Haas Dyson, among others, articulate the importance of opening up both the contexts and contents of learning, many times classroom practices reduce the complexities of navigating such diverse contexts. Equally important, students in the 21st century need to become "active, critical, and creative users not only of print and spoken language but also of visual language," according to the National Council of Teachers of English's *Standards for the English Language Arts* (1996, p. 5). Traditional notions of reading based upon printed materials are no longer appropriate, as we understand that today's students must develop "multiliteracies" (New London Group, 1996), enabling them to adopt new ways of talking, thinking, acting, and being within and outside of our classrooms. A growing number of scholars call for the integration of popular culture into the curriculum, but there is less attention to the reluctance of teachers and administrators to build relationships between the cultures of school and of youth. Scholars such as James Gee (2003), Ernest Morrell (2004), and others offer insights into the promise and the complexities of drawing on popular culture and media studies. What needs to happen is to change views of what counts as literacy and to give students both power and powerful texts.

In this essay, reservations for importing popular culture into the classroom fall into three areas: (1) curricular issues surrounding the use of popular culture, (2) the complexities of moving popular culture from out-of-school contexts and into the context of the classroom, and (3) representations of youth within discussions of teaching with popular culture. Oftentimes, discussions of using popular culture as a bridge to traditional curriculum ignore the need to change that traditional curriculum or examine the complexities of such an import. It is authentic literacies that have a place in the curriculum and not simply an importing of what the youth "own." Our goal is always to move students to work that they cannot do on their own. What is at issue is what we teach students to "do" with texts—intellectually, culturally, socially, and politically. Conversations should center on helping youth decide which texts are worth reading and producing, helping them learn how to read—where, why, to what ends and purposes. What is vitally important in discussions of curriculum is understanding and expanding on what children and adolescents do with texts.

CURRICULAR ISSUES

While some scholars argue that popular culture demonizes youth, others argue that such constructions shape the desires of youth. Central to this narrative is that popular culture places commercial consumption at the center of identity formation. Popular culture plays a significant role in learning about oneself in relation to the social world. Thus, some parents and teachers worry about the effects of popular culture on youth. Circulating around these discussions are concerns that too much sex and violence, too many drugs and dangers may negatively affect identities of children and youth, promoting compelling ways of being in the world. There is a grave concern that representations of youth will influence the actions of real-life youth. There are teachers, administrators, and parents who express concern for the impact of such gratuitous violence on children and adolescents and thus voice arguments to ban such content from the curriculum.

Others see a need for a pedagogical approach as a means to disrupt these harsh constructions. Such an approach constructs youth as passive victims of ideological manipulation. With either of these discussions, there are but two choices for teachers: (1) ban popular culture from the classroom or (2) critique it. According to Donna Alvermann (2010), David Buckingham (2003), and other scholars, this approach situates popular culture as an object for analysis in order that youth will not be duped. While these scholars would have teachers move beyond this pedagogical approach, much of the practice in schools has not. Understandings of the studies of popular culture have expanded beyond an approach of critique to include studying the pleasures and using it as a bridge to traditional curriculum, which brings me to another major concern.

Popular culture is often used as a bridge to traditional curriculum. As noted previously, many scholars argue to disrupt traditional boundaries between in-school and out-of-school practices and popular culture is often characterized as the material that can serve that purpose. Scholars argue for the use of popular culture as a means for students to insert themselves into the curriculum by representing their culture and linguistic identity. Yet teachers often see this argument as reduced to a way in which to take students where they are and lead them to where they should be, using popular culture as a bridge to traditional curriculum. A quick database search for articles on popular culture in the classroom will lead you to a plethora of materials that suggest popular culture is a pedagogical tool to lead students to traditional content. Across the disciplines, popular culture is a valuable means to reach unchanged curricular goals. Authors note such things as follows: "Demonstrate the ways in which three young children move from popular culture images to critiques of fine art," "The aim of the project was to improve standards in literacy, with academic writing as the focus," "used spoken word to teach academic literacy," "apply analysis of popular culture to learn science," and "using popular culture to teach (fill in the blank)."

In my work in a court-ordered middle school, an internal processing was at work for me that regularly and systematically reestablished a traditional view of literacy that discounted the students' work as proficient producers and consumers of popular culture and denied them as competent members of the classroom community. Field notes chronicle my constant struggles to use popular culture to move students closer to traditional notions of literacy. For example, while I was willing to work with popular magazines, I viewed them as a bridge into more "appropriate reading materials." We started with song lyrics, but I nudged them then to poetry. While innovative practices are abundant in professional literature, in classrooms, there seems to be a more rigid adherence to move students toward the curriculum without much discussion on how to move the curriculum toward students.

In addition to using popular culture texts to move students toward a more canonical curriculum, the study of these materials often denies the very nature of them. The ephemeral and performative nature of popular culture is captured, flattened, and lost. By becoming static, the dynamic interplay between the text and context becomes static in order to examine it. While current practices in media studies call for an understanding of popular culture as a cultural phenomenon, the "cultural" aspects are so often reduced to include only attention to the culture of the youth in the classroom with little or no attention to the larger culture that produces and circulates the popular culture. In other words, popular culture becomes simply another text, albeit a text that youth can relate to, a text to be studied as a text severed from the historical and cultural context that produced it. In science, arts, social studies, and literacy classrooms, popular culture is not studied as popular or as culture. For the most part, popular culture becomes infused with meanings and analyzed for structures that the teacher finds relevant to her discipline. Classroom discussions may start where the learners are, but they quickly move to where the teacher wants them to go. And an understanding of what happens to popular culture when it enters the classroom is missing from the larger conversations of using popular culture in the classroom. Popular culture is often banned because of its contents or employed because of its potential to connect to the learners in order to move them to a conventional curriculum.

COMPLEXITIES OF IMPORTING POPULAR CULTURE INTO SCHOOLS

Schools as learning sites come infused with institutional meanings for both the adults and the youth. What happens to popular culture when it becomes a part of the "doing of school"? David O'Brien, Kelly Chandler-Olcott, and a few other scholars are opening up discussions of what happens when popular culture enters the classroom context. For many youth, "doing school" is not associated with engagement, pleasure, or creativity. Further, this is precisely the reason given for importing popular culture into the classroom. Yet making unsanctioned practices (popular culture) a part of the sanctioned curriculum changes them. Something that has been controlled by the youth themselves moves out of their control, thus changing its very nature. Once teachers move popular culture texts and practices into any official curriculum, youth no longer own popular culture; it is stripped of its subversive nature, the very thing that makes it desirable. Does importing popular culture into the classroom hold the potential to move students further out to find other unsanctioned practices for which to call their own? How does assigning it and assessing it co-opt the very nature of popular culture? What makes out-of-school practices so desirable is that they are not assessed; they are not controlled by an authority. They need not satisfy someone else's notions of pleasurable or acceptable or correct. Attempting to empower youth through using texts that connect to their out-of-school lives may, in fact, situate youth in more powerless positions. The con of using popular culture in the classroom is that what is potentially pedagogically productive by the very act of using it renders it ineffective.

Equally concerning, David Buckingham (2003) and Cynthia Lewis, among others, have noted the lack of attention to the potential mismatches between youth and adults in terms of their pleasures, desires, and practices. Teachers may hold very different assumptions about use, attention to cultural tastes, and technological savvy. Little attention is given to the ways in which popular culture may be interpreted differently by middle-class, middle-aged white teachers and African American youth, for example. Moreover, the gap between youth and the adults with whom they work in institutional settings is often characterized as a gap in technology use rather than one of cultural tastes.

The contents of the curriculum are permeated with institutional ways of doing. Importing popular culture into the education institution without any attempts to change the institution has the potential to move youth further away, rather than closer, to engagement and learning. The context of schools must not be undervalued or ignored in these discussions. In fact, the liberal gesture of including popular culture in school activities may do more harm than good when it comes to connecting to the lives of youth. The images, representations, and texts of popular culture are often the very tools youth use to resist the dominate discourse that marginalizes them. Youth culture needs to be tapped not co-opted.

There are important identity issues to consider as well. There is a strong and complex link among cultural identity, language use, and school tasks. Children and adolescents are developing critical beliefs about themselves as learners and at the same time they are constructing multiple dimensions of self. Recognition of the role of popular culture in identity work for young people is reflected in much research on youth culture and media literacy. Relationships and representations of self and others are central to the development of one's identity. Such research shows how children and adolescents draw from the social, cultural, and ideological processes as meditational tools to form their desires, relationships and identities. And curriculum might help young people negotiate this terrain. Yet a disregard for the complexities of importing popular culture into the classroom may make available only two roles for youth who are marginalized in school contexts. Adolescents come to see themselves as helpless in school, as passive failures unable to take control of their learning or they view themselves as powerful resisters who are unwilling to be co-opted. Teachers must be very mindful of these notions so that using popular culture does not become yet another means to marginalize and disenfranchise their students.

Equally concerning is that the popular culture imported into the classroom remains for the most part based on printed text. Song lyrics dominate much of the pedagogical practices with less attention to the uses of other media. Is this because teachers are more comfortable and competent with printed text materials? Perhaps. There is a great need for teacher PD that integrates principles of teaching with effective strategies for digitally mediating student learning. Perhaps popular culture remains based on printed text because many schools do not have the technological infrastructures to engage in more complex popular culture media study. Discussions of the economic disparities of schools do not usually appear in discussions of popular culture in the classroom. In addition to social, cultural, or moral issues surrounding these conversations, curriculum and classroom practices are constrained by the material conditions of communities and schools.

REPRESENTATIONS OF YOUTH

Moving beyond the content of the curriculum and the context of schools, I am concerned with the representations of youth in current literature on using popular culture in the classroom. There is an unsettling homogeneity of youth that undergirds discussions of importing popular culture into the classroom. The construction of the technological-savvy, disenfranchised youth leads us to ignore other diversities within classrooms. In the literature, there is usually an explicit nod to diversity with comments such as "Urban youth will benefit from this pedagogical approach" and "Youth at risk will find a way to connect through the use of popular culture." Yet such discussions deny the much broader diversity of youth. Do we agree on a singular image of "urban youth"? Do all youth engage in instant messaging, blogging, and other digital media tools? I admit that I had been lulled into accepting this assumption that youth today are both technologically savvy and interested in popular culture.

Recently, when I began interviewing 11- and 12-year-old girls as a way to discover in what ways literacy practices may have changed in the 10 years since I had written *Just Girls: Hidden Literacies and Life in Junior High* (Finders, 1997), I anticipated that I would write about the fanzines and text messages that had gained in both popularity and accessibility. Disrupting these assumptions, both the middle-class white girls and the girls of Hmong dissent that I studied noted that they used the Internet for homework assignments, but they did not use it for much more. Where were all of the techno-savvy youth I had been reading about? While I only interviewed a very small sample, what I found most interesting is that popular culture did not seem to have the overpowering influence that I had come to believe dominated youth culture.

CONCLUSION

This essay does not argue for a return to a monolithic view of curriculum that excludes the language and cultural practices of students. It is simply an attempt to complicate the issues surrounding popular culture. It is never as simple as finding texts that youth enjoy and bringing them into the classroom. Whether they are engaging with fiction or fanzines, hip-hop or video gaming, students are at a crucial period of developing identities, tastes, and preferences that will carry them into adulthood.

Discussions of popular culture need to move beyond a debate over whether to import popular culture into the curriculum and classroom instruction. To this end, discussions need to move beyond the content of the curriculum, beyond any simplistic notion that popular culture can be a bridge to learning. Such a shift brings a focus on building multiple worldviews and identities and on examining how to actively engage with everyday literacies, popular culture, canonical texts, and political acts that will be required in these very precarious times.

FURTHER READINGS AND RESOURCES

Alvermann, D. (Ed.). (2010). *Adolescents' online literacies: Connecting classrooms, digital media, and popular culture.* New York: Peter Lang.

Alvermann, D. E. (2011). Popular culture and literacy practices. In M. L. Kamil, P. D. Pearson, E. B. Moje, & P. P. Afflerbach (Eds.), *Handbook of reading research* (Vol. IV, pp. 541–560). New York: Routledge/Taylor & Francis Group.

Beach, R., & O'Brien, D. (2008). Teaching popular culture texts in the classroom. In J. Coiro, M. Knobel, C. Lankshear, & D. J. Leu (Eds.), *Handbook of research on new literacies* (pp. 775–804). New York: Erlbaum/Taylor & Francis Group.

Bearne, E., & Wolstencroft, H. (2005). Playing with texts: The contribution of children's knowledge of computer narratives to their story writing. In J. Marsh & E. Millard (Eds.), *Popular literacies, childhood and schooling* (pp. 72–92). London: Routledge/Falmer.

Buckingham, D. (2003). *Media education: Literacy, learning and contemporary culture.* Cambridge, UK: Polity.

Burn, A., Buckingham, D., Parry, B., & Powell, M. (2010). Minding the gaps: Teachers' cultures, students' cultures. In D. E. Alvermann (Ed.), *Adolescents' online literacies: Connecting classrooms, digital media, and popular culture* (pp. 183–201). New York: Peter Lang.

Deleuze, G., & Guattari, F. (1986). *Kafka: Towards a minor literature* (D. Polan, Trans.). Minneapolis: University of Minnesota Press. (Original work published 1975)

Finders, M. (1997). *Just girls: Hidden literacies and life in junior high.* New York: Teachers College Press.

Gabler, N. (2011, January 30). Everyone's a critic now. *The Observer.* Retrieved February 2, 2011, from http://www.guardian.co.uk/culture/2011/jan/30/critics-franzen-free dom-social-network

Gee, J. (2003). *What videogames have to teach us about learning and literacy.* New York: Palgrave Macmillan.

Gogol Bordello. (2010). *Immigraniada (We Comin' Rougher)* [Multimedia]. New York: Columbia Records. Retrieved May 15, 2011, from http://www.youtube.com/watch?v=5oioNZSPqRM

Hagood, M. C., Alvermann, D. E., & Heron-Hruby, A. H. (2010). *Bring it to class: Unpacking pop culture in literacy learning.* New York: Teachers College Press.

Hall, S. (1981). Notes on deconstructing "the popular." In R. Samuel (Ed.), *People's history and socialist thought* (pp. 227–240). London: Routledge & Kegan Paul.

Kaiser Family Foundation. (2010). *Generation M²: Media in the lives of 8- to 18-year-olds.* Retrieved from http://www.kff.org/entmedia/upload/8010.pdf

Kamil, M. L., Pearson, P. D., Moje, E. B., & Afflerbach, P. P. (Eds.). (2010). *Handbook of reading research* (Vol. IV). New York: Routledge.

Labbo, L. (1996). A semiotic analysis of young children's symbol making in a classroom computer center. *Reading Research Quarterly, 32,* 356–385.

Leander, K. (2007). "You won't be needing your laptops today": Wired bodies in the wireless classroom. In M. Knobel & C. Lankshear (Eds.), *A new literacies sampler* (pp. 25–48). New York: Peter Lang.

Leander, K., & Lovvorn, J. (2006). Literacy networks: Following the circulation of texts, bodies, and objects in the schooling and online gaming of one youth. *Cognition and Instruction, 24,* 291–340.

Lefstein, A., & Snell, J. (2011). Promises and problems of teaching with popular culture: A linguistic ethnographic analysis of discourse genre mixing in a literacy lesson. *Reading Research Quarterly, 46*(1), 40–69.

Lenhart, A., Madden, M., Smith, A., & Macgill, A. (2007, December). *Teens and social media (PEW Internet & American Life Project).* Washington, DC: Pew Charitable Trusts. Retrieved September 18, 2011, from http://www.pewinternet.org/PPF/r/230/report_display.asp

Mahiri, J. (2010). *Digital tools in urban schools: Mediating a remix of learning.* Ann Arbor: University of Michigan Press.

Morrell, E. (2004). *Linking literacy and popular culture: Finding connections for lifelong learning.* Norwood, MA: Christopher-Gordon.

National Council of Teachers of English. (1996). *Standards for the English language arts.* Newark, DE, & Urbana, IL: International Reading Association and National Council of Teachers of English.

New London Group. (1996). A pedagogy of multiliteracies: Designing social futures. *Harvard Educational Review, 66*(1), 60–92.

Ranker, J. (2006). "There's fire magic, electric magic, ice magic, or poison magic": The world of video games and Adrian's compositions about *Gauntlet Legends. Language Arts, 84,* 21–33.

Sefton-Green, J. (2003). Informal learning: Substance or style? *Teaching Education, 12,* 37–52.

14

Are online and other virtual means of curriculum and instruction the future of education?

POINT: John Castellani, *The Johns Hopkins University*
COUNTERPOINT: Peggy Whalen-Levitt, *The Center for Education, Imagination and the Natural World*

OVERVIEW

Through various times and spaces people have occupied many possible worlds. Some worlds are actual and others virtual. On occasion, the virtual subverts the actual or real; at other points, lines between the real and virtual blur (Deleuze, 1994). A fine book is a virtual world extraordinaire, and when a reader unfurls its pages at the best times and in the most intimate spaces the book world becomes an actual one. The Little Prince draws a boa constrictor; King Arthur draws a sword. Narcissus draws a drink from a mirrorlike pool, and when he does, he encounters penultimate virtuality: his own face in reflection. It is the lines of a face that William Butler Yeats wrote of looking for "before the world was made." And if another mirror is introduced to the reflecting pool at a precise angle, then virtual worlds are multiplied ad infinitum.

A fine painting is likewise a virtual world that darts through actual ones. Vermeer's Woman, forever suspended, writes a letter while wedged between light and dark. This is a longing space no different than Virginia Woolf's *A Room of One's Own*. The virtual woman is as solid and as unmoving as a Cézanne Apple or a Brancusi Bird or a Peto stamped letter (a trompe-l'oeil illusion that deceives the eye). And music is drawn from the virtual: Bach's *Mass in B Minor* from angels and bird song, and James Joyce's Dublin from street-noise words.

Of course, movement can even be of the virtual, as well: Japanese dancers evolve from a tree, a mime as gardener with a pocket watch slowly marking, capturing time. These staged spaces are of the theater, and from it Cinema took dramatization to a new level; for instance, Jean Cocteau was an outstanding virtualist whose Orpheus crossed time and space, as well as life and death (e.g., in *The Blood of the Poet*). For centuries, philosophy was caught between poles of light and dark until its notions were refashioned for and by free spirits, such as Gilles Deleuze (1994) who created concepts of actual worlds, virtual worlds, ad infinitum.

These possible worlds were once only accessible to the few. Moreover, from these few much was expected and much was sacrificed. For instance, Cézanne spoke of painting as if it was priesthood, and musicians, such as Billie Holiday, endured poverty, pain, and humiliation to perfect their work. But in the 20th century these matters changed. Machines that could create virtual worlds became readily available to the many. For example, the Kodak camera led to the mass production of images by thousands of people. The human voice was captured on cylinders and disks and transmitted through electric wires. Even the virtual reflection of one's face in the mirror changed, became fragmented, as stable notions of individual and group identity were disrupted and old matters of authority (e.g., king and serf; master and slave) dissolved.

The mass multiplication of the virtual reached a zenith in the 1960s when pop artist Andy Warhol took ordinary mass produced images from Campbell's Soup and transformed those into seemingly endless rows of canned repetition on wall-sized silkscreen. At about the same time, Xerox copying machines and Polaroid cameras allowed for an even greater and faster mass production of images, including those of printed texts.

In spite of this dizzying pace and accumulation, yet another peak in virtual production soon followed through the popularizations of still and moving digital technologies. By the 1990s, products of these digital technologies were increasingly transmitted via websites and e-mail through telephone wires, later by larger cables, and then without wires through air. By the 2000s, even more sophisticated digital tools were available to larger numbers of people and solidly became part of the expression of popular culture in the United States (see the essays by Donna E. Alvermann and Margaret Finders in Chapter 13 of this volume). These tools and related processes provided ways for various people such as youth, academics, political operatives, and dissidents to distribute virtual communications in assorted forms, some of which were manipulated, copied, pasted, remixed, and hybridized with reasonable ease and little effort (Hagood, Leander, Luke, Mackey, & Nixon, 2003). As of late, many of these virtual forms are entirely mobilized through real-time sharing networks, smart phones, portable computer pads, and so on.

Indeed, nearly everything that is part of the actual world has been transformed to simulated digital environments that can be accessed on the fly. For instance, commerce, sex, libraries, gambling venues, breaking news and weather and traffic reports, and video gaming are readily available for online participation and consumption, sometimes through spaces such as Second Life, where people join to a virtual 3D network and create their own avatars or digital proxies who can buy, sell, trade, design, romance, and interact in other ways on what they call the "grid" or a virtual reality global space. Second Life claims over 20 million registered members, and there are millions of users in similar virtual spaces, such as SimCity.

Other actual world services are likewise touched by virtual technologies, such as financial brokerage and health care, and biotechnology and astrophysics are leading areas for developing virtual models. By extension, virtual simulations have become a fundamental part of the advanced education in these subject areas, as well as others, such as engineering and architecture. Take, for instance, the use of virtual flight simulators, through which fledgling pilots can hone their skills without the costs and dangers of actual flight time. Out of these developments, many people believe that the time is ripe, or perhaps overdue, for this level of online virtual world technology to be available for public schooling purposes. In the point essay, John Castellani (The Johns Hopkins University) assumes this position. For example, he argues the merits of online virtual technologies in providing equal access to quality subject area materials for populations of students who have often been marginalized. In addition, he points out that new technology is part and parcel of everyday life in many homes and workplaces; thus, to best prepare children for the future, public education needs to provide them with instruction in the tools of which they will be called on, sooner or later, to use.

However, other scholars suggest that the trend toward the uses of online virtual reality and similar new technologies may indeed connect people but in artificial and distanced ways. In this respect, Peggy Whalen-Levitt (The Center for Education, Imagination and the Natural World) carefully unpacks notions of what it means to be human in the contemporary, actual world and how education is much more than what could be transmitted by a machine, no matter how sophisticated it is. In part, she draws her thoughts from cultural historians and philosophers, as well as her own experiences with nature and from her work in the education of the whole human child. Moreover, interspersed in her essay, Whalen-Levitt weaves narratives to describe subtle human–earth connections, which involve relational ways of knowing. This underscores her stance that *we of the human community* need to discover new pathways for developing compassionate and imaginative qualities to better educate ourselves and others for the future.

A. Jonathan Eakle
The Johns Hopkins University

POINT: John Castellani
The Johns Hopkins University

Technology has changed the manner in which we approach work, school, and personal relationships and most importantly the way we solve problems. Indeed, nearly every single part of society has been influenced, changed, or enhanced by the use of technologies that have facilitated with whom, where, and in what manner people interact. Moreover, online technologies, such as web spaces, communication venues, and other virtual technologies have made it possible to do things which have to date not been possible. For example, real-time online communication technologies such as Twitter, MySpace, and Facebook have been used to promote cultural change and even political revolutions.

The ability to solve problems is a key to being human and actually one of the main features of being human that separates us from other organic creatures. From the beginning of time, humans have used tools to extend the range of solutions to problems like creating fire to getting man to the moon and beyond. What is known about tools then over all this time? If you have used a tool to successfully solve a problem, when the same or a similar problem arises, you will likely use that same tool, unless a new tool is available. People are even more likely to use a tool if that tool was easy to use, solved the problem in a reasonable amount of time, and has become a part of one's overall toolkit. Technology developers are providing us with tool after tool; electronic calculators to computers offer an extensive array of tools, and the opportunities we have because of access to technology are the reason using online technologies for teaching and learning is critical to human development and learning.

In his book *The World Is Flat: A Brief History of the 21st Century,* Thomas Friedman (2005) argued that "people don't change when you tell them they should. They change when they tell themselves they must" (p. 462). He also suggested the world has changed according to the manner in which the current marketplace operates, ways people communicate, and the overall interactions people have throughout the world as they live, learn, and experience life as well as mediate conflicts in society.

During recent international and national conflicts, such as in the Middle East, for instance, these new technologies were often the only means available to circulate messages among people protesting their governments. This is because with so many outlets for communication, it is impossible for any one person or regime to control when and where information is disseminated or received. Satellite, cell, and online technology has made it possible to expand the audience to which any one person would have had access in prior years. In many respects, online and virtual technologies are the present as well as the future of interaction and communication and by extension the future of curriculum and instruction in education.

According to the noted constructivist scholar Lev Vygotsky (1978), overall higher psychological processes are mediated and developed through the historical and social dimensions through which life experiences occur. The cultural artifacts that societies have developed throughout history—for example, communication symbols, divergent languages, art, music, science, physical tools, and so forth—reflect the way in which we understand the world and create meaning in collaboration with others. This collaboration is where learning occurs when one person can take something read or experienced to individuals with common interests and can influence how one understands the teaching and learning experience.

Living in the 21st century requires the integration of technology tools into everything we do, from making travel reservations to using online applications with mobile technologies and, more importantly, utilizing the accessible and online teaching and learning tools to solve problems and expand our knowledge of the world in which we live. We use technology to do everything from turning on the TV and ordering movies to monitoring communications in cyberspace to detect and respond to threats to national security both within national borders and those risks beyond those boundaries. However, this trend toward the use of novel technologies has not been accepted or integrated into all areas of public and private education. This is especially evident when considering the newest Web 2.0 tools that are used for virtual, online, or other means of educating children, as well as adults, in and out of schools. So herein lies the conflict between society and present-day schooling.

ONLINE AND VIRTUAL LEARNING TOOLS

Online and virtual learning tools have assumed a ubiquitous presence in our society; however, many areas of education have yet to understand the role that technology has in the curriculum as a foundation for learning core curriculum content as well as the arts. For instance, in some schools in the United States, there are over 120 languages spoken by students and their families. Even though online curriculum delivery tools such as Moodle can deliver subject area content in many different languages, meet the requirements of federal law to make learning accessible to students with special needs, assess the learning of academic content instantaneously, and provide students access to virtual objects useful for understanding curriculum content and concepts such as those of NASA's (2011) Astro-Venture, questions about why teachers should be using these tools continue to pervade discussions among educators and other stakeholders in public and private education. While there is little empirical research to support the idea that children growing up in this century have brains that are wired differently, it is true that successful problem solving with a tool that works, as Vygotsky (1978) and others have suggested, reinforces the future use of that tool to continue to solve other similar or related problems. Further, there is evidence that today's children, as well as adults, are increasingly using online and virtual tools to solve real-world problems. For example, physical science concepts can be applied in virtual reality environments to examine if materials used to construct a potentially real-world bridge can bear the load of what might cross it.

Chris Dede (2009) suggested that there are at least three ways that virtual learning tools have changed the way curriculum is offered, (1) allowing the student to be exposed to multiple perspectives, (2) enabling situated learning to occur, and (3) promoting transfer of what is learned in one particular subject area to other domains of knowledge. These constructivist type of teaching approaches are important when considering that collaboration and communication are essential skills that need to be embedded within the curriculum. When considering the global workplace in which students of today will be working, it is important to think about exposing these students to other cultures, ways of thinking, and how cultures are solving problems common to being human and being alive. As the Internet has provided us with an explosion of digital content, we can now see things that would have been impossible even 5 years ago. While it is important to continue looking at the manner in which virtual and online tools are integrated within school curriculum, the learning strengths and preferences these media develop in users are important to how students see and interact with the world in which they live and learn.

INTEGRATION OF TECHNOLOGIES INTO CURRICULUM

Online and virtual technologies are very powerful tools; however, they do not deliver themselves. There must be a thoughtful and creative person with the understanding of how to teach actively by considering the ways in which these tools can best be used. As a result, there continues to be a problem with the integration of technology into curriculum. This is largely due to the omission of such online and virtual tools as curriculum is developed, delivered, and assessed by educators. Further, one of the significant reasons that the U.S. National Education Technology Plan listed for why educational technology has thus far failed to live up to its promise is that there is inadequate training for the teachers who should implement technology into their classrooms. Thus, the question of the reason to use online and virtual technologies in education is really one about why teachers are not using the new technologies of which many of their students are accustomed and in many cases have developed expertise. And, in the least, these cutting-edge technologies are ones that all students should be learning to use to be successful now and in the future. This indicates that the educational system is failing in part because the sophisticated technologies that many children, youth, and adults use in their personal and work lives are not readily available for use in many public school settings, especially the most impoverished ones.

To be sure, and as Michael Fullan (2001) reported in his study of educational change, such change is never simple, "putting ideas into practice [is] a far more complex process than people realize" (p. 5). The reason that educational change efforts often fail is because they fail to consider the culture and context of schooling as a result of the changing world around which curriculum is delivered. Nonetheless, new technology advocates encourage the growth of technology in schools. They claim that the use of technology enhances teaching and learning environments, provides for more constructivist types of learning experiences, and fits more closely with the way that our society lives and learns. Therefore, from the first days of schooling to higher education and beyond, the field of education should be embracing virtual and online technologies as fast as the technology industry is producing and integrating cutting-edge tools into society. However, those who object to the use of new technology not only caution against the use of virtual and online tools for teaching and learning but often they are the most vocal advocates for more traditional types of teaching methods.

Some of these advocates of tradition argue that technology can actually harm young children. In one sense, traditionalists believe that what is new might distract from what has been determined over time to work in teaching and learning. A result of spending time, resources, and energies on new technologies—and for that matter anything new that has not been proven effective by measurable means—teachers and students may well fall behind in their efforts to meet No Child Left Behind (NCLB) (2001) state testing requirements, which traditionalists do not think is a risk worth taking. In fact, such risks threaten the very existence of the way teaching and learning is conducted in schools and even the jobs of educators who are not willing to embrace new ways of thinking and acting. Technology dissidents go as far as to state that the use of technology for learning and living has been oversold and underused (Cuban, 2001).

ACCESSIBILITY

The Telecommunications Act of 1996 was a seminal moment in U.S. educational history, ensuring that all schools and libraries have access to universal communications services. Internet access in public schools increased from less than 3% in 1994 to over 94% in 2005, and the ratio of computers to students, schools using broadband and wireless Internet services, and handheld computers have also increased exponentially (U.S. Department of Education [ED], 2008). With this rise in computer and Internet connectivity, there was also a push from the business community to develop the Partnership for 21st Century Skills (P21), which is based on the issue that students entering the workforce are not doing so with the media, communication, and collaboration skills necessary for success. However, many students around the country continue not to have access to the online communication tools available to those who can afford them. As a result, there continues to be what has been described since the 1990s as a digital divide, and the students who need these tools the most to be successful within an individually inspired capitalistic society still do not have access to them.

By way of analogy, if children suffer from malnutrition, there is one sure place where they can get free or reduced lunches: school. Thus, for children to learn to feed themselves in their futures—by use of new technologies that are necessary for living productive 21st-century lives—public schools are again the one sure environment where this can take place. If you go to a grocery store or bank, get on a bus or subway system, you are forced to use technology to move around. Even moving from one state to another on bridges and through tunnels requires the use of technology. After all of the effort to make telecommunications accessible to those rural, urban, and suburban environments where such access has been historically denied due to cost, there is no reason to believe that all educators would not use available online resources and virtual tools.

In addition to the ways in which online and virtual learning tools enable diverse learners to access curriculum, the tools have significantly increased the ability of students with special needs to participate in active, stimulating, and accessible teaching and learning environments where they have not been able to participate in the past. Digital text delivered through online course management tools is one of the most powerful ways to help implement curriculum in classrooms to ensure that all students benefit from teaching and learning. These students include those who have English as a second language (ESL) as well as students with disabilities using technology tools to access curriculum content.

For some of these students, traditional printed text curriculum is difficult to access. For example, students who have difficulty seeing text can manipulate digital formats, such as increasing the font size, changing the color, and/or converting the text to an audio file that can be read aloud. At the same time, most online delivery platforms allow information to be posted in a way that students can preview the content to be learned, engage differentially with the tools they need to access the curriculum, as well as review content by accessing presentations, recorded lectures, lecture notes provided by a teacher, and so forth. Additionally, accessible digital text makes using assistive technology easier, using digital content helps to address the principles of Universal Design for Learning (UDL) while providing minimal if any disruption to the overall teaching and learning process. While some Web 2.0 tools do not meet the federal requirements for accessibility, content management systems (or learning management systems) do meet these requirements. Many of these content management systems have promoted their ability to meet federal requirements in a seamless manner that does not alter the teaching and learning process.

ASSESSMENTS

Another significant way that online and virtual technology is changing teaching and learning is through the use of computerized assessments. In addition to preparing students to become proficient users of technology to solve problems, for better or worse, they also must be prepared to take tests online. Statewide assessments, as well as the SAT among many other evaluations, are all being offered in digital formats. However, many students who take online tests have not been prepared to do so. This can be an unnecessary barrier for them as paper-and-pencil tests fast become things of the past.

In addition, an important component of delivering curriculum is evaluating how learning is occurring in the context of formative and summative assessment. These are two ways that can be significantly altered and enhanced by using technology and are important for understanding how learning is occurring in context. Both asynchronous and synchronous discussion on a curriculum topic can be captured in digital text format and then it can be "mined" to observe useful, as well as useless, learning paths that can be taken to solve problems. In addition, electronic assessments embedded within a virtual task can provide an electronic view into how a problem might be solved by a student and the merit of that student's choice. The use of formative assessments has also greatly expanded through the use of student response systems in virtual and online learning environments. Presently, states are moving toward electronic online statewide assessments, and while the content of these assessments may stay the same, the way in which questions are delivered, like in order of difficulty with the GRE, improves the way in which an assessment system can respond to a test taker based on the questions that are being answered correctly or incorrectly.

CONCLUSION

The United States has a vital economic and social interest to ensure that new technologies are integrated into teaching and learning environments. These technologies are forever evolving, and without great care taken in, and attention given to, the curriculum and instruction of schools to address these fast-paced changes it is within reason that students, perhaps even the nation, will be left well behind others. Nonetheless, we have the technological tools and human, as well as material, resources to participate in a global marketplace where students educated today can be prosperous. Wherever and whenever instruction occurs in the United States, consideration must be given to the online and virtual learning tools that can be used to promote teaching and learning. New tools are being created daily. A new application to solve a current problem is being developed as this article is being read. If these tools can in any way be used to enhance the way children and youth learn, they should be used with thought and pointed integration into teaching and learning experiences.

COUNTERPOINT: Peggy Whalen-Levitt
The Center for Education, Imagination and the Natural World

No reasonable person would argue that there is no place for online learning and virtual reality within the field of education today. But to argue that online and other virtual means of curriculum and instruction are the *future* of education is to diminish the deeper potentialities of education and to beg the question of reality itself that must be addressed as a foundation for any meaningful approach to schooling.

Today, many human children are born into an electrified, electronic world so insulated from the clouds and the stars, the meadows and creeks, the rising and setting sun that the natural world is more of an abstraction than a reality for children. What every child has for centuries experienced—a feeling of inner relation with the outer world—is now threatened with extinction in many societies. Cultural historian Thomas Berry (1999) referred to this separation of the human from the natural world as an "autistic situation." In 2005, writer Richard Louv struck a deep chord in the American psyche with his book *Last Child in the Woods: Saving Our Children From Nature-Deficit Disorder*.

To more fully understand how we have come to this juncture in which the human is separated from the natural world and the natural world is objectified by the human, stepping back and taking a look at the broad sweep of time can be beneficial. While we have come to think of history as a human affair, the human and the universe actually evolve together in a creative process. The emergence of human presence in the unfolding universe story brings with it a new capacity for the universe to reflect upon and celebrate itself. As explained in more detail later in this essay, the future of the earth is in the hands of the humans who inhabit it. On the shadow side, human presence brings with it the capacity for the universe to destroy itself.

EVOLUTION OF CONSCIOUSNESS

At the beginning of human presence on Earth, some cultures believe that human beings lived within a dreamlike consciousness in relationship to a universe permeated by spirit. We have only to hear the prayers and chants of indigenous peoples to experience conversations of deep intimacy with the universe.

Over time, the human being has evolved from this dreamlike consciousness to an awakening of consciousness in relationship to the earth. Gradually, the human being developed the capacity for clarity of representation and sharply delineated concepts. A shift in consciousness began in the 1600s when Galileo, in the interest of developing the scientific method, reduced reality to only those properties that could be mathematically measured, and Descartes introduced a view of material reality as a mechanism. Slowly, a veil was drawn between the human being and the sacred dimension of the universe.

After 400 years of observation and reflection, a scientific understanding of how the universe came to be and how it has evolved is now available to us. But this scientific understanding, based in our rational, logical, and analytical intelligences, has marginalized our imaginative, intuitive, and contemplative ways of knowing, both in and out of school. Our ability to objectify the world around us has inclined us to view that world as an "object" of study. And this distancing, as we have seen, has led to a great desolation of the earth for human use and exploitation.

If we look at the evolution of human communication over time, we see a similar movement toward abstraction. From the pictogram; to phonetic writing; to the printing press; to the telephone, film, TV, and the computer; we see an increasing dislocation of the human being from a direct participation with the world. With each of these transitions, the human community moves increasingly from an immersion in the natural world toward the capacity to make ever more abstract and distanced representations of that world until, ultimately, the human community participates almost exclusively in a technologically constructed reality.

THE MAP AND THE TERRITORY

Furthermore, as these technologically constructed worlds become ever more "real," the human race begins to lose its way. As scientist and philosopher Alfred Korzybski (1931) has said, "the map is not the territory." When we come to the juncture where this distinction is obscured, we need to take pause.

What difference does this difference make? When a human being awakes at dawn to see the sky transformed from the darkness of night to a slowly rising light, he or she experiences more than a physical world. The heart may expand with awe as the light grows over the horizon, and the human being may have a sense that the world is more than just inert matter but rather is a place of depth and creativity unfolding in time. This world of depth and creativity cannot be replicated with technologies and cannot be "captured" in photos or forms of virtual reality. The inner qualities of this world can only be fully experienced by the attentive presence of a human being at a single moment in time.

Online educational programs and simulations of reality, no matter how interactive and scintillating they may be, still keep students swimming in a mediated world. Lacking the presence of the "lifeworld," a term used by philosopher Edmund Husserl to refer to the living reality that sustains all life, they cannot lead students to an experience of the depth of the world. One of the dangers of online education and virtual reality, then, is that they can create a barrier to one's conversations with this living world of depth. They draw children away from the phenomenal world and vie for their attention in persuasive ways. Inundated with these abstract forms of communication, children may begin to lose their ability to know the difference between *real* and *virtual*. In our technological and fast-paced world, the more subtle capacities that enable human beings to feel a sense of belonging to the universe lie dormant.

DIGITAL CONSCIOUSNESS

In order to understand this issue more fully, one needs to look at the computer itself as a trajectory toward the mechanization of human thought. One might begin by asking what dimensions of the human being can be embedded within the computer and what dimensions cannot.

The word *computer* was initially used to describe a person who engaged in arithmetical calculations. According to the *Oxford English Dictionary* (OED), the word was first used in 1897 to refer to a mechanical calculating device. Today, the word is commonly used to refer to a programmable machine that is an extension of logical and quantitative dimensions of human thought. While the computer has infinite applications, all meanings embodied in computer programs are ultimately reduced to finite, logical structures. When a child sits down in front of a two-dimensional computer screen, separated in time and space from a human teacher and the phenomenal world, the child is ultimately entering into a logically constructed world that bears the stamp and codes of an adult programmer. If the program is interactive like Logo, the computer language developed for children at the Massachusetts Institute of Technology (MIT), the child *becomes* the programmer whose primary activity is the translation of meaning and significance to a logically constructed program.

The dimensions of the human that cannot be embedded in the computer are aspects of soul, imagination, intuition, contemplation—all those qualitative leanings that defy the programmed precision of the machine. Given these limitations, one has to wonder how it is that the computer has been embraced with such exuberance as the future of education.

The beginning of the 21st century is a significant historical moment when the evolutionary task of the human is to discover what it means to be human on a much deeper level than we have been able to imagine through the consciousness of the scientific and technological age that has preceded this time. We are able to know the world on a deeper level than with the abstract ways of knowing we have inherited. We also can recognize the confinement of this abstract tradition of knowledge and find a way to reinvite the fullness of reality back into education and recognize the perils inherent in continuing down the pathway of technological and information-based schooling without seeing its limitations.

INTERLUDE

On the threshold of the winter solstice in 2002, the foothills of North Carolina were blanketed with ice, followed by a winter chill that lasted for days. Throughout the bioregion, the foothill residents were cut off from man-made sources of warmth, light, and communication and were given an opening, in space and time, to move into a more primal relationship with the earth. These residents experienced anew the rhythms of chopping wood and placing logs on the fire throughout the night, the glow of candlelight, and the spirit of human community thrust out of modern routines into an essential presence to the moment. They learned, many of them for the first time, what it is to be cold as the expression "chilled to the bone" took on new meaning.

For many, this storm and its aftermath were taken to be an irritating interruption of their schedules, goals, and all else that they considered important. And surely, as the dark days wore on, it was a physical hardship. But rarely are human beings given an opportunity, one they would hardly choose, to dissolve the habitual patterns of their technological way of life and ponder their relationship to darkness and light, to cold and warmth. In this icy interlude, the residents caught a glimpse of their beginnings as human beings on this earth, of natural dwellings heated by the hearth, of the human energy expended for food and warmth, and of the intimacy of sharing stories around the fire.

This "trial by ice" helped the residents become more aware of the full presence of the natural world; helped deepen their appreciation for human comfort, for the simple pleasures of warmth, light, and the companionship of others; and guided them to give themselves over completely to each moment. On a deeper level, it brought the residents into a contemplation of the great cosmic forces of darkness and light that are considered at this time every year.

Ultimately, what the residents experienced was a shift in background and foreground as the electronic world receded and the phenomenal world came to the fore. And it is something like this shift that now needs to happen in the realm of education. In order to consider how forms of online education and virtual reality might be used mindfully in the education of our children, we must first ask this question: "Have we established a ground of being for our students in the phenomenal world?" For it is the phenomenal and relational world that we now need to revive in balance with our more abstract ways of knowing.

THE NEW SCIENCES

Support for this shift in perspective is garnered from the new sciences, as the worldview shaped by Galileo and Descartes gives way to new understandings of reality. What is the new image of reality that implies this reorientation of education for the future?

First of all, we now have a picture of the evolution of the universe, the earth, and humanity as a developmental, creative process unfolding in time. To many, the universe now looks more to us like an ongoing creative event than a "great machine." This evolution from the primeval fireball; to the Milky Way galaxy; to the planet Earth that gives rise to plant, animal, and human life evokes a sense of wonder and awe in many of us as we allow ourselves to become fully present to its mystery.

New understandings and reflections on this cosmology reveal that the universe now becomes aware of itself through human presence. The universe unfolds through a cosmic, imaginative process that includes the human as participant. It is also evident that humanity now holds the future of the earth in its hands.

In addition to this historical perspective, we begin to understand the universe as a community of reciprocal relationships at every level of existence—what Thomas Berry (1999) called a "communion of subjects." Far from the spectator role of objective science, modern physics reveals the inseparability of the observer and the observed. The picture of reality that emerges is one of an interdependent whole—a reality one can only know by being in communion with it.

The implications of this new view of reality for education are profound. From this perspective, children must be supported in their moments of deep connection to the universe. Moments of cosmic awakening in childhood are more common than we might think. Edith Cobb (1998), in her groundbreaking book, *The Ecology of Imagination in Childhood,* documented moments of cosmic consciousness in autobiographies of creative individuals from antiquity to the 20th century. Through these accounts, one can see that these creative individuals, when they were children, readily sensed the inner qualities of the world around them and sensed themselves to be part of a larger, creative process.

In the context of this new reality, the limitations and allurements of mechanical computer thinking as the focus of education must also be acknowledged. While children might learn *about* the new sciences through computer programs, this indirect knowledge is no substitute for being brought into a reciprocal relationship with the lifeworld itself. To experience the world as a communion of subjects, children need to be brought into an intimacy with the world around them through direct experience. To participate in the world as an unfolding creative process, children need to be able to bring their own spiritual, playful, imaginative, and intuitive selves to the unfolding drama. The new cosmology is not an outline written in stone; it is an ongoing event established moment by moment in time.

A new epistemology is being formulated: an epistemology in which knowing is more like the "I and Thou" relationship described by Martin Buber than an accumulation of objective facts and knowledge that serve the economic order of the world. The new epistemology suggests a radically new mode of consciousness: one that calls for the development of *inner* capacities for a compassionate human presence to the natural world, one that moves us from a mind sharpened by critical inquiry toward a mind warmed by a loving heart and stimulated by the soul's imaginative powers, and one that embraces a sense of the natural world as a numinous reality unfolding in time.

The education of children takes on a different form from this perspective. In order to align ways of knowing and educational practices with this new view of an evolutionary and relational reality, the approach to education must now become more oriented to the development of contemplative and imaginative capacities in the child. This new form of education seeks to develop a soul mood of reverence, validates feelings of awe and wonder, acknowledges the numinous dimension of the universe and the inner life of the child, reenvisions what it means to know the world, and asks this question: How might the whole human being be cultivated in relationship to the fullness of the world?

TOWARD WHOLENESS

Visions of wholeness are now emerging in diverse educational circles in recognition of the shift that needs to take place. The Contemplation and Education Initiative is now forming at the Garrison Institute in Garrison, New York. Similarly, in the fall of 2009, the Mind and Life Institute sponsored a conference titled "Educating World Citizens for the 21st Century: Educators, Scientists and Contemplatives Dialogue on Cultivating a Healthy Mind, Brain and Heart." The conference was framed as a two-day dialogue between the Dalai Lama and a wide range of panelists including Daniel Goldman (*Ecological Intelligence),* Linda Darling-Hammond (professor of education, Stanford University), Richard Davidson (professor of psychology and psychiatry, University of Wisconsin), and Linda Lantieri (director of the Inner Resilience Program and author of *Schools With Spirit: Nurturing the Inner Lives of Children and Teachers).*

Goldman (2009) began by speaking about evolution and the planet, noting that the 20th century was a century of great human discovery but also a century of destruction—a destruction that is continuing into the 21st century. He said that the present educational system attends to the physical and material, but it is now time to promote compassion and inner values in the schooling of our children. Lantieri (2009) concurred that there is a need for educators to find ways to cultivate in students those things of mind and heart that are intentional, mindful, and deep.

In seeking forms of education that are in alignment with these new realities, one can look to Montessori, Waldorf, Krishnamurti, and Quaker schools that have for many years recognized a lifeworld of inner depth and meaning. Maria Montessori understood the importance of grounding knowledge in direct experience and created a cosmic education curriculum that helps children consider their "cosmic tasks." Waldorf schools offer an evolution of consciousness curriculum that supports the development of fluid, mobile, and imaginative modes of thinking throughout the grades. Krishnamurti schools offer the practice of silence and dialogue in their study centers, side by side with more academic ways of knowing. And Quaker schools have long created a space for silence where the inner life of each child is deeply respected.

The new schooling of children that is called for in our time is a schooling that engages children as living beings in a living world. It is a form of schooling that begins with the teacher in an inner schooling of consciousness. The teacher must become conversant with inner realms of imagination, inspiration, and intuition. Only then can the teacher guide the child to a place where fascination and entrancement with life are evoked. There is no computer that can replace the teacher in this work.

FURTHER READINGS AND RESOURCES

Berry, T. (1999). *The great work: Our way into the future.* New York: Bell Tower.

Clarke-Midura, J. (2010). Assessment, technology, and change. *Journal of Research on Technology in Education, 42*(3), 309–328.

Cobb, E. (1998). *The ecology of imagination in childhood.* New York: Spring.

Cuban, L. (2001). *Oversold and underused: Computers in the classroom.* Cambridge, MA: Harvard University Press.

Dede, C. (2009). Immersive interfaces for engagement and learning. *Science, 323*(5910), 66–69.

Deleuze, G. (1994). *Difference and repetition* (P. Patton, Trans.). New York: Columbia University Press.

Friedman, T. (2005). *The world is flat: A brief history of the 21st century.* New York: Farrar, Straus and Giroux.

Fullan, M. (2001). *The new meaning of educational change* (3rd ed.). New York: Teachers College Press.

Goldman, D. (2009, October). *Envisioning the world citizen.* Conference on Educating World Citizens for the 21st Century: Educators, Scientists and Contemplatives Dialogue on Cultivating a Healthy Mind, Brain and Heart. Washington, DC: Mind and Life Institute.

Hagood, M. C., Leander, K. M., Luke, C., Mackey, M., & Nixon, H. (2003). Media and online literacy studies. *Reading Research Quarterly, 38*(3), 386–413.

Ketelhut, D. J., & Schifter, C. (2011). Teachers and game-based learning: Improving understanding of how to increase efficacy of adoption. *Computers & Education, 56*(2), 539–546.

Korzybski, A. (1931). *A non-Aristotelian system and its necessity for rigour in mathematics and physics.* American Mathematical Society, American Association for the Advancement of Science Annual Meeting, New Orleans, LA. Reprinted in *Science and Sanity,* 1933, 747–761.

Lantieri, L. (2009, October). *Compassion and empathy.* Conference on Educating World Citizens for the 21st Century: Educators, Scientists and Contemplatives Dialogue on Cultivating a Healthy Mind, Brain and Heart. Washington, DC: Mind and Life Institute.

Louv, R. (2005). *Last child in the woods: Saving our children from nature-deficit disorder.* Chapel Hill, NC: Algonquin Books.

NASA. (2011). *Astro-Venture.* Retrieved March 5, 2011, from http://astroventure.arc .nasa.gov/DAP/DAP.html

Palmer, P., & Zajonc, A. (with Scribner, M.). (2010). *The heart of higher education: A call to renewal.* San Francisco: Jossey-Bass.

Sardello, R. (2004). *Facing the world with soul: The reimagination of modern life.* Great Barrington, MA: Lindisfarne Press.

Swimme, B., & Tucker, M. E. (2011). *Journey to the universe.* New Haven, CT: Yale University Press.

Talbott, S. L. (1995). *The future does not compute: Transcending the machines in our midst.* Sebastopol, CA: O'Reilly & Associates.

U.S. Department of Education, National Center on Educational Statistics. (2008). Table 108: Number and internet access of instructional computers and rooms in public schools, by selected school characteristics: Selected years, 1995 through 2008. *Digest of educational statistics.* Retrieved from http://nces.ed.gov/programs/digest/d10/ tables/dt10_108.asp

Vygotsky, L. S. (1978). *Mind in society: The development of higher psychological processes.* Cambridge, MA: Harvard University Press.

Court Cases and Statutes

No Child Left Behind Act of 2001, 20 U.S.C.A. §§ 6301 *et seq.*

Telecommunications Act of 1996, Pub. LA. No. 104-104, 110 Stat. 56 (1996).

INDEX